# SPANISH
# SAHARA

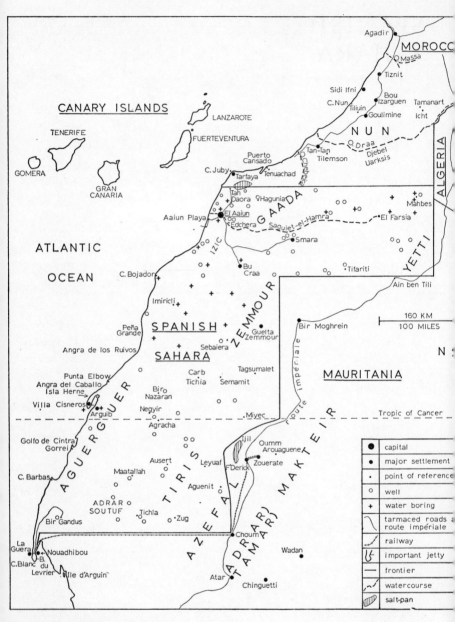

Fig. 1. Map of Spanish Sahara

# SPANISH
# SAHARA

by John Mercer

London   George Allen & Unwin Ltd
Ruskin House   Museum Street

First published in 1976

ISBN 0 04 966013 6

Printed in Great Britain
in 10 point Times Roman type
by W & J Mackay Limited
Chatham

*To Susan*
*for help with the work*
*and companionship on the journey*

# Illustrations

JACKET

*Spine* The territory's only rock-engraving of rain, in the Leyuaf Cave in the Tiris.
*Front* 'The Lybians, towards Cape Blanc, go in this posture in search of their Enemies', extract from *Travels* by Jean Mocquet 1601). The Spanish Army moving up into the desert during the 1957–8 fighting.

FIGURES

# Introduction

This general study attempts to provide a broad summary of knowledge on Spanish Sahara. It has drawn heavily on Spanish publications and, to a lesser degree, on those of French specialists working in the surrounding territories. It is also hoped that the resulting synthesis will both give a useful background to research and suggest still-unexamined fields of enquiry.

The territory is three-fifths the size of Spain, or the same area as Great Britain. The administration's most recent population estimate is of 59,777 Saharauis and 16,648 Spaniards, a figure officially said to include all military personnel; this is one person to $3\frac{1}{2}$ sq km, the most lightly populated state in Africa. The boundary is political, the region's geographical limits being most naturally the Draa River and Anti-Atlas mountains to the north and the Senegal River and the Sudan to the south. In practice, study cannot be limited to the Spanish territory, since all aspects, except those following on Spain's presence, extend beyond the frontiers. It will also be necessary to describe the histories of Spanish Southern Morocco and of Ifni, respectively relinquished in 1956–8 and 1969, since their pasts were closely involved with that of the desert territory. Similarly relevant is the development of the frontier towns of the adjacent states of Morocco and Mauritania, especially of the latter's port of Nouadhibou.

The book will show that, for most of the period since late medieval times, human activity in the coastal desert has been in two quite distinct cultural streams, African and European; contact has been either accidental, as by shipwreck, or has been for gain, by force or trade. The Spaniards, present since 1884, have in the last two decades found it politically expedient to bring about a limited intermingling of the two cultural streams; the Europeans' culture will only be described in so far as it has become a part of that of the Saharauis.

However, during the same period the coast has been replaced, as the zone of conflict, by the inland boundary: on one side the colonial administration and its supporters, on the other those Africans who would prefer to see the Saharauis independent or a part of one of the adjacent states. To the Spaniards, possession of the territory is a matter of pride and a source of phosphates; further, its loss would allow Morocco to concentrate its claims on Ceuta and Melilla and would also lay bare the Canary Islands. So, in the middle of the 1970s, Spain has stayed to share with Rhodesia and South Africa in the final stage of the European colonial cycle. For a while longer, the future of the Saharauis remains unresolved.

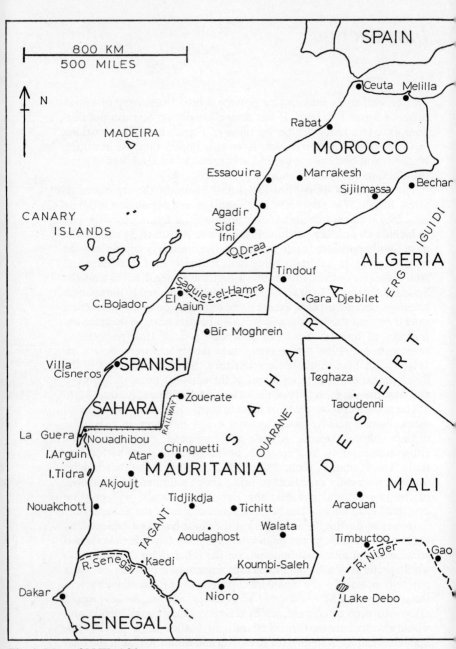

Fig. 2. Map of N.W. Africa

# Chapter 1

# Geology and the Landscape

'A Sandy Plain . . . Inhabited only by Wild Beasts,' wrote Le Maire of the western Sahara in the seventeenth century. 'These Desarts reach to Mount Atlas on the North, and to the country of the Negroes to the South . . . from East to West they can't be passed on Horseback in fifty days. By this way, the Caravans of Fex pass to Tombut, Melly, Borneo . . . When a storm rises . . . the Sand Buries Men and Camels, and often the Stuffs, and filling up the Pits by the way, the Passengers Dye with Thirst; as there is no beaten Path there, they make use of the Compass as at Sea.'

This chapter will describe the natural features of Spanish Sahara, a part of the Sandy Plain. A section giving the map coverage is included for those travelling through this vast and often empty territory. Chapter 11 discusses the mineral prospection and mining by Europeans and Americans, together with a section on the salt-pans and wells.

## Solid Geology

Africa itself, in summary, is built upon a rigid pre-Cambrian basement of crystalline rocks which have been both highly metamorphosed and intruded by plutonics of various ages. Upon the basement lie many long sedimentary sequences, marine and continental according to region. Volcanic activity has been concentrated in the equatorial zone. Erosion has led to peneplanation of most of the continent, though with some subsequent rejuvenation; thus, though generally stable since the pre-Cambrian, regions of Africa have undergone massive tectonics, such as raised the Atlas mountains in the Tertiary period. The coastline, following the continent's separation from the rest of the Gondwanaland block, and lesser subsequent alterations, has remained effectively unchanged since the Cretaceous.

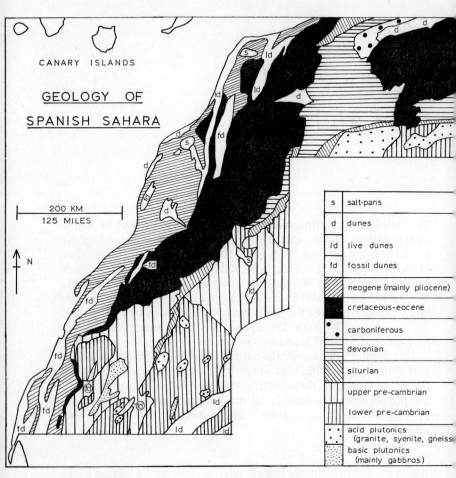

| s | salt-pans |
| d | dunes |
| ld | live dunes |
| fd | fossil dunes |
| | neogene (mainly pliocene) |
| | cretaceous-eocene |
| | carboniferous |
| | devonian |
| | silurian |
| | upper pre-cambrian |
| | lower pre-cambrian |
| | acid plutonics (granite, syenite, gneiss) |
| | basic plutonics (mainly gabbros) |

CANARY ISLANDS

GEOLOGY OF
SPANISH SAHARA

200 KM
125 MILES

N

Fig. 3. Sketch-map of the Geology of Spanish Sahara

Looked at overall, Africa is now a vast plateau with a few widely separated mountain ranges.

Spanish Sahara has a typical African sequence, though the area is without vulcanicity and was barely affected by other than the earliest tectonic movements. The pre-Cambrian basement, probably over 2,500 million years (m.y.) old, is exposed across a third of the territory, an interior zone some 900 km along its NE–SW axis and up to 350 km broad in its main region, the Tiris in the south-east. The latter is a meseta which slopes down gently from 350–250 m above sea-level to the littoral zone. According to Alia (1946), the Tiris is a planed-down NE–SW anticline, linked to the Araouan–Taoudeni syncline in N Mali and to other formations to their north. The Spanish Sahara basement rocks are highly metamorphosed sediments divisible into two groups, one of earlier gneisses and the other of later schists and slates. Intruded into these are extensive plutonic rocks, both acid and basic, mainly granites, syenites, diorites and gabbros. The basement has undergone complex pre-Cambrian folding and faulting, with some zones rising and others sinking, but was too rigid to be affected by the later tectonics; these did however act upon the north of the territory, as will be described. In general, the older Spanish Sahara formations are oriented NE–SW, including the coastline and its two massive fractures at Villa Cisneros and La Guera. Peneplanation stage has been reached by the basement, but the hard intrusives, though often highly eroded too, do frequently provide sharp relief, commonly as abrupt black humps or as ridges stretching NE–SW and, like the Kudia Zug, standing a few hundred metres above the hazy roses and sepias of the Tiris meseta. These formations' important iron deposits will be described in the chapter on prospection.

The Palaeozoic marine transgression of the lower, northerly part of the continent covered all or most of the territory; though the pre-Cambrian basement is visible over the south-east, this is due in part at least to the erosion of the Palaeozoic cover. The main area of Palaeozoic sediments to remain exposed lies in the north-east, inland of Smara; from Ordovician to Carboniferous in age (500–280 m.y. ago), they consist of quartzites, slates, sandstones and limestones. The earlier, Ordovician and Silurian, penetrate into the N Tiris, showing a metamorphism which increases southwards until they are hard to tell from the basement; the later sediments, Devonian and Carboniferous, hold abundant and well-preserved fossils, for example the brachiopods in the Upper Devonian around Smara. The Ordovician–Carboniferous sequence was deposited by a retreating, increasingly-shallow sea. To the south-east of Smara there is an extensive

area of plutonic granite of Carboniferous age. The Hercynian tecton-
ism (about 280–250 m.y. ago) affected the Ordovician to Middle
Devonian of the Zemmour zone, resulting in a labyrinthine relief,
now highly eroded; otherwise the Palaeozoic sediments lie more or
less horizontally, with little folding.

From the Carboniferous (ended 280 m.y. ago), the Palaeozoic
territory was dry land under intensive erosion and by the Cretaceous
it had reached peneplanation stage. At this point the Cretaceous–
Eocene sea in turn overwhelmed the thick, lower-lying palaeozoic
deposits, covering a coastal arc running the length of Spanish Sahara
and at its maximum of 200 km broad at Cape Bojador, together with
the Tindouf Depression in the north-east. The eroded Palaeozoic
sediments, often dark in colour, are overlaid unconformably by the
light-coloured deposits of this later sea. These are of shallow, littoral
type, mainly sandstones, marls and limestones, easily separable by
their various characteristics, especially the changing colours; good
sections are to be seen in the Saguiet-el-Hamra watercourse and on
the inner, eastern face of the Villa Cisneros peninsula. The deposits
are rich in fossils, especially of fish and molluscs; drilling during the
recent phosphate and oil prospections has also yielded foraminifera.
These Cretaceous–Eocene sediments, effectively as horizontal as
when deposited, result in an angular landscape of extensive flats, or
*hammadas*, separated by slopes, with the more resistant layers deciding the land-forms.

The Tindouf Depression, the most complicated feature of the
region's geology, shows the full sequence of the described crystalline
and sedimentary rocks. The Depression straddles NE Spanish
Sahara, the adjacent parts of Mauritania and Algeria and the eastern
end of Morocco's Tarfaya province. Alia (1945) studied the formation in the now-Moroccan sector and in the north-east of Spanish
Sahara. The result of a major pre-Palaeozoic sinking of the continental
basement, the ENE–WSW Depression's outer rim is built of Pre-
Cambrian rocks, visible for example on the south in the cover-eroded
Yetti–Eglab zone; the northern margin, amongst the Anti-Atlas, is
less clear. Within these and overlying them unconformably come the
Palaeozoic sediments; on the north side, good examples are the
Moroccan *djebels* of Janfra, Zini and Uarksis, an arc of mountains
concave to the south-east; in the south the sequence, differing a little,
can be seen along Alia's Erguegua–Smara and Tifariti–Farsia tra-
verses. The limited Cambrian sea left deposits in the northern zone
only. Carboniferous sediments are lacking in the south. Another
difference between the two zones is that the northern sediments are
folded and tilt outwards until the Lower Devonian, thereafter dipping

to the south, whereas the southern deposits tilt inwards throughout, increasingly so as one goes towards the centre of the basin; the comparative instability of the northern zone, on the edge of the African basement, may be the reason. The centre of the depression holds the horizontal Cretaceous–Eocene sediments – the Tindouf Hammada. The north-west marine deposits, also upon the crystalline basement, lie in a second, equally-vast pre-Palaeozoic basin, the NNE–SSW Aaiún Depression; stretching into the Atlantic, with a depth there of perhaps 3000 m, its further border appears to be formed by the E Canaries. Between the two basins there is thought to lie a 'threshold', the Smara Arc, a curve, concave to the south-east, surfaced with early Primary deposits corresponding to the time of the highest Palaeozoic sea-level.

The retreat of the sea during the Eocene (ended 38 m.y. ago) was followed by a comparatively short phase of erosion, closed by a new phase of marine transgression beginning in the Miocene period (26–7 m.y. ago); though the rock materials and colours resemble those of the previous high sea-level, the division is marked in the beds by a clear unconformity. The new transgression, which encroached at the most a hundred kilometres into the present territory, left shallow-water deposits, correspondingly; these are sandstones, marls and limestones. They are so fossiliferous as to be in places little else but consolidated shells, particularly of pectens, oysters and various gastropods; teeth of Miocene fish (*Hemipristis serra* and *Sphyrna prisca*) have been found in a sandstone at the coastal well of Agdul, north of Argub. There are also reef-like limestones, probably formed by lime-secreting weeds. Inshore sediments of Pliocene age (7–2 m.y. ago) follow upwards; pale tones of yellow and red, fossiliferous, they are often simply banks of barely-consolidated sand, up to 15 m thick. The resulting landscape is a scaled-down version of the exposed Cretaceous–Eocene terrain; it descends gradually to the present coast.

The sediments of the last transgressions have most often been studied along the Villa Cisneros peninsula; now averaging 20 m above sea-level, this is joined to the mainland by an isthmus in places only 2 m above the tide-line. Monod (1945) gives the sequence recorded in 1911 by the Catalan Font y Sagué:

(5) On the top, thin bands of red clay with sub-fossil snail *Helix duroi*

(4) A metre of lime-cemented sands with perfectly preserved littoral fossils, some with traces of colour; these and the layer below include many still-living molluscs and fish, the most common of

the latter being *Carchorodon rondeleti*, a shark known since the Pliocene

(3) Yellowish or reddish limestone, in places with oyster conglomerate. Monod puts this level in the Pleistocene (began 2 m.y. ago) though earlier geologists had suggested the Miocene

(2) Quartzose sandstone, ferruginous, multi-coloured, with silicified wood. The explorer Quiroga (1886) recorded abundant trunks, opalised, up to 2 m by 25 cm in size, giving them a Pliocene age

(1) Blue-green or blue-yellow gypsiferous marls. Monod dates this and the layer above as Pliocene.

Late Tertiary dry-land deposits corresponding to the lower zones of the described marine sediments have been located in the centre of Spanish Sahara by Alia (1954). These form the *hammadas* of Negyir, Carb Tichia, Semamit and Carb Afdira, at the level of Villa Cisneros; they mark the boundary between the pre-Cambrian zone and that of the later northerly sediments. The sequence, fossil-lacking, consists of variably coloured clays and sandstones, often ferruginous as on the coast. In places these lie upon the superficially similar Cretaceous–Eocene deposits and are distinguishable from them by their lesser consolidation and lack of siliceous levels; in their lowest strata they in fact include material derived from the older sediments. A hundred kilometres further east, the Agsumal–Tagsumalet humps also show Miocene continental *hammada*, but directly upon the pre-Cambrian; the protected surface of the latter is now some 70 m above the surrounding peneplain.

Sedimentary sequences dating from the Cretaceous can be seen in some of the territory's sunken salt-pans. Hernandez-Pacheco (1942) studied the north side of the Tah *sebkha* on the frontier above El Aaiún. The base of his section now averages 50 m below sea-level, the top 25 m above; the lowest 20 m are grey marls passing up into 45 m of yellow clays with small oysters at the beginning, followed by a 5 m bed of marine sandstones and limestones, with various lamellibranchs, which is probably Pliocene. These are sealed in by the present surface, a few metres of desert travertine.

The Quaternary period saw the cutting of four or five coastal terraces during moments of stationary high sea-levels, comparatively minor transgressions. According to Hernandez-Pacheco (1961), the highest or Sicilian, tilted, stands at 120–100 m and is to be seen as a vast flat running inland from the present cliff's edge; the surface rock is a cross-bedded sandstone 2–4 m thick, rich in littoral and beach molluscs. A typical example occurs at Peña Grande, 200 km north of Villa Cisneros. Consolidated beach deposits near the Ausialet well to the south of C. Bojador, at 85–50 m, are described as Milazzian. A clearer terrace, Tyrrhenian, at 35–30 m, extends over great stretches of the coast, for example around Jatut-el-Bar some 80 km north of Villa Cisneros; the bed is 3–4 m thick and rich in fossils, such as pectens and oysters. The next terrace, at 18–15 m, First Monastirian, is visible just to the north of C. Bojador; it holds little but whelks and has been much eroded. Finally comes a very recently cut water-level, now at 4–3 m above the sea.

The other Quaternary development has been the dunes, divisible into two groups. From El Aaiún southwards, the coastal plains hold long narrow zones of consolidated Pliocene–Pleistocene sands, the best-known being the Aguerguer between Villa Cisneros and La Guera; much eroded by the trade winds, the undercut jagged humps, sometimes travertine-coated, at present stand a maximum of twelve metres above the plain. These cemented sands, now brown, lie conformably upon the Tertiary marine sediments; they contain battered shells and can often be followed horizontally into the strata of the Quaternary raised shorelines. The other group of sands is made up of those alive today, such as the yellow crescentic dunes which block the course of the Saguiet-el-Hamra at the lower end of El Aaiún. Small patches of active dunes can be found all over the territory but are extensive only in the north-west and, as the notorious Azefal, in the south-east below the Mauritanian Adrar.

*Landscape*

Three ranges, the Moroccan Atlas, 4,165 m, Guinea's Fouta Djallon, 1,538 m, and the Algerian Ahoggar, 2,918 m, enclose a plain some 2,000 km across and averaging 400 m above sea-level. The NW coastal corner is taken up by Spanish Sahara, its coast 1,062 km long, its inland frontier zigzagging over 1,570 km, resulting in an area of 266,000 sq km; the territory's highest point is in the south-west, 435 m, the summit of the Amarrasit massif in the Adrar Soutouf. Riley, wrecked on the coast in 1815 and held captive by the nomads for two months, described the essence of the territory: 'A smooth surface, consisting partly of solid rocks . . . and in some places of soil, baked down as hard as marble . . . a light reddish brown'.

The stepped stony plains, roughly divisible into the lower or *reg* and upper or *hammada*, rise slowly from the coast towards the interior, with a maximum of about 400 m in the broken-up Zemmour massif. In the north the lower slopes of the Moroccan *djebels* break up the flats, in the south the Tiris plateau is enlivened by the dark spikes and ridges of the granitic *guelbs*, with the tall cliffs of the Mauritanian Adrar, 500 m average, defining the South-east corner of the frontier. Outside these areas the traveller will often find himself upon a flat brown stony plain, utterly featureless in all directions, other than for the lakes, ravines and hills of the mirages; in the words of one of Alia's guides, it is 'a land where a glass of tea at a distance can equally well look like a camel or like a hill', for lack of any object for comparison. A tree, usually the white-spine acacia, can be seen at thirty kilometres; the focus of excitement and speculation, it changes its shape, grows larger, smaller again, and is at last reached. A tree, a *real* tree! Greedily the traveller looks ahead, to be disappointed, for there is *nothing* in front now. The nomad, often in his own new Santana Land-Rover, will be sent into a frenzy by a running speck on the horizon: one of the last gazelle, not fast enough at 70 kph, to be gradually shot to pieces with bird pellets. Though the massive exquisitely-shaped dunes, *erg*, are limited to the coast and to the south-east's whitish Azefal, extensive sandy zones occur in many places and are difficult to cross in vehicles.

Sunk into the land are a few watercourses and many salt-pans. Of the former, which run rarely but then are usually in spate, the Saguiet-el-Hamra is of importance. Its name means 'the red channel', after the colour of its walls; it rises at El Farsia, 350 km from the sea in a straight line, and, draining some 65,000 sq km, has a bed four kilometres wide in its lower reaches. At El Aaiún its course is usually blocked by a dazzling spread of fused crescent dunes, blown in by the trade wind, so that after rain the town looks out upon a rubbish-festooned lagoon enlivened by flocks of shelduck and flamingoes. Otherwise the drainage network is poorly developed; after rain in the Tiris, for example, much of the water lies in sheets until it evaporates.

The many salt-collecting depressions, *sebkhas*, seem of various origins. Some are merely hollows without drainage. Those inland, such as Ijil, are probably due to early tectonic movement, those on the coast to more recent subsidence; underground erosion by water has also been suggested. Bights such as the bays of Villa Cisneros and Nouadhibou have probably been through a salt-pan phase. The best-known coastal *sebkha* is Tah, the Collapsed. It covers 375 sq km at the west end of the Moroccan frontier, with a length of 35 km and a width of up to 15 km; the treacherous bed of clay and shining salt, a maximum of 55 m below sea-level, can be reached by climbing down cuts in the steep, terraced sides, 75 m high. The archaeologist Almagro (1945) noted that at least the north-west pans of Taruma and Um Seikira appear to have sunk since the Neolithic, since their 'now-uninhabitable' beds have sites upon them; more definite perhaps is his report of a tumulus-tomb, at Um Seikira, which has seemingly been left fractured and on a terrace by subsidence.

*Shore*

The coast has been shaped by various factors: the generally horizontal nature of the sedimentary rocks and their various consistencies; the changes in sea-level, ultimately the recent three-metre rejuvenation; severe erosion by the sea and the NNE–SSW trade winds; sand deposition; and, to a very small extent, by freshwater erosion, for example at the mouths of the Saguiet-el-Hamra and Wadi Craa. Down to C. Bojador the low coastal plain slopes on to an interminable beach, but, further south, to C. Leven, comes a zone of rarely-climbable cliffs, up to 125 m high, these falling however to a third of this height along the southern half of the territory's coast. Distinctive features are few.

Set back on the notorious cape, the tall slender Bojador lighthouse is at present dedicated to Henry the Navigator, his mariners the first Europeans to pass that point, in 1434; sand-drifted brown and buff cliffs, up to eighty metres high, stretch southwards, the contact zone of the lower clays and upper sandy sediments being marked by green plants around minute springs, inaccessible.

Some three hundred kilometres further south, the Villa Cisneros promontory, with its low, embayed isthmus, is about forty kilometres long; it has a great beach on the outer side, and, on the inner, cliffs eroding so fast that a fallen block on the shore below was once seen to show car-wheel marks. At the back of the bay, ten kilometres wide, is the flat-topped rocky islet of Herne, twenty metres high, joined to the land by sand at low tide; some historians have proposed that it was the Cerne Island described in Hanno's 'Periplus' of the fifth century.

Notorious in legend and history, this shore has been the end of many ships, the most famous the *Meduse* on the Arguin Bank, the most recent the Spanish grain-ship, the *Monte Altube*, in 1972, just north of Tarfaya: the hazards are unyielding wind and current, a shallow and violent sea, in places with reefs, and fog, a shapeless or deceptively-shaped coastline – for example False C. Bojador – and even abnormal refraction and a magnetic anomaly, both effective when offshore. Wrecks litter the coast, with the masts of a German World War I merchant-shipping raider, sunk by a British cruiser, visible off Punta Durnford, near Villa Cisneros. Bays are totally lacking over the northern third. The first inlet reached, Peña Grande, is much used by fishing boats. Below the Villa Cisneros bight comes the bag-shaped Gulf of Cintra, twenty kilometres across, with fishermen's seasonally-occupied shacks; just around the southern tip lies the abandoned fish-meal and seaweed-processing factory of Gorrei, its sheltering promontory marked by a vertical whale-bone. Finally, the weathered C. Blanc peninsula, with a humpy topography of decomposing and shapeless fossil dunes interspersed with rippling hillocks of fine yellow sand. Its point is faced by a slope of white sand, 25 m high, at the foot of which a few rare monk seals fish and sun themselves. The Spanish have a poor anchorage in the La Guera hook, the Mauritanians fairly good harbours at Point Central and Nouadhibou within the Baie du Levrier; this is a triangular bay as long as that of Villa Cisneros but with a mouth 20 km wide. The inner, eastern half of C. Blanc, scourged for much of the year by the sand-wind, consists of salty mud-flats leading into weedy shallows with paddling herons and pelicans.

## Sea-bed

The land formations continue below the sea, the immediate bed usually of gently-sloping sands upon sedimentary rocks. The result is an extensive continental platform – one of the world's best fishing grounds – with the 200 m depth only reached off La Guera at 120 km to the west, the widest shelf between Casablanca and the Senegal. Off Spanish Sahara it is narrowest at False C. Bojador, becoming 500 m deep at 20 km, with depths of over 2,500 m between there and the eastern Canaries. A steep slope, up to 1:7 off the Saguiet-el-Hamra mouth, reported from about the hundred-metre mark, has been proposed as the limit of a late Tertiary or early Quaternary phase of land recovery. In the Villa Cisneros bay the bottom averages 10 m deep at the level of Punta Argub: the town's anchorage can only be reached through tortuous channels in the sand. The B. du Levrier is much the same. The Arguin Bank is only 10 m deep when 40 km out from C. Arguin; probably due to differential erosion of the sedimentary rocks of the bed, there are also abrupt drops to as much as a hundred metres, to the detriment of the fishermen's nets. The current Africa Pilot records that a channel 15 m deep has now been cleared to the Point Central ore-loading jetty, though a sunken French cruiser, the *Chasseloup Laubat*, apparently continues its half-century as a hazard in the B. du Levrier.

## The Sea

'Beyond this Cape [Bojador] there is no race of men . . . nor is the land less sandy than the deserts of Libya . . . and the sea is so shallow that a whole league from land it is only a fathom deep, while the currents are so terrible that no ship, having once passed the Cape, will ever be able to return', or so the medieval mariners assured Prince Henry. The terrible current, now the Canary Current, is the 38°–20°N part of the clockwise North Atlantic current, in the SW-going sector between Portugal and the C. Verde Islands; its rate averages 11 nautical miles a day off Spanish Sahara, this and its direction varying with the zone and the surface-driving trade winds. Between C. Draa and C. Juby, ships get an oblique onshore pull with the perpetual south-east-going swell behind them – and, as the Canary narrows are approached, the current can increase to six knots.

Sea temperature is in turn affected by the Canary Current. First, the water brought from the North Atlantic is cold; second, to compensate for the slight slope in sea-level resulting from the trades-induced displacement to the south-west of surface water, deep cold water moves back below the surface to the coastal region – notably in the Guera zone – and incidentally brings nourishment to the myriad fish of the continental shelf. The result is a sea cool for its latitude, with the mean surface temperatures irregular:

|  | *February* | *May* | *August* | *November* |
|---|---|---|---|---|
| C. Juby | 17° | 17° | 21° | 20° |
| C. Bojador | 18° | 18° | 22° | 20° |
| Villa Cisneros | 17° | 19° | 21° | 20° |
| La Guera | 17° | 18° | 21° | 20° |

Lower salinity than in the north is another result of these factors; it averages thirty-six grams per litre, almost two grams less than around Tenerife, for example.

*Freshwater Resources*
Surface water is limited to the El Aaiún lagoon and to other temporary pools such as the *daya* of Teli and those of Guelta Zemmour; the famed *guelta* are three basins in the Palaeozoic rock, one above the other, lasting the local people at least six months if filled by a rain-storm. The salt pans also collect rainwater. There is often good water under the dry river beds. It has been suggested that a third of the territory's rain evaporates, a third runs into the sea, the last third filters into the ground.

The water-table varies with the region, the many factors including climate, topography, permeability, strata-sequence and underground inter-connection with other areas. The zone of the south-east base-ment has the worst forms of all of these, though it does hold some good water, as the few wells show, for example at Zug, the most remote, sunk twelve metres into the granite and yielding 40 cu m a day; in this region, water is most likely to be found at the base of dykes and outcrops.

The level Palaeozoic table-lands, in the north-east, receive most rain and, as this often falls on winter nights, filtration downwards is comparatively good; however, only the Silurian–Devonian transition zone and some parts of the Carboniferous have the right strata sequence, so the water is deep down except towards a slender arc of outcrops running from west to north-east of Tifariti.

The post-Palaeozoic sediments do have the conditions and the water. The lowest water-levels lie amongst the detritus of Jurassic and Lower Cretaceous age which formed in the valleys of the folded and raised Palaeozoic sediments of the interior; more water-tables exist amongst the permeable-impermeable alternation of level beds of Cretaceous to Miocene age, with the later Cretaceous deposits also extending over the earliest, detrital zone in the interior. However, whilst some water is sweet, like that in the later Lower Cretaceous, other deposits are salty, such as the earlier Cretaceous table; a certain vagueness over this may be of political origin, since Spain has made much of its achievement, by 1970, of locating and raising 50,000 cu m a day in a territory which recently produced only a fiftieth as much.

The most important level, the so-called Villa Cisneros Table, lies in fact within the vast Aaiún Depression, in the early Tertiary sediments. Nearest the surface on the rim, inland, and with its deepest point at 900 m under the coast halfway between Villa Cisneros and C. Bojador, the table is vast and accessible, yielding abundant water. It connects over its southern half with the sweet and even greater Cretaceous level and so can draw upon it too. Further, it seems that a fault with block-sinking of the seabed to the west of the Villa Cisneros coast has sealed off the main water-bearing strata, avoiding both loss and the entry of sea-water; on the other hand, a similar fault in the bay itself, causing the peninsula area to be twenty metres below the mainland, has still left the two sides of the water-table in contact over a vertical reach of forty metres. It is estimated that Villa Cisneros now taps a table of 6,000 sq km; the first of its new wells, Hassi Franco, 425 m deep, was said to give 5,000 cu m of good water a day, at a temperature of 36°C and with 80 m pressure – it flooded the town, in fact, on 5 October 1963.

The only natural sign of these water deposits had been the seepage from the faces of the sedimentary sea-cliffs and *hammada* walls; notable examples of the latter are to be seen in each face of the Saguiet-el-Hamra, salty from the right bank and sweeter from the extensive clay zone on which El Aaiún is built. Generally, the territory's water is suffused with salts, the degree varying on either side of palatability. The recent discovery of the vast water deposits is of major importance both to the lives of the settled and nomadic populations –

domestically and in animal-rearing and crop-growing – and to industries such as the phosphate mining.

*Mapping*
For military and prospection reasons, modern mapping of the territory began soon after the Civil War, in 1943–9. Lack of vehicles and fuel meant that an area the size of Great Britain had to be surveyed by camel. The astro team, spending 1943–7 fixing the 200 triangulation points, suffered from severe cold at night; on a traverse of the Yetti zone, twenty-seven of the mapping team's thirty-five camels died. In 1952 there appeared the fourteenth and last sheet of the map, at 1:500,000; reductions to 1:1 m (1958) and 1:2 m (1951) were made. Only the last (1961 edition, showing the newly-marked Ijil and Tarfaya frontiers) is possibly still available; it has been used for positions, distances and so on in this book, with the Spanish orthography retained. Some non-Spanish maps exist, for example one by the US Army at 1:2 m (1968); it gives contours but is otherwise less detailed than those described.

Alia produced the first geological map, 1:2 m (1952), modestly calling it a 'sketch'. It was altered a little by that of the mining engineers La Viña and Munoz, 1:1½ m (1958). However, the prospections of the last two decades have demanded a highly-detailed knowledge of the topography and geology. So, from the late nineteen-fifties, aeromagnetic survey was carried out over the sedimentary zone. The planes, guided by ultrasonic waves, flew up to eleven hours a day, their height and traverse separation being 150 m and 1 km for iron and 600 m and 4 km for oil; the load was half fuel and half gear, the latter including magnetometer and radioactivity counter and their linked stereoscopic camera. The surface and beds were mapped, the latter to a depth of 5,000 m in the north and to 2,000 m in the south.

It seems that, subsequently, the rest of the territory has been aerially surveyed. In 1961 the prospection zone was given a new geodesic grid; this was used for allocating the oil concessions, the 1,100 vertices delimiting the 70 × 35 km rectangles. New geological maps then began to appear, at 1:200,000; fourteen out of the announced twenty-six had been published by 1971.

A new topographical map, at 1:50,000, was under consideration in 1966. In 1968 such a map was announced – Transversal Mercator, five colours, 20 m contours, 1 km grid – but only for a zone on the northern frontier, 27°–27°40′ N to 10°–11°46′ W, perhaps the territory's most militarily sensitive region.

The surveying of the sea-bed by the Spanish was carried out in

1946–53, the result being published as a set of Fishing Charts at 1:500,000, with isobaths at 50 m, 100 m and then to 600 m at hundred-metre intervals. The Africa Pilot is of the opinion that all the charts of the territory's coast should be used with caution, with care in fixes due to refraction, mirages and the magnetic anomaly, this last increasing compass deviation by about $2\frac{1}{4}°$ between C. Bojador and C. Blanc. Doubtless the current prospections for oil in the sea-bed will lead to a modern set of charts.

# Chapter 2

# Natural History

The Portuguese must be credited with the first earnest notes on the region's wildlife. In 1456 Diogo Gomes, of the Arguin Island trading post, visited a nearby islet, a league around, describing 'a multitude of birds of every kind, and on the ground the nests of pelicans . . . these are not as the painters represent them, but have a broad beak, and a stomach large enough to hold a bushel of wheat'. The desert coast and interior have been accessible now for almost a century and a half-century respectively, but scientific study has been all but limited to Valverde's work. Conservation does not go beyond the occasional official edict. Action in 1975–80 could just save the last of the larger mammals from disappearance.

*Climate*
The existing plants and animals, wrote the ornithologist Valverde (1965), suggest there have been no sweeping climate changes since perhaps the opening of Tertiary times. The two million years of the Quaternary brought the territory at least four climatic oscillations, visible in the sedimentary beds according to Alia (1955). The Aguerguer fossil dunes begin with a brightly-coloured basal layer with abundant snails, laid down in a climate more temperate than the present; upon this comes the dune sand of a drier period; this in turn was cemented in a wetter and also erosive period; finally comes the present time of moving desert sands. Alia tentatively correlates the first dry period with the Tyrrhenian marine terrace, making it contemporary with the Great Interglacial in more northerly latitudes and, also, with Lower Palaeolithic culture. The Saguiet-el-Hamra terraces contain limited evidence of these climatic oscillations. A damper phase than the present, a few thousand years ago and perhaps the later one in the four-stage sequence, is shown by the many Neolithic rock-engravings of elephants, giraffes, cattle and other wetter-zone fauna; similarly, the Neolithic camps were made around bowls and watercourses now utterly dry. Finally, these depressions

Table 1: Climate Statistics, Tarfaya and Nouadhibou

| Tarfaya (Averages) | Air Temp. Daily Max. | Air Temp. Daily Min. | Relative Humidity 0600 | Relative Humidity 1200 | Rain Fall, mm | Rain Days With 0.1 mm | Wind Direction (%) 0600 N | NE | E | W | NW | Calm | Wind Direction (%) 1200 N | NE | E | W | NW | Calm | Wind Speed, Knots, 0700, 1300, 1800 |
|---|---|---|---|---|---|---|---|---|---|---|---|---|---|---|---|---|---|---|---|
| Jan. | 19 | 13 | 86 | 74 | 9 | 3 | 47 | 17 | 5 | 3 | 1 | 18 | 46 | 20 | 4 | 4 | 5 | 5 | 11 |
| Feb. | 20 | 14 | 88 | 78 | 5 | 1 | 49 | 11 | 6 | 4 | 1 | 20 | 48 | 15 | 7 | 9 | 3 | 7 | 12 |
| March | 20 | 15 | 90 | 82 | 4 | 1 | 54 | 14 | 4 | 5 | 6 | 11 | 51 | 13 | 4 | 6 | 10 | 4 | 12 |
| April | 21 | 16 | 89 | 81 | 1 | 1 | 55 | 14 | 4 | 4 | 5 | 14 | 57 | 15 | 1 | 11 | 9 | 5 | 12 |
| May | 21 | 17 | 85 | 80 | + | + | 62 | 11 | 1 | 3 | 10 | 8 | 63 | 14 | 1 | 3 | 12 | 5 | 13 |
| June | 22 | 18 | 88 | 82 | 0 | + | 76 | 13 | 1 | 1 | 5 | 3 | 71 | 16 | 1 | 1 | 5 | 4 | 13 |
| July | 23 | 18 | 91 | 85 | 0 | + | 78 | 18 | 1 | 2 | 0 | 1 | 69 | 18 | 0 | 1 | 5 | 3 | 13 |
| Aug. | 23 | 19 | 92 | 86 | + | + | 78 | 16 | 0 | 0 | 1 | 4 | 71 | 16 | 0 | 2 | 2 | 3 | 12 |
| Sept. | 24 | 19 | 93 | 86 | 7 | 1 | 64 | 17 | 1 | 2 | 0 | 14 | 36 | 10 | 1 | 5 | 2 | 16 | 11 |
| Oct. | 23 | 18 | 90 | 79 | 1 | 1 | 56 | 12 | 1 | 2 | 2 | 21 | 58 | 17 | 0 | 3 | 2 | 12 | 9 |
| Nov. | 23 | 16 | 87 | 76 | 14 | 3 | 52 | 6 | 4 | 0 | 3 | 21 | 51 | 13 | 5 | 4 | 4 | 13 | 8 |
| Dec. | 21 | 14 | 86 | 73 | 8 | 3 | 48 | 10 | 3 | 4 | 3 | 27 | 43 | 18 | 4 | 8 | 4 | 15 | 10 |
| Year Average or Total | 22 | 16 | 89 | 80 | 49 | 14 | 60 | 13 | 2 | 3 | 3 | 14 | 58 | 16 | 2 | 5 | 5 | 8 | 11 |

| Nouadhibou (Averages) | Air Temp. Daily Max. | Air Temp. Daily Min. | Relative Humidity 0600 | Relative Humidity 1200 | Rain Fall, mm | Rain Days With 0.1 mm | 0600 N | NE | E | W | NW | Calm | 1200 N | NE | E | W | NW | Calm | Wind Speed, Knots, 0700 | 1700 |
|---|---|---|---|---|---|---|---|---|---|---|---|---|---|---|---|---|---|---|---|---|
| Jan. | 25 | 13 | 75 | 55 | 2 | 1 | 37 | 25 | 28 | 0 | 4 | 6 | 37 | 17 | 17 | 8 | 14 | 3 | 11 | 12 |
| Feb. | 26 | 14 | 78 | 52 | 1 | 1 | 44 | 25 | 19 | 1 | 6 | 3 | 47 | 7 | 3 | 14 | 21 | 2 | 10 | 13 |
| March | 27 | 15 | 82 | 51 | 1 | + | 44 | 38 | 11 | 0 | 1 | 5 | 16 | 2 | 1 | 16 | 22 | 2 | 14 | 18 |
| April | 26 | 15 | 87 | 53 | 1 | 1 | 47 | 34 | 9 | 0 | 4 | 5 | 13 | 1 | 1 | 17 | 30 | 3 | 12 | 19 |
| May | 28 | 16 | 87 | 52 | + | + | 48 | 37 | 5 | 3 | 5 | 2 | 7 | 0 | 0 | 15 | 34 | 1 | 13 | 19 |
| June | 27 | 17 | 87 | 53 | 1 | + | 72 | 20 | 3 | 1 | 3 | 1 | 10 | 0 | 0 | 25 | 22 | 0 | 14 | 21 |
| July | 29 | 19 | 89 | 64 | + | 1 | 55 | 18 | 4 | 3 | 13 | 6 | 11 | 1 | 0 | 9 | 53 | 3 | 12 | 20 |
| Aug. | 31 | 20 | 88 | 65 | 3 | 2 | 47 | 19 | 5 | 3 | 21 | 3 | 13 | 1 | 0 | 6 | 53 | 2 | 11 | 16 |
| Sept. | 30 | 21 | 84 | 59 | 7 | 2 | 56 | 11 | 13 | 4 | 9 | 4 | 9 | 5 | 1 | 5 | 44 | 4 | 11 | 17 |
| Oct. | 27 | 19 | 85 | 57 | 6 | 1 | 69 | 9 | 13 | 2 | 6 | 1 | 4 | 3 | 0 | 9 | 54 | 0 | 10 | 13 |
| Nov. | 25 | 17 | 84 | 57 | 4 | 1 | 49 | 22 | 15 | 2 | 8 | 3 | 9 | 5 | 0 | 12 | 32 | 11 | 12 | 12 |
| Dec. | 25 | 15 | 75 | 56 | 1 | 1 | 37 | 26 | 20 | 1 | 5 | 9 | 19 | 13 | 3 | 8 | 17 | 14 | 9 | 9 |
| Year Average or Total | 27 | 17 | 83 | 56 | 28 | 10 | 50 | 24 | 12 | 2 | 7 | 4 | 33 | 11 | 4 | 12 | 33 | 4 | 12 | 16 |

do still shelter a sparse relict flora from the last more humid phase.

The causes of these oscillations – generally common to the whole Sahara, of course – have been much debated. The desert lies between two more humid climates, the wet-winter Mediterranean and the wet-summer Equatorial, and one or other, if displaced – not to go further into this – would thus bring on a damper phase. If the sub-tropical high-pressure complex were weakened then depressions would be allowed to move in from north or south more often than at present. One long-standing theory linked African pluvials to northern glacials but recently it has been suggested that the linkage should be pluvial-glacial for the north Sahara and pluvial-interglacial for the south Sahara . . . however, the Spanish territory, halfway down the coast, will need further detailed study.

At present the climate is primarily shaped by the stable sub-tropical high-pressure system. As do so many aspects, the weather includes the southern extremity of the Mediterranean zone, the characteristics fading away down the littoral region. The comparatively-cool trade winds and coastal waters are direct tempering influences, counter-balanced by the vast desert to the east, its effect heightened by the occasional *irifi* wind. The tropic's climate sends a wedge of diminishing intensity north through the interior in the autumn, with deflection eastwards below the Atlas.

Saharauis divide the year into *lekhrif*, two autumnal months when the first rains may fall; then *ista*, the three coolest months, perhaps with rain; *tifiski*, two to three months of moderate heat; then the hot, dry *lesaif*, up to five months of summer. By European preferences, winter along the northern half of the coast provides the best combination. The littoral climate grades between those, represented in Table 1, of Tarfaya and Nouadhibou, now Moroccan and Mauritanian frontier towns; there are no reliable long-term averages available from Spanish Sahara itself. Many of the following details are from travellers' narratives.

Barometric pressure, varying little throughout the year, drops southwards as one moves from the Azores anticyclone zone towards the lows of the Equatorial cyclones. The Tarfaya averages range between 1015 mb in August and 1021 mb in January, those of Nouadhibou 1012–17 mb between the same months.

The littoral temperature averages 2°C cooler than is normal for the latitude; Villa Cisneros, with its recorded maximum at 42°C, is no hotter than Rabat. The Tarfaya extremes have been 40° and 5°C, Nouadhibou's 45° and 7°C. The interior is very different, with a day-night variation of up to thirty-three degrees, the extremes being the 70°C recorded by the explorer Quiroga in 1886 and the zero suffered by the Hernandez-Pacheco expedition in the nineteen-forties. The heat roughens the skin, makes nails brittle, dries the eyes. Table 2 gives temperatures for the south-east frontier zone.

Table 2: *Extreme temperatures of each week, 1973, Zouerate, Mauritania*

|  | January | February | March | April |
|---|---|---|---|---|
| Highest | 27 26 28 31 30 | 31 24 25 34 | 34 34 35 34 | 37 36 33 42 |
| Lowest | 11 10 9 13 11 | 13 8 6 13 | 11 12 9 10 | 18 14 13 15 |

|  | May | June | July | August |
|---|---|---|---|---|
| Highest | 43 43 45 44 43 | 37 42 41 44 | 41 46 46 45 46 | 46 43 46 45 |
| Lowest | 14 23 15 20 19 | 18 19 18 18 | 18 19 20 23 24 | 28 21 22 22 |

|  | September | October | November | December |
|---|---|---|---|---|
| Highest | 43 43 42 39 | 39 39 37 33 | 31 37 34 31 | 31 23 22 25 22 |
| Lowest | 23 15 16 16 | 17 14 21 16 | 14 22 18 14 | 12 5 9 10 9 |

Relative humidity drops southwards and eastwards, particularly during the hotter part of the day. Smara's daily range is 72–41 % in January, 77–36 % in August, falling southward during the latter month to as low as 15 % at Atar, just in Mauritania. The *irifi* wind brings this desert dryness to the coast.

Low coastal clouds take the form of strato-cumulus and occasionally cumulo-nimbus; early-morning white cumulus, driven at 100–300 m by the trades, disappears by noon. Above these, around 2,000 m, and going in the opposite direction, there is cirrus and alto-cumulus cloud. On the north coast, the maximum coverage reached is about seven oktas at 0600 hours in summer, the minimum three oktas at noon in spring and autumn; the south coast averages a steady three oktas at all times and seasons. In the interior the sky is usually almost empty. When the temperature is low, as at dawn, the horizon's clouds will glow with colour; in summer the twilight can be struck through by lightning flashes from transient storm clouds. The frequent coastal fog, mist and dew are the result of the temperature inversion caused by the sea rapidly cooling the lowest 500 m or so of the atmosphere each night; a day or two's fog is recorded each month at Tarfaya and Nouadhibou, the least in the north and in summer.

The drought of the early nineteen-seventies, a regularly-recurring event at last discovered by the European and American media, in fact affected Spanish Sahara as severely as any of the desert territories. Around the well of Sebaiera, near the centre of the interior frontier, the author saw many fresh camel-skeletons. By making the State-subsidised life in the towns more attractive, this drought is the Spaniards' crucial ally in their attempt to sedentarise the nomads and thereby bring them to depend upon the colonial administration. However, though at intervals of up to six years, it does rain, for example in 1957 when the Saguiet-el-Hamra overflowed, with fourteen dead and many animals and tents washed away. A usual sequel is a massive outbreak of influenza amongst the humans and deaths from over-drinking amongst the camels. Tracks, including the essential route to Tan-Tan in S Morocco, become impassable. In 1965 the Smara people swam in Wadi Selouan; in fact, the interior seems to get slightly more rain than the coast.

The most famous deluge gave rise to the 'Sea of Daora', a depression crossed by the traveller between the north-west frontier post and El Aaiún. On 4–5 September 1944 the rain turned it into a lake up to twelve kilometres across and averaging five metres deep, marooning a group of Saharauis on a hump and drowning camels, sheep and goats; the army rescued the people in a rubber boat. The Daora *alcazaba*, a mud-walled fort built by the Izarguien tribe in the last century, and the Spaniards' first base in the region, simply disintegrated.

If rain is a curse by its absence, the wind is a plague all too present. The trades, driving the swell down the coast, do however bring their coolness. The feared *irifi*, often compared to the harmattan and sirocco winds, blows off the desert at any season except winter; reaching 100 kph, it lasts from twelve hours to six days, with the temperature usually in the forties and relative humidity down to 10 per cent. A weather observer from Villa Cisneros was once caught by the *irifi* on the southern border: the horizon turned to turbid reds and ochres, the temperature of the July night rose from 25° to 45° in two hours, whilst he, under threat of being engulfed by the driving sand, noted down his increased dehydration as he sweated with fear. The *irifi* forces birds and insects to the shore and, if persistent, the last wild mammals too. Less severe but probably more effective as an erosive agent – on human life as on the rocks – is the sand-wind which blows from Villa Cisneros to the Senegal. Every day during the hotter half of the year, once the dew-compacted surface has been powdered by the climbing sun, the wind gathers the dust and sand, the particles up to 1·5 mm across, driving these into the houses and – but for their face-cloths and, sometimes, goggles – into the eyes of the Saharauis. This wind once gave Villa Cisneros a nickname: 'Villa Neurosos', Neurotics' Town. When the carrying wind is the *irifi*, then twisting sand-columns several hundred metres wide – the legendary *djinns* – come writhing in across the desert, visibility drops to 50 m, with the sun obscured, and the lighter dust settles on passing ships and in the

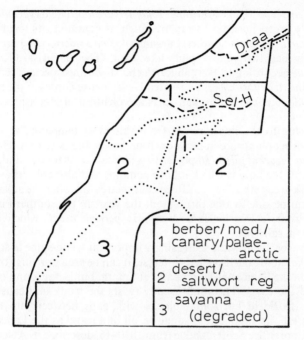

Fig. 4. Flora and Fauna Zones

Canaries. By the side of this, the occasional tornado – such as visited Villa Cisneros for twenty minutes on 26 September 1961, demolishing buildings and injuring many people – might well seem refreshing.

*Vegetation*
Plant life is limited to highly-adapted species in favoured places. Attempts have been made at zonation but the comparatively-uniform territory's flora changes only very gradually from the S. Morocco-Canary species along the north-west coast into the sparse trees and grasses of the plains of the south-west interior, these suggestive of the animal-rich savannas much further south.

Thus, the traveller finds the coastal zone around the mouth of the Saguiet-el-Hamra to be characterised by several euphorbias, notably the cactus-like *E. echinus, dagnus,* a low and rounded grey hump, of thick spike-armoured stalks, which opens out as it gets older, reaching 1·50 m in height; it holds the poisonous euphorbia latex and is not eaten by anything. *E. balsamifera, fernan,* can reach three metres high. Other Canary families include *Limonium, Frankenia* and

*Teucrium*. The thicket-forming *Rhus tripartitum* (*R. oxyacantha*), a straggly green bush up five metres high, is common; its local name is *schdari*. The most southerly argans (*Argania sideroxylon*) are seen; animals eat the yellow plum-like fruit. The tamarisk (*Tamarix balansae* according to Hernandez-Pacheco, various species according to Guinea), or *tarakhe*, is widespread, with dense copses in the mouth of the Saguiet-el-Hamra. Saltworts are plentiful, if inconspicuous in this area.

Moving to the interior *regs* from this most temperate zone, the commonest plants are in fact now found to be the saltworts. The *afsu* (*Aizoon theurkauffii*) is important to animals as a fodder and, even more, for the liquids which it both contains and also collects as dew; the dark green stalks, up to fifteen centimetres tall, offer the advantage of maturing one by one throughout the year. In the southern half of the territory's interior it is *Nucularia perrini*, *ascaf*, which is the dominant saltwort.

However, by now the increasingly important white-spine acacia (*A. raddiana*) holds the traveller's interest; it can be seen growing strongly down in the Saguiet-el-Hamra and at Smara, but is not found on any part of the coast. The wind usually twists the trunk and causes the foliage to lie in horizontal blocks with gaps between; up to ten metres tall, its silhouette is squat or 'all of a rook' as the Lancashire ship's apprentice Scott, captive from 1810–16, described it. Associated with the *talkha* is another smaller acacia, the *taamat* (*A. seyal*). From about the region of the Sebaiera well, where the white-spine acacia grows in an unbroken if thinly-sown belt many kilometres long, the tree shares the land with sand-drifted tufts of *Panicum turgidum* grass, *murkeba*, and, on rocky ground, of *Aristida pungens* or *sbot*. This zone is a degraded savanna, its peak presumably in a time when the tropical weather was more influential.

In the remaining area, the southern and very barren half of the coast, it is the tamarisk which is perhaps most noticeable, vegetation of a comparable size being rare; a tall feathery ·grey-green shrub where conditions are favourable, it is usually reduced here to a dusty contorted tangle in the centre of a *sbar* or sand drift. It can be seen all over Spanish Sahara wherever there is the least moisture, its thickets sometimes extending several kilometres. The salt-loving plants of the northern *regs* extend obliquely south-west to cover this coast also.

Adaptation is seen in many forms. Some plants have an extremely rapid absorption and growth cycle, allowing them to take advantage of momentarily suitable conditions; this brief pasture is known as *acheb* to the nomads. Roots to six metres down have been developed by *Alhagi camellorum*; other plants, for example *Aristida pennata*, have a vast horizontal network. To reduce evaporation, the surface-size of the leaves has usually been cut down, these even turning into the more useful spikes, with the chlorophyll deficiency being counter-acted by making the stalks green as well; in some cases the leaves' skins are very thick, in others they are coated with a moisture-retaining varnish. Yet others have water reservoirs, such as *Nitraria retusa, guerzin,* or like the euphorbias preserve their moisture in the form of latex; *E. echinus*'s domed and compressed shape also keeps evaporation to a minimum.

Habitats vary from the optimum conditions of, say, the Saguiet-el-Hamra mouth, with shelter, underground water and coastal humidity, to the bare *regs* of the interior. The talus around a Tiris *guelb* will usually shelter more plants than does the surrounding meseta; in addition to the acacias, there may be a spread of green to yellow *ilif* gourds (*Citrullus colocynthis*) or the white-flowered *teilun* (*Pancratium trianthum*) to reward the traveller. The dunes have their own vegetation, for example *Euphorbia paralias*, sea-spurge, at El Aaiún beach. Temporary pools, such as that by the capital, bring to life a lagoon flora, including weeds and rushes.

However, the most widespread of the better habitats is the *grara*, a shallow bowl holding alluvium a shade damper than the surrounding plain. The depressions are usually a maximum of 300 m across, but can reach a kilometre. The plants take up position, in concentric rings, according to their preferred moisture level. In the C. Bojador area, the centre of a *grara* would usually hold rushes and grasses. Around this a scattered to dense ring of *Rhus*. With the ground becoming stony, a zone of *Lycium intricatum* or *gardec, Atriplex halinus* or *legtaf,* and other saltworts. Finally, on stony land, *Euphorbia echinus*. The territory's *graras* are important, since they provide permanent, widespread habitats for the wildlife and soil-patches worth sowing with barley for the nomads.

In addition to their value as food for animals and humans, many wild plants are of use to the nomads. To mention here only the acacia, the territory's most memorable tree, it has been tapped for its resin, for export as gum and also for local use in eye trouble, blood clotting and stomach complaints; the wood is chewed to relieve the *iguendi*, brought on by too much salty water; the bark has been used as a scalpel; the berries to give a dye. Increasing sedentarisation makes urgent a study of the nomads' use of plants.

*Animal Distribution*
Until hunted to its imminent extinction from vehicles, by the Spanish,

the bulk of the west Sahara's animal life was to be found in the territory (Valverde 1957). The chief natural factors at present deciding the species and their distribution have been described: habitats with the few natural water supplies, climate and the sparse vegetation. The territory, up to 500 km wide in the north and 350 km in the south, does not quite reach into the Sahara's most lifeless region. Spanish Sahara lies in a transition zone between three overlapping faunal groupings:

(1) From the north, the Palaearctic or, more locally, 'Berber'. This group dominates the *Rhus graras*, tamarisk thickets and euphorbia plains of the north-west, and reaches up the Saguiet-el-Hamra and is important in the Zemmour; typical species include the ground squirrel and the ruddy shelduck. The group's most southerly mammal is a white-toothed shrew (*Crocidura whitakeri*), extending to Villa Cisneros, whilst the golden eagle occurs right down the interior into Mauritania.

(2) The saltwort zone, made up of the northern interior's *regs* and the rest of the coastline. This desert region holds both north-easterly forms such as the Central Asian *Eremophila bilopha* and Saharan species such as *Rhamphocoryx clotbey*, both larks (Valverde 1957). It is the main zone for the houbara bustard. No mammals or other large terrestrial animals seem to have their distribution centres in this inhospitable area, though many from the other two zones can be found in it, especially at favourable times.

(3) The *Acacia-Panicum* savanna of the south-east is the centre for the last of the two species of gazelle and, until their recent extinction, was the final retreat for the oryx, addax and ostrich; the broken-up zones sheltered the mountain sheep, also probably now extinct. To some extent this concentration will be the result of the animals being hunted in the other and more accessible parts of Spanish Sahara, but all five forms do continue south-eastwards beyond the territory.

Nevertheless, there are species which ignore this three-zone division. For example, a relict gecko (*Geckonia chazaliae*) covers the entire coast, whilst the spiny-tailed lizard (*Uromaxtis acanthinurus*) is common right up the interior half, the western limit of its extensive Sahara range. This suggests faunal zones depending primarily on influences from the sea and the eastern desert.

The territory's species live in a network of relationships. Weather conditions, gluts and famines, human interference – such influences send impulses right through the biotope. Though little studied, the most obvious recent occurrences have been recorded: a simple example, the 1952 rodent plague, of unknown cause, had an adverse effect on the hare, ground squirrel, gazelle and man, with only the barn owl, increasingly rapidly, noticeably the better.

## Land Mammals
The territory's rock-engravings, fully described in the next chapter, depict the larger wild animals of the last wet phase: in addition to most of those present into the 1940s, there were four species now long-vanished: antelope (*Alcelaphus*), elephant, rhinoceros, giraffe. Lion, hippopotamus and the ovoviviparus crocodile probably also occurred.

Prior to their motorised slaughter from the 1940s, at least thirty-five different mammals had been recorded for the territory during the preceding hundred years. The six ruminants, seven carnivores, wild boar and badger-like ratel are described below. Less studied locally are the legendary *ganfud* or hedgehog (?*Aethechinus algirus* and ?*Paraechinus deserti*), a widespread hare (*Lepus* sp.) with *L. aegypticus* identified at Villa Cisneros; the ground squirrel (*Atlantoxerus getulus*); five jumping rodents (*Gerbillus riggembachi*, *Dipodillus* sp., *Meriones mariae*, *Pachyuromys duprasi*, *Jacullus j*, all at least in the south); three northern mice or *far* (*Mus* ?*musculus* at El Aaiún, *Elephantulus rozetti* at C. Juby and in the Mauritanian Zemmour, *Eliomys mumbianus* at Villa Cisneros); the brown rat (*Rattus norvegicus*), also called *far*; three white-toothed shrews (the northern *Crocidura whitakeri* down to the tropic, the southern form *C. lusitanica* in the lower Saguiet-el-Hamra, with *C. bolivari*, at Villa Cisneros, being a new species claimed by Morales in 1934 on the grounds of its size, over 85 mm, and peculiar second upper premolar); three differing bats (?*Pipistrellus kuhlii*, a northern species, at El Aaiún). In addition there were lions at least in south Morocco and the now-Mauritanian Zemmour into this century. However, it seems most charitable to assume that the wolves of the current Africa Pilot (1967) were the effect of the 'abnormal coastal refraction' on the territory's jackal, a mistake also made by Scott in 1810.

The largest ruminant, *Addax nasomaculatus*, was last recorded on the Craa flats near Villa Cisneros, in 1940: a photograph shows an army lieutenant standing proudly beside a row of fifteen corpses. The *lemha*, with tall spiral horns and powerful body, used to graze everywhere except the north and Zemmour massif. This antelope still exists in Mali; when the writer was in the Ijil area in 1974, a motorised hunter returned having shot some eighty addax. The sabre-horned oryx (*Orix algazel*, *O. tao*, etc), locally *urkh*, once current up to C. Bojador, was last sighted by the geologist Alia in 1955: a flock of ten or so to the south of the Negyir hills.

In 'Wad Seyghi', Scott saw 'a large beast, almost like a cow,

covered with hair of a grey colour, with large horns, thick at the root
and spreading outwards, a very short tail, and feet like those of a
sheep . . . eaten by the Arabs, who call it *row-y-and'*. The mouflon-
like *arrauit* (*Ammotragus lervia*) is in fact a mountain sheep. Said to
be everywhere in 1949, and still present in 1955 in the hills of the
southern interior, it was by then being persecuted in the absence of
the other disappearing 'more noble' game, Valverde seeing remains
of twenty in one military post.

The brown and white gazelles are all small, the short horns almost
straight in the Moroccan *Gazella cuvieri*, or *kharmus* – seen in the
lower Saguiet-el-Hamra in 1949 – and undulating in the two typical
Spanish Sahara species. The larger of these, the *mohor* (*G. dama*) was
down to a few hundred in 1965 and is perhaps extinct by now in the
territory. The little *guersal* (*G. dorcas*) was seen, up to three at a time,
by the writer in 1974; on the coast between Villa Cisneros and La
Guera, they were probably driven there by the drought, in the same
way as a few hundred went on to the Villa Cisneros peninsula in 1954,
to be shot by the residents. In 1955 they occurred everywhere but the
north-west, in bands of up to twenty, Valverde counting 150 individuals in a twenty-kilometre traverse of the *Aizoon*-covered *reg*; the
author crossed both this and the acacia zone of Sebaiera, on a line El
Aaiún-Ijil, but saw no wild mammals of any species. The gazelles dig
small scoops to sleep in, browse during the day and, when frightened,
first take a long step, then make a leap of three to five metres, then
repeat the alternation up to ten times and finally break into a gallop,
reaching about 70 kph; difficult to see until they start to run, their
white markings then flash in the sun. Their natural enemies are the
leopard, faster at up to 110 kph, and the jackal and hyaena, both
slower than the gazelle.

With the extinction of the plant-eaters goes the reduction in their
predators, of course. The jackal (*Canis aureus*), *dib*, probably still
occurs all over the territory, and Valverde mentions a friend who
killed fifty in 1953–5 on the Villa Cisneros peninsula; hunting at
night, the jackal will eat dead fish, locusts, fruits of *Rhus*, beetles,
leather straps, lizards and all the more defenceless animals, according to place and season. The striped hyaena (*Hyena h.*), *debaa*, was in
1886 said by the explorer Quiroga to be the region's most common
animal; it is now probably mainly on the southern coast, where the
author saw one in the dunes, with small groups around the interior
camps and particularly at Guelta Zemmour. With much the same
habits, the jackal and hyaena are bold and intelligent; they dig water-
holes up to a metre deep, follow lorry-tracks to find a camp around
which to scavenge.

Of the three foxes, the *zaaleb* (*Vulpes pallida*) is the largest, and occurs over the whole territory, with the writer seeing one on the southern coast; it eats big insects, *Rhus* fruit and carrion. Morales (1945) refers to a little Barbary fox, *Poecilitis lybica*, seen at Gleibat Tararat in the south Tiris in 1943; this is perhaps the small fox Valverde (1965) describes as having huge ears and tail, living in rocks and hunting the big desert spiders by smell and hearing on the plains. He is definite that it is not the well-known *fenec* (*Fenecus zerda*), a minute pale-buff fox, with enormous ears, found at least in the sandy regions of the very south; of its speed, the Saharauis sing 'One dog comes nowhere, the *aguerchi* laughs at two whilst three still make him smile . . . four get him running and five really make him hurry . . . with six dogs after him he dies'.

It is uncertain whether either of the two cat species remains in Spanish Sahara. The big *fahel* (*Acinonyx jubatus*, called leopard, cheetah, lynx or ounce) has been seen intermittently and Valverde said it still existed in a dozen rocky places, mostly northerly, in 1955; a group of four had just been seen at Sebaiera, retreating south into the Gor Ait Usa hills. A wild cat, *Felis lybica*, was said by Morales (1945) to be all over the territory but Valverde (1955) could only positively identify it in the Saguiet-el-Hamra; it has been killed at Guelta Zemmour. The mongoose, *Herpestes ichneumon*, may occur in the Saguiet-el-Hamra, since it is still found in the lower Draa and the Mauritanian Zemmour.

The wild boar (*Sus scrofa*), *khaluf*, has been reported once, in the north-west, in a tamarisk clump near the Daora well; this is a south Morocco species. An unexpected animal is the badger-like ratel (*Mellivora capensis*), a savanna-dweller from the south, with a range up the territory into the Anti-Atlas; the Saharauis say the *enduf*'s choice foods are the bush *Launaea arborescens* and the spiny-tailed lizard, this being dug out of its burrow at night.

*Reptiles and Amphibians*

There are at least thirteen snakes and eighteen lizards, in individual numbers the most common animals. The reptiles seem little affected by fluctuations in conditions; they are thought to have been long installed in the region and thus to be highly adapted, with at least *Geckonia chazaliae* peculiar to this one coast.

In 1930, the nervous Vieuchange said he saw a snake as thick as his arm and almost six feet long on his way from Tiznit to Smara – perhaps the territory's cobra (*Naja haje*), *el tzenin* or 'the black one'. The viper *Bitis lachesis*, *monnarub* or 'hare-eater', is another large, dangerous snake of the north-west, a region inhabited also by the

Moroccan viper (*Vipera lebetina*) and the black-tailed viper (*Cerastes vipera*). But the snake of which the Saharauis are most afraid is the *lefsa* or horned viper (*Cerastes c.*): one found under a rock by the author's companion, at Aslein bu Kersch near Smara, was fifty centimetres long, with little 'horns', its body a pale grey with pale brown diamond markings. There are also eight inoffensive *Psammophis* species, all said to be called *bucerrig* by the Saharauis; Valverde (1965) has identified one as the egg-eater *Dasypeltis scaber*, a true savanna form.

The territory's only endemic species, the helmeted gecko, *Geckonia chazaliae* or *arrub*, is thought to be of Tertiary implantation, like the scorpion *Buthus occitanus* (*Androctonus amoreuxi* also occurs); the gecko lives the length of the coast within twenty kilometres of the sea, hunting insects at night on the *reg*. There are three other terrestrial geckos and two climbers; one of the latter, the *talegleg* (*Tarentola ephippiata*) is a savanna species, with tenacious jaws, sucker feet and a flat body adapted to rock-cracks. The powerfully-built spiny-tailed lizard (*Uromaxtis acanthinurus*), *eddab*, is black with yellow bars; it likes the heat and dryness of the interior, digging a spiral two-metre burrow deep into the soft soil, and has been found to cohabit with an unidentified 13 cm scorpion.

The most fearsome lizard, a metre long, is the interior's slender *oran*, *Varanus griseus*. This highly-organised creature kills rodents, other lizards and also snakes, including the vipers: it is said to cover itself first in the venom-neutralising juice of the *muschlud* (*Pergularia tomentosa*), then attack the viper with blows of its long whip-tail, stopping to renew the juice during the combat. This lizard will attack a camel if hungry. The possibilities of the *muschlud* as a snake-bite antidote would be worth investigating.

The territory's most common vertebrate family holds the several small diurnal *Acanthodactylus* species, important in the food chain. So too are the three *Agama* lizards; *A. bibroni*, yellow, red and blue, can be seen sitting on top of the *dagnus*, and is also called *arrub*. *Lacerta lepida* is part of the Berber group of the north-west. A chameleon (?*Chamaleon c.*), *el libuya*, has been caught at El Aaiún. The coastward half of the territory holds three sand-diving skinks; *Sphenops sepsoides*, the *serchmala*, has almost no feet, a bevelled snout and scale-protected eyes.

There are also a frog and a toad, both unidentified, in the damp parts of the north-west. Here it can be mentioned that the El Aaiún lagoon contains leeches, predaceous on the frogs, and the adaptable crustacean *Apus sudanicus*.

*Birds*

The west coast of the Sahara is a main migration route from the North Atlantic to the Tropics. The birds go south in the autumn with the trade winds behind them and the summer's reserves of fat to carry them through, returning in the spring when the coast's food supplies such as plants and insects are at a maximum and travelling at night when the trades are slackest. There is also a resident population; this too is the result of past and present climate, vegetation and other animal life. Some 176 bird species have been reported from Spanish Sahara, fifty-seven of these probably nesting.

The resident Palaearctic or Berber species can be divided into three groups. The north-west *graras*, watercourses and temporary pools hold the ruddy shelduck, Barbary partridge, coot, black-winged stilt, avocet, rufous and spectacled warblers, magpie. The coast around Villa Cisneros is reached by the lark *Galerida malabarica*, the Sardinian warbler, pied wheatear and, probably, the stone curlew. Four pedators cover the territory into north Mauritania: the golden eagle, little owl, kestrel and Egyptian vulture. Seven of these northern species can also be seen in the upper Saguiet-el-Hamra and the Zemmour hills.

The birds most often found in the desert can be zoned according to the distance they keep from the coast. The easternmost group are the sand-grouse *Pterocles coronatus*, and the crested lark, desert warbler and white-rumped wheatear. The long-legged buzzard and three larks (*Ammomames cinctura, A. deserti, Rhamphocoryx clotbey*) reach to within fifty kilometres of the sea. The coast is included in the range of the spotted sandgrouse, a swallow (*Hirundo obsoleta*), another lark (*Eremophila bilopha*), the desert wheatear and a red-tailed wheatear (*Oenanthe moesta*). The trumpeter bullfinch and houbara bustard occur in the Canaries, the desert crow and the bifasciated lark in the C. Verde islands – where they are rejoined by the lark *Ammomames cinctura* – with the cream-coloured courser reaching both archipelagos. This group of variously-adapted birds is characterised by a light-brown upper colouring, helping avoid detection, and a conspicuous underside shown off in flight to signal the individual territories. Some of these desert species are found far north too – the courser to the Marrakesh area – so that the Berber-Desert groups' overlap is some 1,500 km.

The birds typical of the savanna include the vulture *Torgos tracheliotis* and a lark, *Erimopteris nigriceps*, and, until killed off, the ostrich, recently reaching up to the Saguiet-el-Hamra.

The environment poses many problems to the birds. Unspecialised habitats are few and dominated by predators, notably man. Water may have to be obtained from a diet of juicy fruits or as dew or by following the camels at the temporarily-moist well troughs. The ground heat means that some nests have to be protected or raised up. Neither tents nor domed architecture provide nesting places for house-seeking species. The vastness of any sudden climatic deterioration kills the less adaptable; the *irifi*, for example, is preceded on the coast by waves of desperate birds, often driven to try to drink seawater.

The temporary pools, apparently havens, end as traps for many. The El Aaiún lagoon, for example, usually covers three kilometres by 300 m of the watercourse, with dense tamarisk and *Nitraria retusa* scrub. Many aquatic birds soon bring it to life: little grebes, avocets, stilts. The huge ruddy shelduck can number sixty individuals, one of its few remaining colonies anywhere. These birds nest, only to see the young taken by predators or killed by local people as the lagoon dries out; the helpless creatures retreat to the centre, dive to try to escape. The nearest freshwater habitat will then be 250 km away, along the Draa.

The three largest birds, the stork, flamingo and ostrich, are respectively transient, resident and extinct. The white stork, *blarich*, avoiding the coast, flies up and down the territory in spring and autumn in thousands, stopping a while if there is a locust plague; as the slave-catching Portuguese paused to note in 1445, it nests far to the south, from whence one with an arrow-head in it recently got back as far as Spanish Sahara. The flamingo, *en-nani*, has permanently-occupied colonies, reaching a hundred and more birds, in sheltered shallow water at intervals down the coast: the Puerto Cansado lagoon just north of C. Juby, then behind Herne Island and at La Sarga, both in the Villa Cisneros bay, and around Nouadhibou in the B. du Levrier. A few nests and eggs have been reported but whether young have been raised is uncertain. Some of the flamingoes seen are migrating between the north and Mauritania.

Until the appearance of 'a motorised army on a war footing', as Valverde puts it, the Spanish Sahara probably had the western desert's greatest concentration of ostriches. By 1955 these were reduced to a few bands in remote and favoured places such as the acacia valleys of the Negyir hills. In 1965 the *naam* was almost extinct and has now disappeared. Its preferred diet was thistles torn up entire, the colourful colocynth gourds and plenty of pebbles, and on this an ostrich would live for forty years, striding across the savanna and along the watercourses.

*Hunting*
This falls into three groups, primitive, modern and in the name of science. The Saharauis of the past, much of the time hungry, hunted everything edible. Animals needing stalking, such as gazelle, were crept up on by a hunter in a pale-coloured hood, a speciality of the Delim tribe; or a man might lie on the ground under an earth-coloured cloth, or nude, whilst another drove the quarry towards him. Once shot a creature's head was turned towards Mecca whilst, with a prayer, its throat was cut. The primitive guns, with cartridges so valuable as to be divided into two or three, and the difficulties of the chase ensured that victims did not exceed young animals. Birds like the Barbary partridge were caught in traps – a stone slab which fell when the bird knocked down a stick. Riley described the ostrich hunts of 1815: the horsemen would make them run with the wind, since against it the birds outlasted the horses, and caught them up and shot them after about three hours. Ostrich feathers and eggs were a prize, eventually illegal but always on sale, openly, in the Spanish posts; these birds had the misfortune to lay when the desert was accessible to man, in the rainy months of October and November, and to have a lengthy incubation period.

Although laws have long been passed setting up a licence system, game reserves, close seasons and so on, these have been utterly ignored, with civilians, military and police in stripped-down Land-Rovers ranging at will. In 1974 the author found himself present at the hunting of some of the last gazelles, in the south-east; using a shot-gun, a Spanish fisherman fired eight cartridges of bird-pellets into one animal before, dazed and bleeding, it would halt. Those which escape can be expected to have permanently damaged hearts. When there were still flocks the aim was to keep them together so as to kill them all. The predators are hunted too: the disappearing *Acinonyx* for its cubs, both cats and the large fox for their skins; on the central *reg* the author was offered a fox's pelt in exchange for diesel oil. The jackal is killed for simple amusement, as when the Saharaui driver of the author's long-distance taxi chased one, in his headlights, almost over into a ravine. The ostrich, able to take rifle bullets at fifteen metres without flinching, unless hit in a vital place, and locally known for its ability to run long distances with its entrails trailing, was theoretically protected by large fines; yet it fell at up to thirty at a time at *official* hunts laid on for dignitaries.

'In the next few days we shot all three from the fort's windows,' wrote Valverde (1957) in his section on the rare desert fox. He saw only seven ground squirrels, including at El Aaiún 'a family formed of at least five young and an adult female. We got four. Two days later,' he adds, apparently surprised, 'at the same place, and with the same sun, there were none'. In 1955 he shoots several ostriches, to see what they had eaten; in 1965 he deliberately knocks over one of the only two groups he sees with the bonnet of his jeep, taking three chicks. His last line on the now probably extinct *Gazella dama*: 'Its meat is excellent'. Valverde's book – the main work on the territory's zoology – has plate after plate of dead, dying, hunted or captive animals.

*Marine Fauna*
As described, the C. Blanc waters are the richest in W. Africa in plankton, reaching 100,000 organisms to the litre. This results in turn in the coast's concentration of fish; the main species will be described in the section on the fishing industry. The only freshwater-dwelling fish are the mullet which swim up the Saguiet-el-Hamra during spates; as the El Aaiún lagoon dries out they are collected in sackfuls. In the sea south of C. Blanc, tropical creatures such as turtles become common. On the Spanish Sahara coast itself, records are limited to an otter (*Lutra l.*) in the mouth of the Saguiet-el-Hamra in 1945, to a surprisingly-large bottle-nosed dolphin (*Tursiops truncatus*), 4 m 82 cm, off Villa Cisneros in 1933, and to an undated reference to the rough-toothed dolphin (*Steno bredanensis*) off C. Blanc.

The monk seal (*Monachus m.*), protected because of its feasible world-wide extinction, occurs right down the coast as far as Arguin Bay. It is a large seal, dark brown on top, whitish below. Its first European hunters, the Portuguese of 1436, found a colony of some 500 seals in the Villa Cisneros bight. The largest-known present concentration is at Las Cuevecillas, not far north of La Guera; in November 1954 this was a base for about 200 animals. A few years before this, the coast's friendly seals had been watched at close quarters by underwater divers (Cousteau 1958); a pup, its favourite food found to be octopus, was removed to Marseille zoo.

# Chapter 3

# Prehistory

The Catalan geologist Font y Sagué was the first to study the region's prehistory, examining the Villa Cisneros area around the turn of the century. Soon after, the B. du Levrier was investigated by French archaeologists. Subsequently, Spanish Sahara's sites have been pillaged by the military, the huge collection made two decades ago by General Vasquez now notorious amongst Spanish prehistorians; the continuing removal of the many rock engravings of animals complements the extinction of the living fauna. Spanish archaeologists have made collections in the territory since the Civil War, with Almagro (1946) the only synthesis.

However, there has been almost no methodical field investigation along modern lines. French work on the Draa terraces suggests the Saguiet-el-Hamra could produce a sequence, probably in conjunction with the raised shorelines. No stratified sites have been reported, but at least the Devil's Cave, in the south-east at Leyuaf, is worth investigation; wells and salt-pans are other possibilities. The ancient fauna is known only from the engravings. The flora is unknown; however, the wells and the few caves should hold stratified pollen. Some sites yield charcoal, allowing C14 dating; thermoluminescence dating on sherds kept moist in wells and caves would be possible. The Canaries, with many caves, provide Early Metal Age material, partially dated, with African affinities; the prehistory of the nearest island, Fuerteventura, 100 km off the coast of Spanish Sahara, has been studied in relation to that of north-west Africa (Mercer 1973). However, it is all but impossible for foreign investigators in any field to obtain access to the territory; for example, in 1973 the writer was refused a visa to carry out a rock-art survey.

As a result of the absence of scientific evidence, a cautious survey of the available material, supplemented by the work carried out in the surrounding French-speaking territories, is all that is possible. Spanish Sahara is anyway a transition or interaction zone, so that clear-cut groups and phases are not to be assumed. Warring nomadism

Table 3: Simplified correlation of available evidence on quaternary events, based on Alimen (1957), with interpretations from Zeuner (1958) and Biberson (1954–66) and the addition of data for Spanish Sahara (see text)

| Sea Levels | Beach in Morocco | Beach in Sp. Sahara | Glacials and Pluvials | Glacials acc. Zeuner | Man in N.W. Africa | Stone Industries | | | |
|---|---|---|---|---|---|---|---|---|---|
| | | | | | | R. Draa (Biberson) | North Mauritania | Sahara (Excl. Draa N.M. & S.S.) | Spanish Sahara |
| Flandrian (Z: Epimonastirian) | 2 m | | Post-Glacial + Wet Phase 5500–2500 BC | Wurm I–II Inter-Stadial | Negroids decrease Negroids increase | Neolithic (Affinity with Sahara) | Neolithic (as Sahara) | Neolithic: Capsian Trad., Saharan, Sudanese | Neolithic (As Sahara) |
| | | 3–4 m | | | Homo sapiens | ? Aterian + ? Final Acheulian etc. | ? Pre-Neolithic Microlithic | ? Pre-Neolithic Microlithic | |
| | | | Wurm + Last Pluvial (Two Peaks) | | | | Aterian down to 22°N. | Aterian + Levallois-Mousterian | Aterian |
| Ouljian (Z: Late Monastirian) | 5–8 m | | | Riss–Wurm Inter- | Neander-thaloids | Final Acheulian with Levallois Technique | Adrar Levallois-like Industry (Biberson). | Levallois-Mousterian | Levallois-Mousterian (duration unknown) |
| Grimaldian Regression | | | | | | | | | |
| ?: Main | 15 m | | | | | | | | |

| Marine stage / Regression | Sea level | Sea level (alt) | Glacial / Pluvial | Interglacial | Hominid | Sequence | Sequence with Pebble Tools (these earlier?) (Biberson) | Sequence |
|---|---|---|---|---|---|---|---|---|
| Tyrrhenian | 30 m (Z: 25–30 m) | 30–35 m | Riss + Pluvial | Mindel–Riss Inter-Glacial | *Homo erectus* over Maghreb-Chad Region | Chellean Hand-axes with A.P.T. (these earlier?) | (Biberson) | Chellean |
| Post-Sicilian or Roman Regression | | | Mindel + Pluvial | | | | | |
| Sicilian (Milazzian) | 60 m (55–60 m) | ? | | Gunz–Mindel Inter-Glacial | | | | |
| Post-Calabrian Regression | | | Gunz? | | in Morocco | | | |
| Calabrian (Z: Sicilian) | 100 m | 100–120 m | | | *Homo habilis* in Algeria 1¼ m.y. ago | Advanced Pebble Tools | ?Pebble Tools (Biberson) | |
| Villafranchian Regression | | | | | | | | |
| (Z: Calabrian) | | | | | | | | |

has probably always been the rule, leading to cultural inter-weaving over vast regions. Only artefacts seen or illustrated recognisably will be discussed.

The sites are to be found along the coast, there usually as shell middens, and up the Saguiet-el-Hamra and around the desert wells; the flint-bearing marine transgression zone is one vast knapping floor. Table 3 is an outline of the main events of the Quaternary period in the region, based on the limited evidence available; not only is it subject to local revision but to the currently-unceasing reconstruction of the global theories.

## The Early Stone Age

'Pebble tools', simple quartzite spheroids dating to at least $1\frac{1}{2}$ m.y. ago, have been found at Ain Hanech in Algeria; they are presumed to be the work of *Homo habilis* (Australopithecus), the earliest known artefact-making hominid, about four feet (1·20 m) tall and fifty pounds in weight, chinless, with massive jaws, prominent eye-brow ridges and a sloping forehead fronting an ape-size brain. Evolved pebble-tools on the Draa River just north of Spanish Sahara are the earliest evidence of tool-makers on the desert littoral. The last pebble-tools to be made in Morocco are now found in apparent association with 'Chellean' hand-axes; these chopping-digging tools are in fact found occasionally in Spanish Sahara itself, for example on the B. du Levrier, at Smara and at Bir Tagschent (Figure 5, No. 1). The territory's early tools are made of primary rocks such as the quartzites and eruptives of the Tiris.

North-west Africa's next, more advanced hominids and their arte-facts take the forms of the Maghreb-Chad *Homo erectus* (*Atlanthropus*) skeletons – five feet (1·50 m) tall, with a more man-like face and brain than *H. habilis*, perhaps ancestral – and the associated well-shaped hand-axes of 'Acheulian' type. This period, producing the whole Acheulian tool sequence, lasted several hundred thousand years, until about 50,000 BC at least. The hand-axes have been found in Spanish Sahara, at Bir Nazaran and Bir Tagschent (No. 2); the nearby Mauritanian Adrar sites of Azrag and El Beyed have yielded the Late Acheulian cleaver as well.

It seems that the Sahara region was by now well into its present desert phase, since the Acheulian tools are usually concentrated around still-recognisable water points. This probably led to a cultural separation of the Maghreb and its adjacent northern desert from the region south of the Sahara, as is suggested by the subsequent tool sequence, described next.

On the Draa River, the last Acheulian tools show the 'Levallois' technique, a link with the 'Levallois-Mousterian' tools found on many post-Acheulian working floors right across the Sahara. These artefacts, generally attributable to a Neanderthaloid possibly evolved from *Homo erectus*, have been reported in unusual isolation from the Djebel Zini, now part of south Morocco (Jorda 1955). In Spanish Sahara, the Cuesta del Gaada has been found to have typical Mousterian points and side scrapers, Levallois cores and, also, some blades, as did the Zini sites; a Mousterian disc-core was found at El Aaiún (No. 3); Crova (1912) reported Mousterian tools from the B. du Levrier.

Credited with the invention of the bow and arrow, the subsequent lighter-weight 'Aterian' industry may have been evolved by the users of the Levallois-Mousterian techniques – which continue alongside the new artefacts – with the hominids of the two groups being perhaps a single line of Neanderthaloids. The Aterians hunted over the Nile-Atlantic zone, their period including a phase shown by pollen analysis to have seen the Ahoggar mountains covered with Aleppo pine, Atlantic cedar and Mediterranean shrubs, suggesting woods and humid savanna where there is now desert (Almagro 1968). The characteristic tool, often of flint, was a point, its inverse trimming limited to the tang; it is occasionally found in Spanish Sahara, as at Auinat Lecruf (No. 4) and on the fifteen-metre terrace of the Saguiet-el-Hamra, for example at Tucat-en-Haila. The industry's south-west limit is the Mauritanian Adrar; it is in fact rare on the west Sahara littoral.

On the Maghreb coast, the Neanderthaloids were absorbed and replaced by 12,000 BC by the eastern-origin Oranian blade industry and its Mechta-Afalou human type, the region's first Caucasoid – *Homo sapiens* of Combe Capelle affinities – but in the desert there seems no undisputed evidence for the presence of pre-Neolithic blade industries. Thus, the Aterian is presumed to have survived in the Sahara until the Neolithic; recent C14 dates suggest that the earliest facies of this had reached the south-central desert, the Enedi-Ahoggar, as early as 6000 BC.

---

Fig. 5 (overleaf). Stone tools, Nos 1–4 (redrawn from Martinez 1944, no scale given), 5–9 ($\frac{1}{4}$); engraved ostrich-egg shell, No. 10 ($\frac{1}{2}$); stone arm-ring fragment, No. 11 ($\frac{1}{2}$); stone bowl, No. 12 ($\frac{2}{7}$)

Fig. 6 (overleaf). Common axe shapes, Nos 13–16; pots, Nos 17, 19 (Martinez 1944), No. 18 ($\frac{3}{16}$); common arrowhead shapes, Nos 20–9

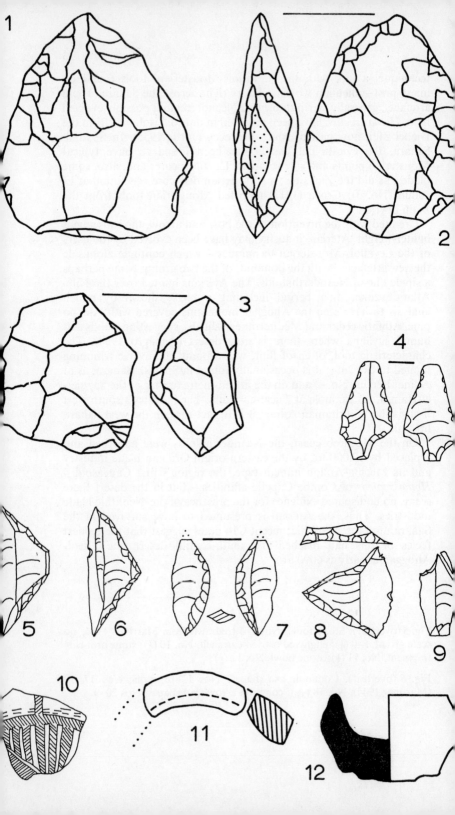

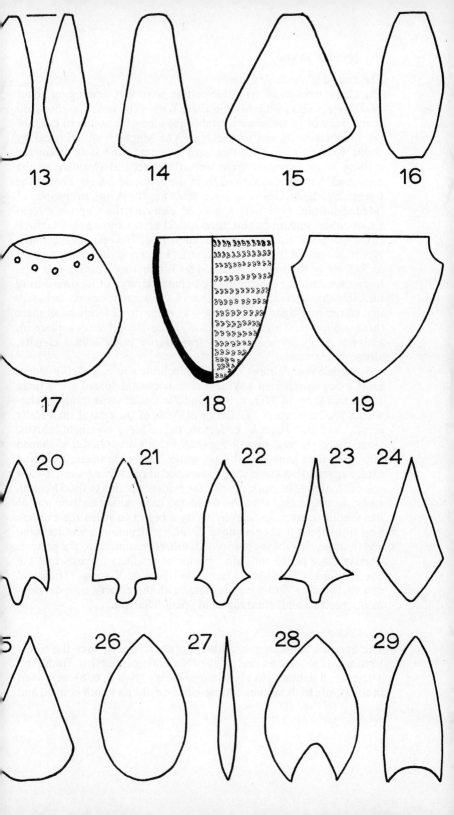

13     14     15     16

17     18     19

20     21     22     23     24

5     26     27     28     29

## The Arrival of Neolithic Culture

The characteristics of Neolithic culture were first developing about 10,000 years ago in the Middle East. Within the next few thousand years many of its traits were established along the southern coast of the Mediterranean and up the Nile. The Maghreb was reached by about 4000 BC, the Neolithic here superimposing itself upon the existing blade cultures; these were the described Oranian on the coast and, having also arrived from the east, and having hunted the Cyrenaica-SE Algeria zone since 8000 BC, the 'Capsian' people, of 'Mediterranean' type plus a negroid element; the Capsian's Neo-lithicised descendant culture then spread across the whole Maghreb to the Atlantic coast. From the Sudanese Nile, a second, differentiated Neolithic crossed the Sahara, recent C14 assays giving datings as old as 5000 BC to the west of the Ahoggar Mountains. Thirdly, and as is to be expected, the Sahara evolved characteristics of its own during the Neolithic period. The Neolithic of the western desert, including that of the now-Spanish territory, was made up of facets of all these three groupings. This dissemination of the Neolithic took place in, and was probably aided by, a temporarily more humid climate, already mentioned.

Spanish Sahara's most common Neolithic site is a shell-midden. Font y Sagué reported a Villa Cisneros coastal spread some three kilometres long, of *Murex*, *Arca* and *Turritella*; some mounds, elsewhere, are made up of *Mytilus* or of shells of the typical snail *Helix duroi*. Much dug about by collectors, the middens once held hearths, stone tools, pottery, ostrich egg-shell – both decorated and shaped into body ornaments – and food waste. This wide range, including axes, suggests that these camps were the normal living sites, even if seasonal, of the Neolithic people; the evidence points to food hunting and gathering rather than to animal and crop raising as their way of life. Neolithic traits look likely to have begun to reach the extreme west from about the beginning of the fifth millennium, some declining and disappearing during the second, others continuing to the present. The typology of the following groups of artefacts suggests that the two immigrant Neolithic currents, northern or 'Capsian Tradition' and southern or 'Sudanese', together with the desert's own developments, reached and intermingled in Spanish Sahara.

## Neolithic Stone Tools

The Spanish Sahara's microlithic flintwork, spread over the whole territory, is similar to that of the 'Neolithic of Capsian Tradition'. These small delicate steeply-trimmed forms (Nos 5, 6, 8) were used in composite tools such as cutting-blades, drills and both pointed and transverse projectile heads; with them is found a typical waste product, the so-called micro-burin (No. 9). The same geometrically-shaped tools also occurred in the Maghreb blade-cultures but in the desert are commonly associated with Neolithic relics and sometimes even bear the flat Neolithic flaking (No. 7). The microliths are usually accompanied by a normal range of large flintwork – blades, scrapers and perforators being the most common – and, in a La Guera *grara*, by many minute 'choppers' made of small quartz beach-pebbles flaked at one end.

An important Saharan grouping is the typically-Neolithic flat-flaked arrowheads, generally bifacially-worked. Most shapes are found in Spanish Sahara, though usually unifacially trimmed, almost exclusively so in the south. The territory's wide range (Nos 20–9) is in fact composed of variations on two types, leaf-shaped and barbed-and-tanged, the latter perhaps the most modern Saharan form; sometimes the points have serrated edges for better holding. Their fascination to collectors has blurred distribution patterns. For example, it is difficult to assess the significance of the somewhat similar trimming – most or all of one face and the tang of the other – of both the earlier, widespread Aterian point and of many of Spanish Sahara's Neolithic arrowheads, or of the almost total absence in the territory of the two points sometimes proposed as the Sahara's oldest Neolithic types, the hollow-based (Nos 28–9) and lozenge forms (No. 24) – but it would be natural that Aterian traditions should have survived longest in the western desert, since Neolithic penetration will have been from the east and down the coast.

The remaining division is that of the large stone tools, many polished, usually of massive rocks such as, in Spanish Sahara, the Tiris plutonic diabases, diorites and porphyrites; rolled beach stones were sometimes chosen. The group seems most common in the south. The polished axes (Nos 13–16) ranged from 172 mm–182 gm to 22 m–7 gm, apparently. The smaller axes were perhaps toy or votive; in 1942 the Saharauis were flaking toy camels and horses out of flint. Polished chisels of sedimentary rock, taking advantage of the flat layers, are found occasionally. Grooved stones were used for polishing and sharpening these tools and also for shaping needles and piercers. Beach cobbles used as pestles-cum-hammers, showing polishing and battering, were common; anvils were often found and were unstandardised, mortars were rare. The present author saw two dish-querns in sandstone on the *grara* working floor near La Guera, presumably for grinding wild or sown grain, or perhaps roots. Flat schistose discs four to eight centimetres across occur frequently on C. Blanc. Crova mentions stone balls, perhaps projectiles. There were stones on which red and yellow colours had been prepared. Not immediately distinctive, these tools will need detailed study if they are to be of use in reconstructing the region's cultural evolution.

### Other Neolithic Artefacts

The territory's carrying, cooking and drinking vessels were of three materials – ostrich eggshell, pottery, stone – in addition to the *guerba* water-skin, evidenced in the Sahara from 3000 BC according to Lhote (1967) and doubtless far older.

The rims, sides or bases of the emptied ostrich eggs might be engraved with abstract decoration, varying from rows of dashes, through the chevron, to complex patterns (No. 10, La Guera, found by the author), or, around C. Juby, with animals such as fish, the addax and the oryx (Fig. 7, No. 3); the southern pattern shown was made by pressing a small point into the shell, producing lines of dots, whilst the oryx (Grébénart 1973) was sketched out with a thin continuous line which was then deepened by a series of V-notches. The ostrich not having lived north of the Sahara, the use of the eggs does not extend to the northern Maghreb sites; the decoration's origin – parallel to that of the earliest rock-engravings, described shortly – is thought to lie in the Neolithic of Capsian Tradition culture, its diffusion centre, Cyrenaica–south east Algeria, at the east end of the zone of engraved shell.

A second, small group of vessels consists of a dozen finely-carved, polished stone bowls. These have been found in a Morocco–Tassili–north Mauritania triangle, including a C. Blanc fragment made in the area's whitish limestone and a bowl (No. 12) from a tomb at Guelta Zemmour, this described shortly.

Pottery is common in the middens and detailed study thus possible, with caution due to the probable longevity of styles – Jordá (1955) reports 'Neolithic' sherds repaired with copper, from Villa Cisneros, Martinez (1944) a Moslem-like crescent on a sherd. Two important groupings are by the egg-shaped pointed base (No. 18, C. Blanc, author's reconstruction) and by the bag-like round base (No. 17, Hanish, Martinez, 1944); shouldered forms of each exist (No. 19); hanging holes, above or beside each other, were common. Apart from the suggestive similarity to the local ostrich egg, the conical-base pots have parallels in the Mediterranean Neolithic zone; the globular vessels, however, appear to belong to the Sudanese Neolithic. Decoration, common, was incised, including the use of a comb, or pressed in with knotted strings and other tools, or stabbed: including the simpler eggshell patterns, designs were a combination of lines, columns and blocks of dots and variously-angled dashes, the latter sometimes forming chevrons and zigzags. On C. Blanc at least, a distinctive feature was the cross-hatching and other decoration of the upper faces of the broad rims, with the bodies themselves, occasionally with traces of a red slip, highly ornamented too. Jordá (1955) reports cardial or shell-impressed sherds from the coast and also from the Devil's Cave, inland, at Leyuaf, whilst Martínez's expedition brought back a pot resembling a Bell Beaker – these respectively suggest the Neolithic and Early Metal Ages of the Mediterranean and Iberia, but are clearly not typical of the desert's culture. The region's distribution patterns need to be worked out. Here it can be mentioned that net sinkers of fired clay and spindle whorls shaped from broken sherds are to be found on the sites but may well be recent.

One customary grouping appears undescribed – it must exist – from Spanish Sahara, the bone and ivory tools. The Sudanese Neolithic sites to the east, many around now-dry lakes and watercourses, yield decorated harpoon heads and domestic implements. The use at Villa Cisneros of the pointed, fossil teeth, up to 4·5 cm across, of the shark *Carchorodon*, is hardly comparable.

Finally, before the rock engravings, the *art mobilier*, in this case all body ornaments. Linked perhaps to the bowls are the carved stone bracelets, sometimes found in Saharan tombs; rare in Spanish Sahara, a fragment from a ring, eight centimetres across, of fine grain dark green magmatic rock (No. 11, found on C. Blanc by the author) appears to have been much valued, since the broken faces have been ground flat and polished, whilst the outer side bears deliberately-scratched lines, seemingly from a third phase of use to judge by the patinas. The many perforated beads suggest necklaces were common, the materials being ostrich eggshell, fish otoliths and polished vertebrae, cowries and easily-bored stones; at Gaseiba Adam, the white pebbles were of many shapes, including barrel, cylinder and olive. Large beads in stone and shell have been described as pendants. There are also squarish bevel-edged plaques lacking holes.

## Rock Engravings

Though numerous, the territory's reported engravings are limited to the length of the Saguiet-el-Hamra and to three sites in the southern interior. Smara, not perhaps coincidentally the modern focus of the region's nomads, is the centre of the main concentration, the engravings cut in the dark Devonian slate; many slabs have now been taken away. In the south, 200 km south-east of Villa Cisneros, there are carvings on the southern face of the peak of the central Gleibat

Mosdat outcrop. Another hundred kilometres east, near Ausert, an undated burial ground, mentioned by Jordá (1955), has an engraved monolith and other decorated stones. Finally, and as far east again, the mentioned hills of Leyuaf, or 'the Benign', oddly hold the big Devil's Cave, called after the noises made in it by the wind; not described in detail by Jordá, it yielded the cardial ware and its floor is pitted with 'offering holes', with wall engravings of animals, a human, a rain representation and also Arab votive inscriptions. Two groups of paintings have recently been announced from three rock shelters in the Leyuaf hills (Biedermann 1974). There are many engravings, comparable to those of Spanish Sahara, just on the Mauritanian side of the frontier, from the Zemmour massif round to due south of Gleibat Mosdat. Though interesting, the territory's engravings are usually artistically poor.

The oldest group, attributed at its most typical to hunters during the first few millennia of the Neolithic, are plain sketches of wild animals, including the four now extinct in the region; these engravings are typically cut with a deep V or U incision and are the most heavily patinated. The species depicted, according to Spanish archaeologists, are the hartebeest antelope *Alcelaphus*, with forward-facing horns (Figs 7–8, No. 23); unidentified antelopes, some chased by a canid (No. 26) – if not a dog (as perhaps No. 27) then a hyaena, also engraved elsewhere – and others alongside barbed-and-tanged arrowheads (No. 18); elephants, including a hunt by a man in a loin-cover (Nos 1, 16, 17); a rhinoceros (No. 5), its upper horn sometimes depicted as longer than its lower (No. 4), and in one case pursued by a hunter, the man with a bow and followed by a woman; many giraffes (No. 13), the addax (No. 7), oryx (No. 3), mountain sheep (No. 8), gazelles (No. 6) including *G. dama*, and an unspecified goat (No. 25); the ostrich (Nos 19–20). A lion once, and perhaps the *Acinonyx* cat and a snake. Fish have been noted near Smara, far from the sea; a species with a barbel (No. 22) may be the red mullet, prolific in the bay of Angra dos Ruivos, named by the Portuguese after this fish, *ruivo*. Although the crocodile and hippopotamus, together with the elephant and the giraffe, were said to live in the Saguiet-el-Hamra in Carthaginian–Roman times, there is only a note of an untraced giraffe engraving, near the watercourse, by Camille Douls late in the last century; the crocodile is said to have lived in south Morocco and south Mauritania until the end of the nineteenth century. Various isolated human figures, some phallic (No. 28), usually naked, have been attributed to this first period too: one man may be dancing, another has spiky hair like a present Saharaui type (No. 28), a third has a noticeably round head, suggesting the Central Sahara paintings of Neolithic negroids. Rain has only been depicted at Leyuaf (jacket), but then 5500–2500 BC was a wet period compared to that since, as is shown by the described fauna, at home in a dense acacia and shrub savanna; this vegetation is independently supported by pollen analysis in the Central Sahara, associated with a radiocarbon age of the fourth millennium. In fact, it was to be the ownership of domesticated animals, rather than the hunting of wild beasts, which would later make the Saharauis call themselves 'the sons of the clouds'.

Strikingly, this group of engravings is not found below the Saguiet-el-Hamra, although the depicted fauna will have flourished down to the Niger: both the limited zone and the comparable style suggest the group belongs to the Neolithic of Capsian Tradition complex, this extending right across the northern desert to the Draa and Spanish Sahara. North-western Mauritania holds many paintings and an advance description of one group of the newly-discovered Leyuaf works makes comparisons with the art of the Central Sahara; the red and white Leyuaf paintings, the first known from the territory's Neolithic, appear to include a mountain sheep and two giraffes.

The usual second division, in the Central Sahara belonging to the fourth and third millennia BC, holds engravings of domesticated animals. However, at the western extreme of the desert the most certain of these seem associated with the group discussed next, the chariots, dated in Central Sahara from 1500–1200 BC at the earliest;

---

Fig. 7 (overleaf). Prehistoric engravings. No. 1, elephant, chariot (Asli, Smara); 2, three chariots (Gleibat Mosdat); 3, oryx (Tarfaya, on ostrich-egg shell); 4, rhino (Chelkha Mairat, Smara region); 5, rhino (Pozo Mecaiteb, Smara region); 6, gazelle (Smara); 7, addax (Pozo Mecaiteb); 8, mountain sheep (Adoloa, Smara region); 9, 10, 'pick' forms (Meran I, Smara); 11, bovid (Asli); 12, antelope (Pozo Mecaiteb); 13, giraffe (Pozo Mecaiteb); 14, violin-shaped 'idol' (Pozo Mecaiteb); 15, man with 'pick' object, and axe-blade (Meran I)

Fig. 8 (overleaf). Prehistoric engravings. No. 16, man with waist-cloth chasing elephants (Pozo Mecaiteb); 17, elephant, violin-shaped 'idol', axe-blades (Lagchaiuat, Smara region); 18, antelope, barbed-and-tanged points (Seluan, Smara); 19, ostrich (Hausa, Smara region); 20, ostriches (Tucat en Haila, Smara region); 21, horse-cum-chariot (Seluan); 22, fish with barbel (Laasailien, Smara); 23, *Alcelaphus* antelope (Pozo Mecaiteb); 24, long-horned bovid (Hausa); 25, goat (Smara); 26, antelopes chased by hyena (Pozo Mecaiteb); 27, canid (Lagchaiuat); 28, two humans (Adoloa)

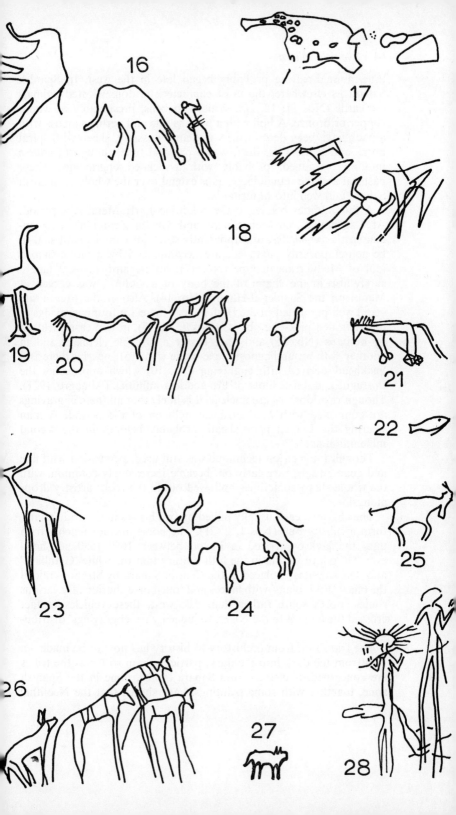

thus, animal-rearing probably began late in the west. In Spanish Sahara as elsewhere, the most characteristic domesticated animals are cattle (Nos 11, 12, 24), some with bells, presumably of wood, copper or bronze. A bull with a pack saddle and perhaps an ass with a pack have been described. A dog and, possibly, sheep with spiral horns and bells. This, then, was a pastoral time, though of course hunting continued, probably with associated engravings. These pastoral and the remaining groups extend over the whole of Spanish Sahara and well into Mauritania.

A few oddities belong to the Neolithic–Early Metal Age period. At Lagchauiat, between Smara and Guelta Zemmour, two un-diagnostic axe-blades, one apparently stuck into an elephant said to be contemporarily engraved, are accompanied by a violin-shaped idol of Mediterranean type (No. 17); an elegantly-stylised face – surely also in the shape of the body of a violin – was carved at Meran on the Saguiet-el-Hamra (No. 14). Also at the Meran site – and well paralleled in the High Atlas – there are four engravings of long-handled pick-like objects (Nos 9, 10, 15), in two cases held up by humans (No. 15) and once beside a possible elephant and in another with an undiagnostic axe-blade (No. 15): nearby there is a 'pickhead'-derived fifth engraving (No. 10) which approaches the Portuguese dolmen idols of eye-goddess affinities (Almagro 1971). Though relationships are unclear, it is likely that all these engravings are connected with Mediterranean religion of the period. A man wearing the Lybian penis-sheath probably belongs in the second millennium BC.

Though the incision technique was still used, percussion with fine and coarse tools, rare early on, became increasingly common, with the whole shape sometimes hollowed out in the rock; artistry drops alongside.

The chariots, each usually pulled by two horses in Central Sahara, form a third group (Nos 1, 2, 21). The horse did not reach Africa until the Hyksos arrived in Egypt, between 1680–1580 BC; however, Herodotus wrote in the fifth century that the white 'Getulians' and 'Garamantes' – placed in the Central Sahara by Strabo – raided the black 'Ethiopians' with lances and four-horse chariots. By various routes, north–south rather than east–west, these vehicles in fact crossed the Sahara to the Niger, to judge by the engravings' distribution.

The transition from prehistory to history has now to be made – a leap from the dark into the dark, particularly in so far as the tribes are concerned. Skeletons from Sahara tombs, none in the Spanish zone, together with some paintings, have shown that the Neolithic

1  The Atlantic coast of Cap Blanc, with the lighthouse. The cliff is made up of sedimentary beds of marine origin.

Consolidated dunes under erosion near La Guera, during a sand-wind. There was a Neolithic camp amongst the stones in the foreground.

2   White-spined acacias and a domed sanctuary at Smara. Behind, Ma el Ainin's *ribat* and, background right, the Spanish Foreign Legion barracks.

An old tamarisk near Golfo da Cintra. An unsurfaced track.

*Panicum* grass, and distant acacias, in loose sand in the Tiris. Tagsumal hill behind.

desert people included a strong negroid element, thought to have migrated northwards and westwards into the Sahara during the sub-pluvial which began about 5500 BC; the Capsian's black people may already have been in the desert. The vigorous Neolithic of Capsian Tradition culture was developing in the Maghreb from 4000 BC. These lines of evidence, together with that of the previous paragraph, can be compared with the belief of the present Saharans that the pre-Arab Sanhaja Berbers colonised the desert by pushing southwards a black people, the 'Bafots', considered to have founded the oases. One possible conclusion is that Neolithic of Capsian Tradition whites – prehistoric Berbers, known to the Romans as Getulians and Garamantes – took the desert and its oases over from the black Bafots, or Ethiopians, perhaps from the end of the second millennium and apparently with the aid of horses and chariots. By this period, the increasing dryness had probably weakened the desert culture. The long-standing subordinate role of the Sahara's negroid population, illustrated later, may date from this time.

Treating now the chariots themselves (Nos 1, 2), there are stylised engravings on a north–south route from near Goulimine in southern Morocco – a town long the trade focus for the littoral nomads – by way of Oued Tamanart, still just in Morocco, to Smara (No. 1 with 'earlier' elephant. No. 21 with horse) and, an obvious branch, down the Saguiet-el-Hamra to El Aaiún; the main route onwards is probably shown by the chariots depicted at Bir Moghrein and in the Adrar, both now Mauritania. Well to the west, the Gleibat Mosdat site, with its legendary well, has at least twenty chariots (No. 2), the stylised drawings showing them to run on a pair of spoked wheels and to be drawn by two quadrupeds; the belled cattle and sheep occur at this site. A Saguiet-el-Hamra engraving is said to show an ox, with liriform horns, pulling a chariot; already acclimatised elsewhere in the desert, the ox would have been better suited than the horse to the increasing desiccation. Such a slow vehicle could only have been used in a supply train or for peaceful purposes. Some 700 km south-east of Gleibat Mosdat, the ox-drawn chariots of Tichitt are dated by C14 to the seventh to fourth centuries BC; the North Africans still had war-chariots at the time of the Greek expedition under Agatocles, 310 BC. In summary, it seems that both the first domesticated animals and the ox-drawn chariot arrived late in the west, perhaps not until the first millennium BC. In Spanish Sahara, horse engravings only occur on the Ausert monolith and, undescribed (Almagro 1971), at Leyuaf; the six haphazardly-placed lively animals on the stone stele rather suggest riding horses, current until recently. The war chariots may have been first conceived in the

Nile Valley, so it is interesting that Smara should have two engravings of boats said to be of Sudanese Nile type (Balbin 1969).

To complete the description of the engravings, and moving further into the historic period, the 'Berber' and 'Arab–Berber' groups need coverage. Roman monuments in the Maghreb, from about 200 BC, include inscriptions in a local or 'Libyan' alphabet; this then had the vigour to spread over the triangle Mediterranean–Fezzan–Niger as the written form of the Berber language, the latter itself of south-west Asian origin or, according to Greenberg (1963), of African origin.

However, following the Moslem invasions from the late seventh century AD, Arabic appeared and began towards its present dominance; the local alphabet gradually shrank in area of use until, known as 'Tifinagh', it is now limited to a few Touareg groups in the central desert. In Spanish Sahara, most of the reported inscriptions occur near Villa Cisneros or around Smara; they are now being studied in detail for the first time (Biedermann 1974). Arabic writings are found all over the territory. Both types of inscription usually consist of proper names, route indications, insults, gallantries and, in the case of Arabic, professions of faith. In addition there are footprints, brand marks, gaming boards and many unidentified signs; the most interesting site for these is at El Farsia, where the bluff by the well bears graffiti in ochre, red and black, the territory's only post-Neolithic paintings. There appear to be no ancient non-African inscriptions.

Animal representation seems lacking in the territory over the last two thousand years. There are thus no pictures of the camel, of eastern origin and first known in Africa on a coin of Pompey's lieutenant, L. Lollius, 68 BC. This animal must have reached the western desert soon after the time of Christ, replacing the ox and the horse, less adapted to the still-increasing desiccation; pollen analysis has shown that the dry phase was well advanced by 1000 BC. Inscriptions in the old alphabet, to the east of Spanish Sahara, are associated with engravings of men riding horses and camels and carrying a round shield current from the first millennium BC; this defence and the javelin replaced the bow and arrow. This suggests that the horse-to-camel transition was probably made by the north-west African people themselves, the ancestors of the present Berbers.

*Tombs and Skeletons*
In the Sahara, the earlier Neolithic burials were in a simple trench in the open or in a cave, sometimes with the red ochre rite; these have not been recorded for the Spanish territory. The construction of megalithic tombs in the Mediterranean, from the second millennium

BC, may have sent impulses, by way of the Maghreb's conical *chouchet* and *bazina* tombs, into the desert. Spanish Sahara has many cairns, almost without scientific investigation; as noted, Almagro reported 'Neolithic' tombs older than some salt-pan subsidence, this so far undated, whilst Martinez (1944) refers to 'necklaces' from the territory's tombs.

An exception has been one of a number of tombs about 16 km south of the Guelta Zemmour military post (Balbin 1973). Key-hole shaped in plan, the cairn consisted of a round mound 6 m across with two 2 m walls, forming a three-sided roofless enclosure, built against its south-east side. The burial chamber was in the centre of the mound: the powdery skeleton was crouched, on its left side, face to the south-west. The enclosure, not connected to the chamber, held a dish quern and a fine limestone bowl, the latter 13·5 cm across and 8 cm deep (No. 12). Just beyond of each of the short walls there was a heap of stones. The excavator felt the tomb was well on in the Neolithic, basing this on a partial similarity to the Maghreb types; the quern and bowl were typologically older and so had presumably been long in the tribe. A skeleton was recovered at a probably-similar tomb at the B. de l'Etoile, on C. Blanc: semi-contracted, it had been a man thirty to forty years old, 161–9 cm, robust, buried with pieces of pottery, shaped bone and snail shells (*Helix*). Such tombs seem to have become Islamised with the Arab immigrations, the corpses being placed on their right sides so as to face Mecca, the head and feet being marked by upright stones.

A second common tomb in the western desert is crescentic. One planned by the author at Oumm Arouaguene, near Zouerate, just in Mauritania, was about 150 m long overall: a centrally-placed cairn, oriented north–south, 20 m long by 9 m wide, and 2 m high, was extended in each direction by a stone wall or 'horn' about 65 m long; it appears to have a Moslem prayer wall nearby. A similar crescentic tomb dug on C. Blanc had a small entrance leading into a corbelled domed chamber: a crouched skeleton lay on the ground.

Modern burials, the body merely covered by rocks, nevertheless have the characteristic of the head and feet being marked by upright stones. Women's graves are additionally indicated by a fecundity stone in the middle, though the author did not see these in the C. Blanc cemeteries; Dangelzer (1911) refers to big head-stones here. In the Reguibat tribes' area, these people's graves are additionally marked by a lengthways line of small white stones.

This is meagre information on the burial customs of so many groups: nomadic Neolithic hunters and pastoralists, with perhaps some sedentary crop-growers in favoured places – as in the Central

Sahara – then the chariot people, next the horse and camel riders, leading on to the present Berbers, and, comparatively-recent arrivals, the Arabs. Racially, it appears that there have been both black and white people in the desert since the Neolithic. The black population has declined since. The white people are characterised by two physical types, ideally: the robust hyperdolichocephalic salient-occiput 'Mechta-Afalou', first appearing in association with the Oranian industry, and the lighter, dolichocephalic 'Mediterranean' who brought the Capsian tools. In practice, interbreeding with outside types has given the Berbers a mixture of physiques, further confused by the Arabisation of the culture of many, discussed shortly.

## The Early Use of Metals

Copper was in use in the Iberia–Maghreb zone by 2500 BC, bronze by 2000 BC. As with the megaliths, the age and extent of these metals in the desert remain undefined. Apart from the Villa Cisneros 'Neolithic' sherds repaired with copper, the territory has only yielded a copper hook, point and fragments, from the B. du Levrier (Crova 1911). Finds in Mauritania are said to be of early Iberian technique (Saez-Martin 1952): a flat univalve axe with lightly-incurved sides – the engraved Spanish Sahara axes are straight-sided – and heads for an arrow and a spear. Although, chemically, surviving better than iron, any copper or bronze would have been re-used indefinitely by the desert people.

Iron was probably introduced to the Maghreb by Phoenicians during the first millennium BC and then carried to the interior in Roman times by travelling artisans. At a later date, iron-working became the speciality of men from black Africa and today, for example in La Guera, the battered Land-Rovers of the richer nomads and the aged boats of the Spanish fishermen are partially dependent on blacksmiths from the Senegal River, possibly in the tradition of the subjected Bafots put to service their conquerors' chariots.

*Chapter 4*

# Berber History to AD 1400

Little pre-Islamic written history exists for the Atlantic coast of the Sahara; the inscribed stones are potentially informative. The region lay just outside that known to the classical Mediterranean historians.

*Phoenician Traders*
From about 1200 BC, the Phoenician merchants, with Early Metal Age culture, began to spread along the Maghreb. They traded with the coastal Berbers – 'Imazighen', 'free-men' or 'nobles', as the descendants of the Neolithic people called themselves. About this time, others of these Berbers were making the chariot expeditions into the desert, its inhabitants comparatively backward and enfeebled by the increasingly-dry climate.

The most famous of the early voyages known to Europe occurred about 450 BC, when the Carthaginian Hanno, in sixty penteconters, ships of fifty oars each, apparently took 30,000 people down the Atlantic coast to colonise 'Cerne Island'; this was said to be as far from the 'Pillars of Hercules', the mouth of the Mediterranean, as was Carthage in the other direction. Of Cerne, Pliny was to remark that 'All the accipiters of Morocco come there to lay'. The port of Lixus, just south of Tangier, was then a trading point for the gold brought across the western desert and so possibly this was the first of many attempts – at a peak in late medieval time – to cut out the Moroccan middlemen. Hanno claimed to have twice sailed further south beyond Cerne, probably in search of the gold's source. A historian referred to by historians at Pseudo-Scylax mentions an expedition to Cerne in about 337 BC.

Following recent French excavations, it is known that Essaouira, once Mogador, was an important Phoenician trading counter, so that its much-fortified islet may well have been Cerne. Earlier, historians such as Carcopino (1948) suggested Herne Island, joined at low tide to the back of the Villa Cisneros bight; the islet is 1 km by 200 m, reaching 25 m above sea-level in the north-east. Recent roadworks are said to have produced no signs of settlement around the back of the bay at least; the suggestive name does not appear on maps until early in the nineteenth century and is probably a corruption by Captain Glas – examining the coast about 1760 – of an earlier 'Ile des Hérons'. The British marine survey of 1821 cosily improved the name to 'Herne', being also responsible for the present 'Punta Durnford', after one of the midshipmen, and for other English names. However, the explorer Cervera recorded that, in 1886, the local name for the islet was 'Me Truk', 'the Abandoned'. There seem no other choices for Cerne until one reaches the Arguin islands, below C. Blanc; here also there is an 'Ile des Hérons', the islet with the pelicans remarked by Diogo Gomes. No north-west African island appears noted for the birds of prey referred to by Pliny, though all will have had bird concentrations, until human colonisation. As to Hanno's furthest point to the south, not clear from his descriptions – though it would have been very difficult for his kind of boats to return from below C. Bojador, historians have suggested the Senegal and the Cameroons.

## Roman Domination

The East Mediterranean's trade with the Imazighen was disrupted when, in 146 BC, the Romans destroyed Carthage. Rome's colonisation, of the whole North African coast, was to be imitated by the post-medieval European nations. In 29 BC, the indigenous people were, first, divided into Protectorates, that of the west being called Mauretania Tingitana and reaching only halfway down the Moroccan coast. Then, in AD 42, this Protectorate was made into a Province; for similar political reasons, Spain began to call the Spanish Sahara a Province in 1958. The Romans were aware of the trans-Sahara gold caravans, of course, but there is no record of their going far into the desert, though Pliny knew of the Draa River; they did carry out punitive raids, from at least 32 BC, on the recalcitrant 'Barbarians' of the interior, driving them into the mountains and, about AD 40, chasing them into the Sahara. There is a strong possibility that the first important colonisation of the Canaries was by people from the Mauretanian Province, shipped there, perhaps as exiles, by the Romans: evidence ranges from a late-Roman amphora recently found off the north-eastern island of Graciosa, through physiques and culture, to the earliest C14 dates, these all in the first centuries AD (Mercer 1973).

With the fourth century collapse of the Romans' empire, control of the Tangier area passed by the fifth century to the Vandal people and, during the sixth and seventh, to the Byzantines. Neither group appears to have influenced the western desert's population, by now once again becoming distinct from that of the Maghreb.

These last few pre-Islamic centuries probably saw the development of a way of life which lasted into the twentieth century: faced with the difficulties of raising crops and animals in the deteriorating environment, the desert Berbers would have become increasingly dependent, parasitically, on the few vulnerable settlements and the cross-desert caravans. They were now ready to evolve towards the camel-riding nomads clearly recorded from the late Middle Ages, towards the way of life based on extortion and robbery in a setting of tribal feuds.

*Oscillations in Imazighen Power*

By the first centuries AD, the 'free men' of north-west Africa were divided into three main groups: the Zenata dominated the Tripolitania–Tunisia interior, the Masmuda held the Moroccan Atlas, the Sanhaja – Zenaga or Azenaga – lived on the vast triangle of desert between the Moroccan Sus, the west Mauritania Trarza and, now in Mali, Timbuctoo. The Sanhaja were a confederation of four main tribes, the Lemta, Gadala, Messoufa and, the most powerful, the Lemtuna. The confederation emerges into history as an ambitious people, animists, their tongue nowadays called Berber and their inscriptions in the old Sahara alphabet, the men veiled. The central Sahara 'Touareg' remain today as the Sanhaja's most pure descendants.

The little information on the Berbers before the arrival of the Arabs can be quickly summarised. Reference has been made to the tradition of their expulsion of the black Bafots from the Sahara. In this or a later expansion, the Berbers – probably the Sanhaja, possibly the Zenata – came to dominate the Senegal–Chad people, memory of this remaining in the name of the Senegal River and in the white kings found in the history of the region's black people. Armed throughout with javelins and round shields, the Berbers seem to have evolved from chariots drawn by horses through horse-riding and, perhaps, ox-carts, to the camel as both mount and pack-animal. It seems that, in the third century AD, the Lemtuna had become vassals of the emerging kingdom of Ghana in the south and, possibly, of the Zenata in the north; by the eighth century the Lemtuna were fighting both Ghana and the Tekrour black people, now the Toutcouleurs.

Just before this, in AD 680, the first Arabs, under Okba, arrived in Morocco, the most far-reaching immigration since that of Neolithic culture. The Maghreb Berbers found the Arabs, Bedouin, more like themselves than the Romans and other invaders had been and, if they resisted further foreign domination, had however little difficulty in assimilating the Moslem beliefs. Apart perhaps from the 'Sudan' expedition of Okba's grandson, AD 732, the first Arab wave did not directly penetrate the desert – but the Berbers themselves spread Islam southwards. The Maghreb traders wanted the gold of the Wangara, the river valleys of the Upper Niger and the Senegal, and also ivory and an Islam-tolerated stimulant, the cola nut; they took down cattle and horses, trinkets and metalware, copper and cowries – and the Moslem faith. An important caravan route was from Sijilmassa, near Risani in south Morocco, to Ghana; the latter was prosperous from its control of the gold and salt trades. The route passed through the Lemtuna territory and in particular went by way of their main settlement, Aoudaghost; a town with 5,000 inhabitants, this lay some 600 km east of the present Nouakchott. At the end of the tenth century, Ghana took over the town, taxing its people, and dominated the southern desert. The Lemtuna now centred themselves on Atar in the Mauritanian Adrar mountains, easily defended.

In the zone of direct and powerful Arab influence, the Maghreb, the eighth century saw the Berbers already breaking away from the eastern dominance, first by the social, fiscal and religious Kharijite revolt of 740 and then by the installation of the first member of the schismatic Idrissites in 786. This dynasty fell in the tenth century, coincidentally with the apogee of the Ghana empire. By this point the whole Maghreb–Sudan area was nominally Moslem. The region, together with Spain, was next to be unified politically under the Berbers.

Early in the eleventh century, a Sanhaja chief went to Mecca. Feeling as a result that his people's practice of the Moslem religion was debased, on the way back he asked a Sijilmassa divine, Ibn Yasin, to come with him to reform the desert Berbers. This puritanism was rejected by his tribesmen. Ibn Khaldun, the fourteenth-century historian, then records how, in 1030, Ibn Yasin and two Lemtuna chiefs retired from the world to 'a hill surrounded by water . . . penetrated to the centre of the undergrowth . . . and, each choosing a place, settled down to a life of prayer'. Many joined them in their fortress, or *ribat*, for religious and military instruction. The site has not yet been located: Hugot (1966) at first thought it was Tidra, an island 150 km south of C. Blanc, shown by his excavations to have had much occupation, but later decided against this as there were no traces of buildings.

At length, about 1043, Ibn Yasin could declare: 'A thousand men are not easily defeated; thus we must now work to maintain truth and, if needs be, to force its acknowledgement. Let us go from here and carry out the task laid upon us'. The 'people of the *ribat*', or

Almoravides, soon forced their doctrines on the other Sanhaja and then divided into two militant streams, to south and north. In each direction there were in fact territorial as well as religious matters at stake, as will be seen.

By 1054 the Sanhaja, under the Lemtuna Abu Bekr, Emir of the Adrar, had destroyed the still-Ghanese Aoudaghost, and in 1076 sacked the negroes' capital, Koumbi-Saleh, 400 km to the south-east; in this they were in fact helped by the Tekrours. One effect was to consolidate Islam, but only as the elite religion of the region; the masses remained effectively animists. Secondly, the focus of civilisation moved southwards, to evolve into the Mali empire of the mid-thirteenth century, and trans-Sahara trade shifted eastwards to routes, from Timbuctoo and Gao, through more stable zones. In fact, though unable to control Ghana for more than a decade, the Sanhaja did bring on the disintegration of the kingdom. However, the bell tolled for the Berbers themselves when, on the Senegal in 1087, a negro's poisoned arrow killed Abu Bekr.

About then the Almoravides held the Maghreb and Spain too. By 1069 the northwards-going Berbers, under Ibn Tashfin, had taken over all Morocco and were founding Marrakesh. Some time prior to this, the Moroccan Sanhaja leaders had been asserting themselves against the eastern Fatimites and this dynasty had reacted by sending an army of primitive and unwanted Hilalian Bedouin to the Maghreb; the first of the 'horde of locusts', in Ibn Khaldun's phrase, had arrived there in 1061, but initially the Almoravides successfully controlled this threat. Secondly, the desert Sanhaja had early on taken over Sijilmassa, then held by the Zenata, and repulsed these rival Berbers' incursions on the Moroccan Sanhaja and their monopoly of the northern end of the trans-Sahara trade. The Almoravides presented themselves to the Maghreb people as their liberators from these threats and from their corrupt rulers and unjust taxes. In Morocco, the Malikite rite, now part of orthodox Islam, is of Almoravide origin. At its maximum, Almoravide influence reached to the E Maghreb and the Fezzan.

In 1085, these Berbers, still led by Ibn Tashfin, crossed to Spain to help the weakened Omayyad caliphate against Alphonso VI, and in fact took over control. By about 1100 the Almoravides nominally commanded from Zaragoza to Ghana, allowing a modern Spanish writer, in one of Spain's many twentieth-century political contortions, to claim that 'Spaniards of all epochs . . . including El Bekri of Huelva in the eleventh century . . . have called Rio de Oro [Spanish Sahara] a "province"'.

Two often-repeated factors brought about the decay of Almoravide power: internal dissent and a rising outside force. The events of the second half of the eleventh century had led to various tribal movements in the western desert, placing a strain on natural resources and human nature. The Sanhaja fought fiercely amongst themselves, notably in 1056 in the Adrar, where the Gadala were defeated by 'the men of the *ribat*', the Lemtuna's leader, Ibn Omar, being killed; El Bekri said that at prayer time one could still hear the calls of the muezzin over the battlefield, a place then shunned. Secondly, in Morocco the Almoravides' crusading spirit was soon lost and they began to act as foreign conquerors. This led their old enemies, the Masmuda Berbers of the Atlas, under Ibn Tumart, to rise in 1125 as the 'Almohades', the 'people of one god'; revenge, power and expansion were always sought under a religious banner. By 1147, after much fighting and with Marrakesh lost, the desert Almoravides' century of dominance was at an end.

Simultaneously the continuing influx into Morocco of eastern Arabs, much accelerated from the twelfth century onwards, disorganised the country and perpetuated the low level of the western trans-desert trade, disrupted in the previous century by the Almoravides themselves. The long-established Sahara crossing had been Sijilmassa–Tindouf–Kedia Ijil or the Ouarane desert–Aoudaghost but the troubles allowed Timbuctoo and Gao to continue to increase in importance, the former for those caravans still going to Morocco and the latter for Tripolitania. This isolated the Sanhaja from the Maghreb.

In the thirteenth century, the Arab warrior immigrants arriving from the east included the Maquil, come to support the Merinides, these being Zenata Berbers risen in turn against the Almohades, the Masmouda Berber dynasty. Halting at first in the Draa–Tafilalet zone, from the fourteenth century the ungrateful hostility of the Merinide dynasty, installed in 1258, led the Maquil to emigrate southwards as far as Mauritania; the main group was the 'sons of Hassan'. Naturally, there was conflict with the Sanhaja over many issues; a practical matter was the right to use the wells, in the digging of which the Berbers were very active. The Sanhaja were merchants and shepherds, well enough materially, pious and education-conscious – both boys and girls were taught – yet still very much divided within their confederation. The Arabs, poor and relatively backward, were fighters. However, they made some alliances, notably with the Gadala. From about 1400 the Hassaniya Arab tribes of the Delim and Oudaia took over control of the desert, setting up emirates; the first occupied the southern part of the present Spanish Sahara, the second were based in north Mauritania. As a result, the fifteenth century was for the desert a period of re-lit Moslem fervour. A Berber converted to Islam not only obtained full social status under the new order, but could also take over the belongings of one of the unconverted . . . all became Moslems. Berbers and Arabs began to intermarry and to interweave their cultures, with the former going over to the Arabic tongue.

One of the last references to the Saharan Sanhaja in their original state was by Ibn Khaldun, who died in 1405. Writing of the Mali region, he said: 'Close north is the country of the Lamtunah and of the other groups of the veiled Berbers (Sinhajah) as well as the deserts in which they roam'. Most of those who, in the desert, still speak Berber, including the 200,000 Touareg and also some north-west Mauritanian tribes, will be more or less full descendants of these Sanhaja.

The Berber assimilation of Arab blood and culture, due partially to compatibility and partially to force of arms and then social expediency, was superficially total in the case of some tribes, less so or not at all in the case of others such as the Touareg. In 1644 the Sanhaja revolted against the Hassaniya Arabs, opening a long war. Their leader was Abou Bakr ibn Omar, the Lemtuna Emir; he was defeated in the Trarza and died in 1650. By 1674 the Arabs had regained control. Since then all the free Berber tribes of the littoral desert have claimed Arab origin – as opposed to merely having become Moslems and culturally and linguistically Arabised – as this has come to give the highest social status. Chapter 8 will discuss the final phase of west Sahara society.

# Chapter 5

# Portuguese and Spanish Incursions, 1434–1638

The long period of 1200–1850, its legacies visible in current African and European attitudes, is sporadically illumined in the case of the coastal Sahara by the widely-spaced chronicles of a few explorers and travellers. Real or imaginary, the many voyages of the first two centuries – mainly by Mediterraneans – are only dimly lit, by notes rather than by narratives. Then, in the mid-fifteenth century, the full Sahara sun is suddenly shining upon real people, at least along the shore between C. Blanc and Arguin Island: the records are those of the Portuguese man-hunts and trading, left by Gomes Eannes and by Ca da Mosto. Next, the torch is held up by the Spanish, in their well-documented 1476–1524 slave-catching and barter action on the mainland opposite the Canaries. Throughout the many centuries covered by this and the next chapter, only force of arms could preserve foreigners on the Sahara coast – for European inhumanity and African barbarity stimulated each other – and this state was in fact to continue until 1934.

*The First Recorded Voyages from Morocco*
The earliest credible report, by the thirteenth-century Ibn Said, relates how another African, Ibn Fatima, set out from C. Nun in southern Morocco and reached a bay abounding in tunny, with white birds on the shore – probably the pelicans again, herons being presumably too well known in the Maghreb to go unnamed – to be wrecked there and find himself in the territory of the Gadala Berbers: a 1320 planisphere shows their lands stretching to Arguin, with their capital between there and the Saguiet-el-Hamra, so probably Ibn Fatima reached the B. du Levrier, the pelicans' northern limit. He had to return overland, as did his next recorded successor, Mohammed ben Ragano: at some time prior to 1337, he sailed to C. Timiris,

just south of Tidra Island. Stranded Moslems were well received by the coastal people, just then becoming Islamised. The early four-teenth century was the time of the Merinides' zenith, with Moroccan pirates raiding the Canaries and probably being driven onto the Sahara coast.

Even when not shipwrecked, the steady wind and current from the north made it hard for sailing boats to return from below the Canaries. However, in late medieval times the map, compass, rudder and quadrant were coming into general use in the Mediterranean and, according to Mauny (1960), by tacking ENE and NNW according to the time of day, boats could get back up to the archipelago.

## The Earliest European Explorers

The first medieval northerners known to have sailed into 'the Sea of Darkness' were the Vivaldi brothers, leaving Genoa in 1291; they hoped to reach the Indies by this route but were never seen again. The next vessel to pass C. Bojador – the Arabic *bou khatar* or 'father of danger' – was a *huissier*, the little galley of Jaime Ferrer, a Catalan who, in 1346, also disappeared southwards. Seated in his boat, he is depicted on the 1375 planisphere of the Jewish Abraham Cresques, leaving '*per mar al Riu de l'Or*'. This logically refers to the Senegal, the upper reaches of which had long produced gold, but the name has since been variously attached to the whole of present Spanish Sahara, or to its southern half, or just to the Villa Cisneros bay, the latter supported by historians who interpret *riu* in the Galician sense of *ria*, sea-loch; however, Cresques was not from the Cantabric coast but a part of the developing merchant marine of Majorca, an island responsible for many more unnarrated voyages during the second half of the century. Amongst the pretended journeys, the best known is that said to have been made by Dieppe expeditionaries to Guinea, 1364–1410.

By 1400 both the Canaries and the coast opposite had been reconnoitred. The islands had been known to Europeans for up to a century, with a slave-catching raid by a Mediterranean vessel under Niccoloso da Recco in 1341; the conquest of the islands nearest Spanish Sahara began in 1402 (Mercer 1973). In the desert, the Saguiet-el-Hamra was known to Europeans by 1350 – it is the only useful information in the fictitious 'Travels' narrated by a mendicant Spanish friar, of this date – and Wadan, 550 km east of C. Blanc, had by then been placed on the Europeans' maps.

## Africans and Europeans about A.D. 1400

As the first detailed narrative of Saharaui–Iberian contact is approached, the driving characteristics of each group can be summarised. The coastal people were the indigenous Sanhaja Berbers and immigrant Hassaniya Arabs: the southern part of the territory, a Gadala preserve in Ibn Fatima's time, was by now becoming the domain of the Delim Arabs, probably by a mixture of fighting, treaty and absorption. As described, it was a time of change in the desert, though the Europeans were probably quite unaware of this. The Moslem religion was fervently practised – as it was then in all Islam – stimulating a strong feeling against 'infidels' appearing on the coast; the Saguiet-el-Hamra was a minor centre for scholars and mystics, growing parallel to the shrinkage of the Arab world, the fall of Granada in 1492 to be the last event said to have sent impulses into the desert. Another very active facet of nomadic life, noted by Ibn Khaldun, was the trade in negro slaves. Though slavery had long been in existence in the region, an organised traffic developed parallel to the main Arab immigrations into the desert, possibly because these had never had ties with the black people to the south and, themselves most immediately from the Maghreb, they could appreciate the commercial value of slaves taken to the north; however, the Almoravide eleventh-century conquest of Ghana may have added greatly to the slaves taken up each year into white Africa; in fact, it is likely that the slave trade has varied greatly in intensity since the Neolithic. Otherwise, life was dependent on the camel, with regular raids and battles as diversions.

The Europeans had various motives for landing on the Sahara coast. Commercial: stimulated by maps such as Cresques' of 1375, showing a pass in the Atlas used by 'merchants going to the land of the Negroes of Guinea', they hoped for gold and slaves and also sought seals, fish and spices. Each nation's territorial enlargement, perhaps with colonisation. Religious influence, coupled to the exaggeration of Christianity's sway in Africa, with a lost Christian kingdom awaiting re-discovery. Adventurers hoped for personal fame, titles and land. In combination with all these there was the search for knowledge, the least zealously pursued in practice.

### The Portuguese Raids, 1421–46

By 1421 Henry the Navigator, the Portuguese Infanta, was sending ships out into the Atlantic, since he was 'desirous to learn new things, particularly of the peoples dwelling in those lands, and to cause injury to the Moors'. He also wished to get at the sources of gold and slaves and to find a way to the Indies which avoided the Turks. Henry's Atlantic ambitions encompassed the Azores, Madeira, Canaries and, preferably with these as a base, the African coast. The satanic C.

Bojador was at last passed – going north, as the trouble had always been to get back again – by his captain Gil Eannes in 1434, in a small single-masted, square-sailed *barcha*. The expeditions of the next twelve years were chronicled by Gomes Eannes, a native of Azurara in Portugal's Minho province.

By 1446, he wrote, some fifty of Henry's caravels had passed C. Bojador, reaching the Senegal River. Though they did operate in the 'Rio de Oro' bight, the focus was the C. Blanc–C. Timiris zone, especially Gete, soon called Arguin, a bare, low islet of sandstone. In practical terms the recorded results were both black and white slaves, gold-dust from the Sudan, seals and fish, an ox-hide shield, a clutch of ostrich eggs served up to the Infanta. Otherwise there was some increase of knowledge, to be balanced against the enduring memory of the incessant treachery, fighting and enslavement. The Portuguese knighted each other on the battlefields, looked forward to divine reward for their Christian labours.

A total of 927 slaves was taken in the period, Gomes Eannes re-marking: 'Oh, if only among those who fled there had been some little understanding of higher things,' then they would have given themselves up 'that they might have saved their souls'. The slaves were mostly caught during surprise attacks, to trumpets and shouts of 'Portugal' and 'Santiago', on the settlements on and around the Arguin and Tidra islands, though the caravels did work the coast as far down as the Senegal. Against the archers, crossbowmen, lancers and footmen, the nomads could only fight with spears and stones, and often fled, abandoning their women and children. Sometimes the captured nomads ransomed themselves for six or seven of their own black slaves. The most successful raid was on Naar Island, in 1443: helped by 'Our Lord God, who giveth a reward for every good deed . . .', the caravels, each flying the Cross of the Order of Jesus, took off 165 slaves, including all the children who had been hidden in the seaweed by their parents, many of these killed or drowned whilst trying to escape. Soon after, these Portuguese saw twenty 'canoes' crossing to an island, but their own boat was very small 'and, moved with pity, although they were heathen . . . they sought to kill but a few', and took aboard the fourteen smallest.

On arrival back in Lagos, in Portugal, where one could see 'houses full to overflowing with male and female slaves', the 235 African survivors were 'poorly and out of condition'. They were put in a field and divided into five lots, the best for Henry who, however, gave away his statutory fifth, for his reward lay in 'the salvation of those souls that before were lost'. A popular public spectacle, some were 'white enough, fair to look upon and well-proportioned, others less white like mulattoes, others as black as Ethiops, and so ugly . . . the images of a lower hemisphere'. All were lamenting, striking their faces with their hands, throwing themselves on the ground. The chronicler indulged in much sentiment over their misery and the separation, there, of husbands from wives, parents from children. However, they were now better off than when they had had 'no knowledge of bread or wine . . . covering of clothes or houses . . . and only knew how to live in bestial sloth'. Nevertheless, getting 'prepared food and coverings, their bellies began to swell' and some died, 'but as Christians'. But once the survivors got the habit of clothes 'they picked up the rags which fell from the coats of the other people . . . and sewed them on their own garments'. This is one of the first examples of the degeneration and low-level assimilation sequence which has usually followed African contact with Europeans over the last 500 years.

The commercial results of these first voyages stimulated many Portuguese merchants to ask Henry for licences to send caravels to West Africa. These boats, covering 100–200 km a day, were twenty to thirty metres long and six to eight metres wide, with three masts each carrying a long pole from which hung a lateen sail; they were armed with bombards and culverins. In 1440, Henry got papal indulgences for those fighting against the Africans; he gave his men a Crusade banner which absolved those who died fighting beneath it.

Back on the Arguin coast, the nomads soon began to move inland or, when encountered, were now in large, daunting bands. Though ineffective fighters at the side of the well-prepared Portuguese, they did kill a number of these; the blundering Gonçalo da Sintra, whose name is still attached to a big bay south of Villa Cisneros, made his last mistake when cut off by the tide on Naar Island. The Portuguese could not go far inland, due both to fear of the nomads and to the climate, lack of horses and the general difficulty of keeping themselves alive in the vast desert. In 1448 they began the first of Arguin's many forts and 'after this year, the affairs of these parts were . . . treated more by trafficking and bargaining of merchants than by bravery and toil of arms'.

The Portuguese had brought back some information on the region. The brunt of their raids fell on coastal hut settlements; the people, good swimmers, owned wooden 'canoes' and, naked and three or four to a craft, apparently used their legs as paddles; the references to nets, well-made of tree-bark thread, shows they were one of the tributary fishing tribes such as that now at least known as the Imraguen. These were seen using donkeys, to carry a large catch of

3   Wild life in the south-west: gazelles (*Gazella dorcas*), a *fenec* fox (*Fenecus zerda*), flamingoes taking off at Nouadhibou.

4 Crescentic Neolithic tomb below Oumm Arouaguene, near the Kedia Ijil, seen along a 'horn' towards cairn itself.

MacKenzie's trading counter on an islet at Tarfaya, Cap Juby. Built in 1878, it is now abandoned.

turtles. Probably they were the tribe who indignantly hacked to pieces a Portuguese catch whilst it was drying in the sun on the shore at Angra dos Ruivos. It was thought that the coastal people ate the liver and blood of dead Europeans.

On the nomads' life, first-hand information came from João Fernandes, left with them for seven months as a hostage, in 1445; he had been a captive of the Moors in the Mediterranean. Though he knew some Arabic, he could not understand that spoken by the Arabs and, by then, by the Sanhaja leaders, none of whom could write; all were certainly Moslems. His clothes, biscuit and corn being taken away, and a burnous given him to wear, he then went with the nomads to their main pasturage, in the interior desert between Taghaza and the Sudan. Moving on at least every eight days, his companions centred their lives around the animals – camels and horse, sheep and goats, some cattle – and on selling negroes to the Moorish and Christian merchants of the eastern Maghreb. The nomads also hunted, and seemingly stole a great deal from the negroes, probably within the local rules of tribute extortion, described in Chapter 8. Fernandes and his companions, and also the dogs and horses, had sometimes nothing but camel milk as food; the band ate wild plants and their seeds. The region produced amber, civet perfume and resin, he said. Desert navigation was by the stars, wind and direction of the birds. The nomads wore skin tunics and shoes; a woman veiled her face before a stranger but did not worry much about the rest of her body. The chiefs were rich, some with gold rings in their ears and even in their noses. The tribes were not subject to the kingdoms of the Maghreb. The chronicler recorded, with understandable astonishment, that Fernandes became on such good terms with the nomads that they wept on separating from him.

Finally, these early Portuguese left a few natural history notes, such as those on the seals and storks and a description of the various fish unknown to them. In the desert they recognised migrant birds from Portugal: 'Quails, turtle-doves, wry-necks, nightingales, and linnets . . . in search of warmth', whilst others they thought went up to Portugal in the winter for food, such as 'falcons, herons, ring-doves, thrushes'. Amongst the birds of the Ile des Hérons they saw 'some hornbills, all white . . . greater than swans, and with beaks of a cubit's length or more . . . like the engrained sheaths of swords, so wrought and with such ornamentation as . . . with the aid of fire to give them beauty . . . the mouth and maw so great that the leg of a man would go into it to the knee'. Clearly, at this time both the hornbill and the pelican were little known in Europe; the second was to be accurately identified in 1456 by Diogo Gomes.

*Portuguese Traders, 1446–1638*

In 1455, soon after its first fortification, Arguin was visited by a Venetian, Alvise de Ca da Mosto, aboard a Portuguese caravel. In addition to the following notes on the Sanhaja, he explained a re-orientation of Portuguese policy towards the Africans: Henry had forbidden raiding in the hope of converting the Sanhaja, who were 'not yet firmly attached to the tenets of Mohammed'. The Infanta had begun the leasing of Arguin to Portuguese traders, these with dwellings and counters on the island; caravels went to and fro regularly. In 1456, following hostilities with Spain over the Atlantic territories, the Portuguese were adjudicated by the Pope all land below C. Bojador.

By 1461 the Arguin fort had been destroyed – either by the Spanish or by the Africans – and rebuilt. Its main source of trade was Wadan, a halt for the slave caravans and six days away by camel; in 1487, the Portuguese are said to have tried to actually set up a counter at Wadan, probably in that case the origin of the 'Christian' or 'Portuguese' wells, legends and other features of the interior. A thousand slaves a year were now being sent to Portugal, these and gold-dust being obtained for cloth and grain. The nomads got the slaves cheaply in the south, sometimes as many as fifteen for a single horse, these animals often being brought down from Morocco due to the difficulty of rearing them in the desert. Ca da Mosto added that 'On all the coast, there are very large fisheries', these Portuguese drying their catches on the shores.

'The first time they saw sails . . . they believed they were great sea-birds . . . when the sails were lowered . . . that they were fishes. Others . . . that they were phantoms that went by night.' The Venetian explained that the Africans could not understand the caravels' speed; and these always attacked in the dark. They themselves, wrote Valentim Fernandes in 1509, had no better vessel than a raft of corded tree-trunks, propelled by pieces of wood used oar-wise at the back, the water halfway up their legs. About 1600, Pory, translator of Leo Africanus, wrote: 'They go to sea in certaine small botes which they call *Almadies*'. The pre-conquest Canary Island people were equally without sea-going boats and were similarly amazed at the first European ships.

Further information was provided on the Sanhaja themselves. They appeared to have no religion of their own, nor kings in the European sense – might and wealth gave leadership. The richer wore the in-creasingly-traded European cloth, with turbans, the poorer went in skins and adorned their hair with a daily unction of fish oil. 'That woman who has the largest breasts is considered more beautiful than the others . . . at the age of seventeen each woman binds a cord around the breasts . . . frequent pulling every day causes them to grow and lengthen so much that many reach the navel'. The Venetian said the Sanhaja only used currency, white cowrie shells, when trading in the interior, probably meaning the south.

Fig. 9. Saharauis, 1601, from *Travels* by Jean Mocquet (pub. 1696)

Sixteenth-century information seems lacking on Arguin and perhaps the trade and fishing continued without important events. In 1601, Jean Mocquet reached the coast aboard the French *Serene*, the ship having been attacked four times by pirates since leaving St Malo. He was told that the Arguin fort was manned by Portuguese soldiers, on friendly terms with the Africans; fish and ostrich feathers were now perhaps the main cargo. Told not to fish that coast by five Spanish vessels – Iberia was then temporarily a single, united kingdom – the *Serene* was finally captured by a ruse, ship and catch being sent back to Spain as a prize. In 1638 the Dutch took Arguin, the local people welcoming the change, because, it seems, they had been ill-treated by the Portuguese.

### The Spanish at Sta Cruz de Mar Pequeña, 1476–1524

Although the Spanish had long been eyeing the coast opposite the Canaries – in 1449, for example, King Juan II gave the C. Guer–C. Bojador strip to Duke Juan de Guzman – it was not until 1476 that an expedition is recorded on this Saharan shore. At this date the four lesser Canaries were in the hands of Diego de Herrera whilst the rights to the three unconquered islands had just passed from him to the Spanish crown since it was beyond his means to capture these. Herrera decided that instead he would exploit the African coast for slaves and other loot, filling two urgent needs, practical and political. Firstly, the Spaniards' treatment of the subjected islanders had by now left Fuerteventura and Lanzarote short of slave-labour and, secondly, Castille and Portugal had spent the middle years of the century disputing the C. Guer–C. Bojador coast, a matter Herrera felt best settled by simply taking over this zone.

The first expedition's six boats came in secretly at midnight at a place called 'Guader', perhaps just a Spanish corruption of *wadi*, watercourse. Hastily, they built a tower, calling it 'Santa Cruz de Mar Pequeña', and garrisoned it, with artillery and its own boats, under Alonso Cabrera. Maps of the period show the site was opposite the eastern Canaries, in which Herrera lived, being either at Wadi Chebica (Rumeu de Armas 1956) or at Puerto Cansado; the latter is a five-kilometre lagoon said to have wells and two ruined towers, a square one on the north beach, a round construction on the opposite shore at the entrance to the narrows. However, twentieth-century Spanish politicians long tried to place the tower in the Ifni region, 250–180 km to the north, to justify and continue the Spaniards' 1934–69 enclave there.

Although a modern peninsular writer describes 'the enthusiasm of the tribes . . . to become Spaniards', within a year or two the tower was under siege by 10,000 foot and 2,000 to 3,000 cavalry; Herrera apparently relieved his base with only 700 men, in five ships, something of a Quixotic distortion. The man-hunts now got under way with the aid of a renegade African newly christened Juan Camacho, said to have planned forty-six raids by the time he died, at a great age, in 1591. The author has described in detail elsewhere (Mercer 1973) the effect on the eastern Canaries of the massive forced immigration of Africans between 1476 and about 1550; although their physique and culture blended with those descended from the prehistoric immigrations from north-west Africa, clear traces of this late medieval wave can be seen in the present place-names and in the Arabic elements in modern speech, additional to those normal to Castilian. As an example of the manhunts, about 1480, and as revenge for the siege, the Spanish attacked the Taghaost area, taking 158 captives.

In Europe, Papal Bulls alternated with treaties. In 1480, the Alcaçovas decision gave the C. Bojador–Guinea coast to the Portuguese; in 1494 the Tordesillas agreement adjudicated to the Spaniards the zone opposite the Canaries, from C. Bojador up to Messa, at least some 650 km in a straight line, together with raiding rights below. However, with Columbus' departure from the western Canaries in 1492, Spain turned her energies to the Americas, so that the African venture was never to receive much official support and so did not become of national importance.

Herrera had died in 1485 and his tower was abandoned at some time in the next ten years. In 1495 his widow, Inés Peraza, wanted to rebuild, again as a private venture, but, handicapped by their lack of formal ownership of the site, she saw the Crown forcibly take over, putting the enterprise in the hands of its Canary governor, Alonso Fajardo. The last island fell in 1496 and, in the same year, and protected by thirty out-of-work veterans of the Canary campaign, the new 'royal tower' of Sta Cruz was begun. The soldiers, forty-four crew and twenty-eight craftsmen were kept fed by three fishermen and had their clothes laundered by a washerwoman, Maria. Boat charter, wages and materials cost over a million maravedis and the tower was up in three months. The garrison then left behind was only seventeen men, armed with lombard cannon, long muskets and crossbows. The tower was planned both as a trading counter – as usual tapping the caravan route for gold and slaves – and as a base for expansion into Africa. However, there was a risk that uncontrollable adventurers along the coast might stir up the Africans, so in 1497 the Catholic Kings declared the tower area a 'peace zone' . . . the manhunts could continue elsewhere.

For a while life in the tower ran smoothly but then Inés Peraza, brooding in the wings, chose the moment when, in 1498, it was being re-victualled by Alonso de Lugo, the victor and Captain-General of the Canaries, to go into action. She persuaded a Portuguese relative, the notorious Diego da Silva, to come with no less than eight ships and – in spite of the Tordesillas treaty – sack the post. This was the first of Lugo's unhappy experiences on this coast. Inés Peraza then seems to have quietly put up a trading tower somewhere else on the coast – most habitable bays now have ruins.

The peak of Spanish activity on the coast, and the moment most often described by twentieth-century politicians, came on 13 February, 1499. Following talks in the Canaries and at Sta Cruz, the leaders of the Ait bu Aita, or Ait bu Tata, a disintegrating Berber confederation holding the Messa-Draa-Icht zone, received a Spanish delegation in their capital, Taghaost, now called Legsabi, and seemingly pledged submission to the Spanish monarchs, then even sending ambassadors to the peninsula. This led to increased Spanish trading with Taghaost; the first use of the African territories for exiles came when a Canary civil servant was sent there for violating the Guanche queen of Adeje in Tenerife.

However, a part of the desert region's people was against the treaty, so the Spanish decided to take over thoroughly with the aid of three more towers: at Taghaost, at its port of 'San Miguel' on the Assaka River, and at C. Bojador. Lugo was offered the expedition and the title of 'Captain-General of Africa', being well-placed to raise the soldiery and finance in the Canaries; the Crown was to take a risk-free fifth of the profits. Preferably pacific, with the people to be well and honestly treated, the expedition was to fight if needs be, *pueda azerles la guerra*. The venture began ominously: the Canary veterans by now preferred their island lands and slaves to further battle, so that Lugo had to use menaces and violence to conscript and then drive them aboard the vessels. The 400 men landed at the mouth of the Assaka, not finding the friendly tribes there as expected. A Portuguese having perhaps stirred up the opposition, a hostile force exaggerated at 20,000 men gradually gathered, the new tower being built at a frantic rate. Lugo, if he did not actually burn his boats, did send them out to sea. At the first assault the trenches, parapets and walls were overcome and, by dusk, three-quarters of the Spaniards were killed, with the redoubtable Lugo left for dead with 'many wounds in the head and body'. The remaining hundred invaders retreated to the beach, spending the night hoping for the return of the boats. But these, seeing the slaughter, had set sail. In the morning the Africans butchered the remaining Spaniards, except the best-dressed, kept for ransom. Some loyal Berbers now appeared and, finding Lugo still alive, took him to Taghaost; a few days later the Captain-General of Africa was carried into Sta Cruz on a litter, to be taken back to the Canaries in a ship lent – the final humiliation – by his old enemy Inés Peraza 'in the national interest', as Rumeu puts it. With him went a few other survivors from the 400 men. Parts of the Canaries, for example Sta Cruz de Tenerife, were left with only women and children. The Crown refusing to share in the costs, Lugo found himself in great debt.

Yet, no wiser, in 1501 the two parties were planning another tower, this time as far up as C. Guer, by the present Agadir. This was to dominate the rich Messa-Guer zone, though the Tordesillas treaty had given provisional rights in the area to the Portuguese. The latter were also then given grounds for complaint when Lugo, in need of funds, went to look for orchil, a valuable dye-lichen, to the south of C. Bojador, a zone in which the Spanish could legally only hunt men. In 1502, then, an exemplary expedition landed at Galevarba, unidentified, somewhere on the Agadir cape and, after this time defeating the Massa tribesmen by the use of artillery, had the tower almost up . . . when a royal command came to abandon the project, a victory for Portuguese diplomacy. So, after two months' fruitless work, Lugo returned to the islands; the Crown's immediate contribution to his fresh losses was to change his title to *adelantado* or Governor of the Canaries. The Massa people long insisted this was a triumph for their arms; in 1505 they welcomed the building of a tower there by the Portuguese.

In 1508 the increasing Moorish piracy in the Mediterranean led the Spanish to occupy one of its strongholds, Peñon de Velez; this came within the 'Kingdom of Fez', a Portuguese area of operations under the Tordesillas treaty. The breach was only healed by Spain giving Portugal its small Atlantic zone of influence, R. Massa to C. Bojador; the Sta Cruz tower was to continue Spanish but trade was to come to it, not to be sought the length of the coast. Henceforth, to trade, raid or fish, other than at the one tower, a Spaniard or any other European would need a licence from the Portuguese.

Now Portugal, in turn, began to think of taking over the region, and even asked Lugo's prestigious help. However, this was a moment of great religious fervour in south Morocco, paralleling the decadence of the reigning Beni Watta dynasty; a Hassan-descended family on the Draa River were being hailed as *mahdis* and, eventually taking over Morocco as the Saadian dynasty, were now gradually incorporating the always independently-minded Sus into their territory by force. The traveller Leo Africanus, in the area about 1512, refers to the Arabs' molestation of the Berbers. The warriors of this new Holy War unsuccessfully assaulted the Portuguese fort at C. Guer in 1511; in 1516 they took over the Messa and Ait bu Aita tribes, together with Taghaost . . . the following year they attacked Sta Cruz, burning it down, only to see the Canary people arrive within ten days and rebuild it. But in 1524 a second assault, without relief from the islands, said to have then been plague-stricken, finally drove the

Spaniards off the desert coast; they did not build again until 1884. In 1527, a combined Portuguese-Spanish massacre of Africans in a coastal settlement brought on a series of attacks against the C. Guer fort, finally destroyed in 1541. Near it, in 1572, the Moors built the *alcázaba* of Agadir.

As did the Portuguese counter at Arguin, so the Spanish action opposite the Canaries had brought in slaves, merchandise and fish. At first these had come from uncontrolled private ventures but, with the Canary conquest over and the Sta Cruz fort rebuilt as 'royal', all African operations became controlled and in some cases monopolised by the Crown. Taking first the man-hunting, in 1500 Lugo began to enforce the no-slaving rule on the C. Guer–C. Bojador coast: in Las Palmas the market in humans thereupon collapsed, its port's traffic declined, island depopulation began. Even the church was complaining, of loss of alms. The only exploitable area, below C. Bojador, was difficult to raid. But, in fact, the royal tower's income was suffering anyway because, reassured, the Africans now traded with private merchants able to land all along the temporarily-peaceful coast. Lugo's abortive tower-building expeditions of 1500–2 partially hid the islands' crisis, but in 1505 the ban had to be lifted and the 'war' – it was justifiable to enslave captives taken in battle – was on again.

In fact, the Catholic Kings and their successor, Charles V, now greatly stimulated the raids. Ferdinand and Isabella gave Lugo a half-share of their own fifth of the profits. The cannon-fodder in the now-regular expeditions was the pre-conquest islanders and, in 1514, they petitioned the Queen for exemption, saying a half of them had died in Africa . . . they were given 'old Christian' status, freeing them from conscription. In 1525, with the tower lost, Charles V encouragingly waived his share. Expeditions might be on behalf of the Crown, by the Adelantado, or private – as when the Canary planters organised themselves into slave-catching co-operatives.

Then, in mid-century, a new, worried note was heard in Spanish circles. On the one hand, the Moorish fleet was seen to be increasing in the area and, on the other, the islands were found to have an alarmingly high proportion of Africans, many free and beyond control. In 1566 the Sanhaja of Sta Ana Island, by Arguin, routed a Canary expedition, keeping its ships. This disaster, with the fears of attack from within and without, led the Crown to limit raids to licence-holders. Then, from 1569 the Moors at last began a counter-offensive, devastating whole islands and taking many as captives into slavery in Africa; at once Philip II declared raiding forbidden, hoping thus to pacify the Maghrebians, now in the ascendant in the Mediterranean too. Nevertheless, in 1579 the Grand Canary employers – owners of sugar plantations, vineyards and farms – asked permission to raid for slaves once again, those from Guinea being too costly and their businesses 'ruined' without them. They explained that one first caught a 'Moor' and then he gave several of his own black slaves in ransom; it would be quite safe as the people on the coast had no boats. The leader of an illegal man-hunt in 1590 was imprisoned, though the last raid, a reprisal in 1593, brought only an official admonishment.

From mid-century also, the growing number of 'apostates' brought the Inquisition into the scene. On arrival in the islands, the captured Africans were under pressure from the church to become Catholics; however, if a ransom was to be demanded, their Spanish captors preferred them to remain Moslem, to ensure they would want to return to Africa. Many of the converts, *moriscos*, took jobs – with Inquisition permission – as agents and interpreters in the raids, or in the exchanges of prisoners and ransoms, or as fishermen, and stayed in Africa. With them 'defected' some of the remaining pre-conquest islanders. In 1552 a Berber took a ship and several dozen of his countrymen back to the desert coast. By 1561 the Inquisition would only license visits to families in Africa if relatives and property were left in the islands; but these were often simply abandoned. Ultimately the frantic inquisitors were insisting upon exit visas for fishermen, traders, everybody, to be told at length by the Crown, in 1589, not to interfere.

The Canaries–Africa trade – to describe this next – had begun before Herrera's tower of 1476, the Berbers and Arabs seeking silver, cloth, grain, raisins and sugar against their usual merchandise, here drawn off the Tindouf halt on the cross-Saharan caravan route or from its terminals in the Sus; at that time, for example, Pisan and Venetian merchants came regularly to buy gold-dust at Messa, as Ca da Mosto remarked. Leather and the high-grade African wax were shipped to Cadiz; the peninsular trade slowly declined with the exploitation of America and the increasingly-difficult African relations. From 1498–1505 the Crown's licence-system operated – it took 50 per cent of traders' profits, though only the fifth on slaves – with its own tower's trade linked to the Casa de Contratación in Seville, focus of the royal monopoly of both the African and American commerce; before and after, the new tower came within Canary jurisdiction. Two valuable raw materials were however declared Crown property in 1497: the orchil lichen and, also, cowrie shells (*Cypræa moneta*), used as money in W Africa. The cowries, collected on the Canary shores, were either bartered on the African coast or sold to the Portuguese for shipment to Guinea; very lucrative work, its peak was passed in 1506. Finally, there were goods which could not legally be traded. Foodstuffs, in practice the basis of the commerce, because these were used by the Spaniards as ransom and so were not to be in good supply. Lugo himself was accused in 1510 of selling wheat to the Africans. Otherwise metals, wood, sulphur and, of course, arms – this last embargo broken by happily-uninvolved states such as Genoa.

Fishing boats from the Canaries and Andalucia were working the prolific waters of the coast by the mid-fifteenth century. The Crown began renting out the rights from 1490. The Spaniards had to stay north of C. Bojador, by the Tordesillas treaty. There was barter and conflict on the shores, where the fishermen had to dry their catch and nets and, once the Moorish corsairs became active, the risk of capture was much increased. In 1564 the English pirate John Hawkins found and attacked forty Spanish and Portuguese fishing boats at Sta Ana in the south. Clearly the waters were becoming free to all, now that the echoes of the arquebuses and collapsing towers had died away.

*Chapter 6*

# Expeditions and Shipwrecks, 1500–1850

With the ascendant Morocco now actively dangerous and the Sahara coast both hostile and comparatively poor, the Europeans preferred the more fruitful shores southwards from the Senegal. There was all but no planned exploration of the territory during this period. First-hand information on the interior comes from two Moroccan trans-desert journeys of about 1512 and 1556. Next, published in 1682 and 1728, two French travel books relate in some detail the history of the Arguin fort from 1638–1724; France was interested in the island as the northern limit of its Senegal zone of influence. Last on the scene were the English and Americans. George Glas had time to publish little, his murder in 1765 immediately following the African and Spanish opposition to his trading post. Next came two shipwrecked sailors' narratives: the naïve yet valuable notes, covering 1810–16, by the apprentice Scott, the first to follow Mungo Park to the Niger bend – and the first to return – and the long chronicle, more aware and scientific, by Captain Riley, 1815.

*Leo Africanus in the Desert, 1512*
'Leo the African' was in fact a well-educated Moor whose family had moved to Fez at the fall of Granada. His extensive travels culminated in his capture and presentation as a slave to the Pope, who on Leo's temporary and doubtless diplomatic conversion, christened him with his own name. About 1512 Leo joined a caravan over the Sijilmassa–Teghaza–Wadan–Timbuctoo route, in the tracks of the scholar Ibn Batuta who, in the eleventh century, had taken two months to Walata, by Timbuctoo; this was the normal time, though fast camels only took twenty-eight days. It seems clear that, though moving east after each invasion of the west Sudan, trade always tended to return to the western route again.

Noting that the Sanhaja covered the zone east of his course across the sands, Leo described various of their characteristics. The aristocracy dressed in bluish cotton tunics with wide sleeves, sold to them by Sudanese traders. Some nomads wore black turbans, with men of the more genteel class covering their faces, except the eyes, with a black veil, only taken down to eat. The women, narrow-waisted and full-buttocked, were friendly to Leo; he noted they were quick to jealousy over their husbands. Female dress was a wide-armed tunic and, draped over the shoulders, a further strip of black or blue cloth; veiled too, the women had many silver rings in their ears and on their fingers.

Camels were the only transport, it seems, and Leo was struck by the way of riding: the saddle fitted between the hump and the head, some men resting their crossed legs on the animal's neck, others using cord riding stirrups. Their goad was of wood and iron, used on the flank. The riding camels had leather thongs through their noses, as reins. When on transhumance, the women rode in a rug-covered basket-like seat, one woman to a camel. Tents were of camel-skin and thick wool, with mats to sleep on.

Leo was impressed by the nomads' ability to manage on so little food: 'In the morning a great amount of fresh camel's milk . . . in the evening a little dried meat boiled in milk and butter, eaten and drunk from their hands . . . then a cup of milk to finish'. They preferred milk to water, and rarely washed. 'Their whole lives, until the day of death, are taken up in hunting and in stealing the camels of their enemies,' said Leo. If few were literate or understood law, all were poets.

This early description of the nomads is still largely correct in the twentieth century. Only new or conflicting details will be quoted from later narratives.

*Sixteenth-century Armies in the West Sahara*
Morocco was of course no more free from imperialist ambitions, once it became powerful, than were the European nations. About 1520 the Songhai kingdom commanded the Tindouf–Fezzan–Segu area, the furthest north of any of the successive Sudanese states. Morocco's first three attempts to conquer the Songhai – and thus dominate the gold trade and the desert salt-mines – took place during the second half of the century, the northern armies not getting beyond Walata at their most successful. Then in 1591 the Saadians, at their apogee, marshalled a force of 500 arquebus-firing cavalry and 1,500 lancers, together with a large body of Spanish mercenaries also armed with arquebuses, and took along 1,000 personal servants and

seventy Christian slaves; the leader was an Islamised Spaniard. Surviving a desert crossing of twenty weeks, this army, said to have been opposed by 80,000 men, took Timbuctoo at the third attempt. Once again a Sudanese kingdom was broken up by the north, and again with as little profit.

The flow of the coveted gold to the Moroccan-held Niger termini ceased. The ordinary people, who had been practising a mixture of animism and the Moslem religion, now reacted against Islam. The vast intervening sands soon made effective Moroccan control impossible; about 1632, the increasingly-Sudanesed administration of Timbuctoo and Gao declared independence. The nomads were again ruling the desert and were also making incursions into the disintegrated Sudan. As usual, trade preferred to concentrate on the east Maghreb. Once again the nomads' source of livelihood was in a decline. Another factor in the decrease in the west Sahara traffic had been, since the mid-fifteenth century, the bartering of slaves and goods with the European ships at Arguin, on the Senegal and to the south.

An unsuccessful Moroccan expedition of 1556 included a thirty-six year old Spaniard called Luis de Marmol y Carvajal. His 1573 book on the region, much of it repeating Leo's writings, included a description of the Delim Arabs. An early translation: 'Dulein having neither Dominions nor Pay, are Poor Robbers, that range amongst the People call'd *Zanhagu* . . . and carry Cattle to Dara to be exchang'd for Dates: They have 4000 Horse and 6000 Foot, and are equally Strangers to Gallantry and neatness of Apparel.' Another translation gives only 500 cavalry out of 10,000 men.

## The Dutch and the French at Arguin

Having captured Arguin in 1638, the Dutch strengthened the fort and began to trade. The English temporarily took over the island in 1665, but Ruyter's victory on the Thames forced its return to the Dutch. These, seeking the gum collected twice a year from the acacias of the savanna, made treaties with the Africans which adversely affected French trade to the south. Le Maire wrote: 'From these *Moors* we have the Gum-Arabick, they gather it in the Desarts of the *Inward Lybia*; it grows on the trees as that . . . from Cherry and Plumb-Trees; they come . . . a month or six weeks before the overflow of the *Niger* . . . five or six hundred Leagues to sell a half Quintal of Gum, and some farther. They ride quite naked on their Camels, Horses and Oxen'. Arguin was supplied by the major local tribes, the Trarza and Brakna, a little later referred to by Labat (1728) as tributaries of Morocco. In exchange for the gum, went on the Sieur Le Maire, the French gave the Africans 'Blue cloth, linnen of the same colour, and a little Iron'. To preserve their monopoly, in 1678 the French attacked and destroyed the Arguin fort.

The Dutch returned in 1688 and rebuilt, so in 1721 the indignant French landed there again. But they found the post defended by some forty Africans who, recalling the previous time the French had taken over, at once shot at the drummer sent to demand their surrender. The French had fortified a huge exterior cistern with sand-barrels and wood taken from the Africans' huts, also outside the fort, and now opened fire with half-a-dozen cannon at middle range on the south bastion. The Africans kept up musket fire but were inexpert with the fort's own heavy artillery. After two days the wall was breached and the French closed in . . . the fort was empty, the Africans and several Europeans, presumably Dutch, having left by ladder and boat for the mainland.

This time the French themselves rebuilt. However, the equally tenacious Dutch at once put up another fort at Portendic, to the south. In this they were helped by the powerful Trarza under their chief Ali Chandora; their regional enemies were the northerly Delim and the Brakna, the latter kept at boiling point by French 'advisers' – already present – and their gifts of food, arms and slaves. The desperate French now had no choice but to attack the Dutchmen's ships, one being found to hold no less than twenty-five tons of gum. The Arguin governor treacherously massacred a number of Africans. Then, still in 1721, the new tenants began to die of scurvy and dysentry, the last six survivors out of forty going for help . . . to Portendic. However, the next French governor at Arguin improved local relations and a diet of traded turtles kept the men healthier. Alas, this promise was soon halted, in 1722, by a Dutch attack, in turn stimulating Ali Chandora to capture a couple of French boats and, with 1,500 men, to besiege their fort. The Trarza chief mined a corner of the building, loosening all the locks and hinges. Food at length ran out and the French agreed to hand over to the Dutch, always much preferred by the Trarza.

The next scene in this eighteenth-century comedy opened with the appearance of an avenging French force, out from Lorient that same December. Its siege of Arguin failed for lack of drinking water but Portendic was found empty and burnt. Here a favourable gum treaty with the Africans exchanged each '*Quintal Maure pesant 700 livres poids de Marc chacun*' for a length of the sought-after blue cloth. Labat noted that the size of the gum measure, which varied from nation to nation, 'is increased by the Europeans as often as possible'. Le Maire described the region's people as 'little, meagre, and of a bad mien and a crafty, subtile Genius', but there is no record of the

Africans' opinion of the Europeans. In 1724, and on the way burning the Dutchmen's rebuilt Portendic a second time, the French Senegal Company did capture Arguin: an altar was built against the wall and a Te Deum sung, secular power being demonstrated by three discharges of musketry and cannon.

At this point, the end of Labat's book (1728), detailed history of Arguin ceases. In 1727 the Dutch officially sold the area *'depuis et compris le C. Blanc'* to France, since they were finding the outpost unrewarding. The English installed themselves at Portendic in 1760, the counter flourishing at the expense of Arguin. The French soon took over the southern counter too, by the Versailles treaty of 1783, trade then slumping. The treaty of Paris, 1814, confirmed French sovereignty over this coast; it was to remain within their sphere of influence for a further century and a half, in fact. After a period of oblivion, in 1880 the two bases were surveyed by the French for possible use as fishing stations, to be part of their expansionist ambitions in the region. The ruins of the Portendic fort were noted by the ichthyologist Gruvel (1909), together with seven rusty cannons; on Arguin, the vestiges of the outpost lie in the north-east of the island.

The goods traded had been little different from those of the Portuguese period. Ostrich feathers had become important and Labat stated that the great troupes of birds were being hunted from horses with spears and bows; it would be interesting to know if the weapon-heads were still of stone. Le Maire commented cautiously over the eggs that 'I can't easily believe . . . that one will feed eight Men'. He does however accept that a local turtle, the green species, is enough for thirty people; the fishermen entangled these in nets 100–20 'arms' long and three deep, with 20 cm mesh, stretched across the inlets.

The nearest trading town was still Wadan, where two slaves would buy a camel but up to ten might be given for a horse. However, the Europeans gradually referred less to slave-shipment from Arguin and Portendic, the bulk of this traffic now leaving directly from the Senegal and the other ports of negro Africa. The triangular trade was now at its height: cheap European goods to Africa, the bartered slaves to the American plantations, the sugar and tobacco from these to Europe. The Dutch dominated the trade in the sixteen hundreds, yielding the lead to the English and French in the next century. European demand for slaves, including their exchange for guns, had lasting repercussions in Africa; both there and in Europe, racial hatred grew in intensity with the trade. Europe and the United States began the abolition of slavery in 1808 but, as will be described, it has continued in the western desert.

## An English Trader, 1764

Focusing again on the coast above C. Bojador, the eighteenth century's best-known incident involved a sea-captain called George Glas, the long-dormant Spanish and the Sultan of Morocco. Glas had had much experience of the Canaries and the coast opposite, with his valuable history and mariners' handbook already written around the area, and in 1764 he took a ship, with interpreters and his family, into Puerto Cansado. There were meetings with three local leaders and, having built another of the coast's many towers, this one called 'Hilsborough', trade began. In need of more men and of small boats, Glas sailed back to Tenerife.

The Spanish, however, still claimed a right to the coast, in spite of 250 years absence and the lack of binding force of medieval Portuguese-Spanish treaties and Papal Bulls upon the English. In 1698, for example, they had rejected an application to settle at Sta Cruz de Mar Pequeña, sent by way of the Spanish ambassador in London, from a group of Huguenots expelled from France fourteen years earlier; permission was refused on religious and political grounds. So, when Glas landed in the Canaries, he was imprisoned for a year for taking over 'State property'. At Hilsborough things soon went badly too, the local people killing the factor and burning the main ship, two launches escaping with Glas' wife and twelve-year-old daughter aboard. After diplomatic exchanges, Glas was released and, taking his gold-dust, sailed for Britain. The ill-luck had followed him up the gang-plank, for the crew mutinied and Glas and the captain were run through and flung overboard, his wife and daughter being thrown after them alive.

In the Canaries, the Spaniards now had an idea – perhaps *they* would set up a base in Glas' place. An agreement was suggested to the Sultan of Morocco. During the last hundred years, the new Alaoui dynasty had been more active in the desert than had the preceding Saadians. In the reign of the Sultan Moulay Ishmail, 1672–1727, many expeditions had been made down through the interior of the present Spanish Sahara to the centre of modern Mauritania; the Alaouis may even have managed to collect taxes in the south about 1735; towards the end of the century the investiture of the Trarzas' emir was at the hands of the Sultan of Morocco. Morocco's claim to the desert at the time of writing is based on such 'evidence of sovereignty in the past'. Conversely, in 1767, the Sultan now wrote to the Spanish that 'The coast from Sta Cruz to the south not being within my jurisdiction . . . I am not responsible for misfortunes which may happen there . . . and those who inhabit the country, nomadic and ferocious, have always attacked and imprisoned the

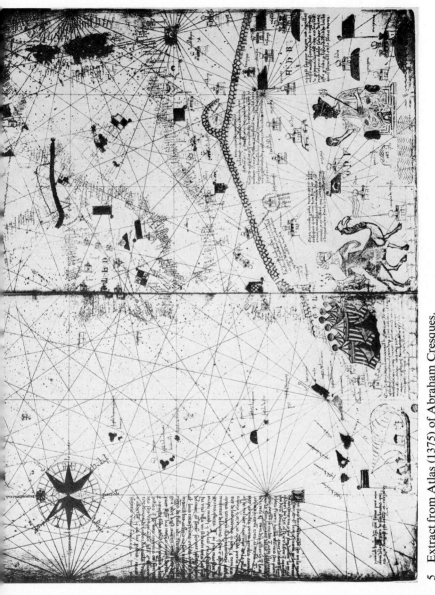

5   Extract from Atlas (1375) of Abraham Cresques.

6 Children, full face and profile, in varied dress. The smaller boys have their hair shaved in traditional style. In the background (upper) are the 12-dwelling hexagons.

(Below) The palace of Ma el Ainin in the Smara *ribat*.

Canary people'. The Meknes treaty of 1799 placed even the Nun River, earlier called the Assaka, outside the Sultan's territory. The Spanish ambassador to Morocco advised that it would be more profitable to fish off Newfoundland and the islanders, seeing they would be without protection, dropped the idea for another century.

*Alexander Scott, captive from 1810–16*

The opening of the century was a time of many recorded shipwrecks, with Gericault painting the pitching raft from the frigate *Meduse*, lost on the Arguin Bank. The first of two English-speaking castaways was Scott, whose ship, the *Montezuma*, left Liverpool for Brazil late in October 1810 and was wrecked on 23 November between C. Juby and C. Nun. In 1811, as the captive of nomads on a pilgrimage, Scott was to reach Lake Debu near Timbuctoo, six years after Mungo Park had passed that way on the journey on which he died; the apprentice, unknown to history, was the first to return alive from this legendary region, leaving a valuable narrative, the only description until that by René Caillié in 1827.

Captured, the *Montezuma*'s crew found themselves in a camp of the Tabaulet tribe, at least 600 nomads in a hundred tents. Scott's master at once set off southwards. Covering about twenty-five kilometres a day, they crossed the Saguiet-el-Hamra – Scott described the mountain sheep there, also acacias – and after seventeen days pitched camp, about thirty kilometres from the coast, in the El Ghiblah area, probably below C. Bojador. From there the nomads often went to the coast for good water, a day each way.

In June 1811 a great pilgrimage to 'Hez el Hezsh' was announced ... Scott, now looking after goats instead of scrubbing decks, heard that he must there become a Moslem or die. Twenty families set out to the south-east interior, taking at least 500 camels, the males laden. Some 2,000 sheep and goats left too, their long legs able to take them fast across the desert; they would come together at a whistle or, more usual, if a horn was blown. These nomads had five horses, used for chasing ostriches for flesh and feathers; a great many dogs, like greyhounds and, apparently, bloodhounds, were used on the hares, foxes and 'wolves', all eaten. If an attack was feared, the tents were pitched in a circle around the animals, the men sleeping amidst the ever-alert camels.

The desert became increasingly barren, varying from sands to clays, now flat and now rocky. After some two and a half months, a place was reached where salt and brimstone were mined, Scott getting an extra-routine beating for nearly suffocating everybody by throwing a piece of the sulphur in the camp fire. Possibly this was one of the Teghaza or Taoudenni mines, now in nothern Mali; the Ijil salt-pan would not have taken so long to reach. The nomads now went six days on milk, camel urine and the stomach water of dead camels; food included roasted locusts and camel skin, the latter first beaten thin between two stones. Taking another month to cross yet further sands – during which time, in a wood, they met people with a domesticated elephant – they at last reached L. Debu.

Mungo Park's boat, according to his guide, had been pursued here by three canoes 'armed with pikes, lances, bows and arrows etc, but no firearms'. Leaving the animals and some of their band behind, Scott and seventy others embarked on the more regular service, being rowed across to 'El Hezsh' in two and a half days by negro slaves; the return fare was three camels each family. The Moslems kissed the ground where they landed, the women saving Scott from a severe beating for not doing so too. The pilgrims said they had reached the tombs, much-frequented, of 'Sidna Ali and his wife, daughter of the Prophet'; the nomads kissed a holy stone.

Back across the lake again, a month later, and safely leaving the Niger bend, the nomads took the chance to catch eight Bambara negroes, in spite of their bows and arrows; the prisoners had three diagonal tattoo marks on each cheek and a horizontal line on the forehead. Working over any rain-awakened pasture, plundering here and there for camels and grain – and avoiding enemy tribes to north and south – the band took a year to return to El Ghiblah. There the negroes were sold to some Wadi Nun people. Scott's nomads were now in high esteem locally, the men with the title of 'Sidi el Hezsh Hezsh' . . . Scott, unconverted, was beaten for this more than before. Clearly the pilgrimage was to some degree comparable to that to Mecca, the *hadj*.

Scott added a description of the nomads. The men wore the *haik* around them, a 'blanket'; the chief and elders, each referred to as 'Sidi', had turbans. The women, slender, fair-skinned when young, very wrinkled with age, had their blankets belted at the waist and fixed at the shoulder with silver clasps; a piece of blue linen covered their heads but they did not use veils. Marriage was simple, the price of a bride – from ten years old – was ten camels. Divorce, he said, was at will. On death, a person was washed and at once buried, bushes and stones being piled on the grave. Children were taught to write on smooth boards in black ink, made of milk and charcoal, using pens of split cane or reed; Scott was a poor pupil.

However, his standing was to rise. He and the other men went on a raid; their arms were muskets and short sabres, the chief with pistols from the *Montezuma*. The successful surprise attack at night was reversed a few days later and Scott's band fled to the mouth of the Saguiet-el-Hamra, living for two months off the shore. Scott, either the bravest or the most expendable, was lowered from the cliffs to collect shellfish. At length, re-arming, they defeated the enemy tribe, Scott having no choice but to kill a man in the encounter and being henceforth approvingly called 'Mahomed the Christian'.

He soon shattered this success. Seeing a brig out to sea, he ran away and hid in a cave, only to be caught and have the soles of his feet beaten with a hot iron rod; they took two or three months to heal. However, in the summer of 1816 (he was twenty-two years old) Scott successfully escaped, the nomads being then in the *till* or north, in fact above the place of his shipwreck. Without food, he followed the coast up to the river Nun region and then turned east into the mountains. Giving himself up at a stone house, he was at length ransomed by the British representative in Mogador. A name well-known to west African travellers in distress, William Willshire sent him a horse and money for food, from funds provided by the Ironmongers' Company of London, and in five days, on 31 August 1816, Scott reached safety.

*'Riley's Captivity in the Great Desert', 1815*
Just possibly, the brig which Scott saw was the American 220-ton *Commerce*, out from Gibraltar in 1815 to exchange wines for salt in the C. Verde Islands. During a fog in the notorious Canaries channel, on 28 August, the captain, the 37-year-old James Riley, heard a roaring but acted too late: 'Surge after surge came thundering on, and drove her in spite of the anchors . . . She struck with such violence as to start every man from the deck'. Riley hastily piled a dozen barrels of water and wine into the launch, together with some casks of bread and salted food and his instruments. Then, caught up by the waves, he and some of the others were carried 300 m and thrown onto a sandy beach. The rest of his dozen men came ashore on a line and they then made a tent out of oars and sails.

Soon a nomad appeared and began collecting up their scattered clothing. Riley described a typical Saharaui: 'Five feet seven . . . complexion between . . . American Indian and negro . . . a piece of coarse woollen cloth . . . from below the waist nearly to his knees; his hair was long and bushy, resembling a pitch mop, sticking out in every way . . . his eyes were red and fiery . . . a long curling beard . . . very old yet fierce and vigorous'. A pair of crones joined him: 'Their eye-teeth stuck out like hogs' tusks', a feature he later said was a deliberate deformation, whilst 'their tanned skins hung in loose plaits on their faces and breasts . . . their hair was long and braided'. With them came 'a girl of eighteen . . . who was not ugly, and five or six children . . . entirely naked'. These nomads were armed with an English hammer, an axe, some long knives slung in sheaths to the right of their necks. Without any choice anyway, Riley tried to make friends by letting them take everything; the crew simply got drunk, their only possible escape. A child made them a fire and they cooked a drowned hen. Night came and the nomads disappeared.

At dawn they were back, the old man now armed with a four metre iron-pointed spear. To unceasing yells from the women, the dozen sturdy mariners allowed themselves to be forced back to the wreck and from there, baling desperately, watched their food, tent and so on taken away on camels, their instruments burnt and the wine barrels emptied – the nomads were good Moslems. Next Riley, not particularly quick-witted, it seems, was enticed ashore and had to have the crew produce a thousand Spanish dollars for his ransom . . . but was not released. More in the spirit of the region, he now ordered a seaman, whom he describes contemptuously as old and poor, to come on shore – then, whilst the nomads were engrossed with their new captive, made a dash for the sea and swam underwater until out of range . . . leaving the old sailor to be killed by the enraged nomads. Riley rationalised this: the men needed his leadership.

The launch patched up again, and carrying a water-barrel for which Riley had dived into the hold, the twelve took off their hats and prayed for the breakers to calm: a channel nearly a mile long appeared in the twenty-foot waves and they reached the open sea. They now coasted southwards for nine days. A pig off the ship had swum ashore but, finding it was a choice between Islamic contempt and Christian voracity, had opted for the evil it knew and swum back to the wreck: it was eaten, raw, and gratefully washed down with urine saved in bottles. 'Some . . . by thrusting their heads into the water, endeavoured to ascertain what the pains of death were. . . .' Hunger drove them to steal the common stores during the night.

On 7 September they were near C. Blanc and, having seen no ships and being unaware perhaps of Arguin's French fort, they landed, finishing off their launch. Supplementing their recurrent diet with a few mussels, they made their way along the broken-up rocks until the interminable 200 metre cliffs gave way to a beach, behind it: 'A barren plain . . . without a tree, shrub, or spear of grass'. The lower ranks cried at the sight, and consumed their tears. Most were so dry they could hardly speak, but they bathed in the sea and felt refreshed. In the night the captain stole some of the cook's water.

On the 10th they were seen, set upon and stripped, the first nomads to reach them demonstrating their rights to those who followed by throwing sand in the air and shouting. But a sword-fight was needed to decide ownership. Soon they were all on the move to the south-east, the start of a new torture for the Americans. Too weak to keep up, Riley was laughed at and beaten. At length he was put on a camel but his legs were so blistered 'that the blood dripped from my heels'. To try to excite pity, he fell off . . . and they made him run behind . . . he tried to find a stone with which to kill himself . . . but there were none.

The nomads next held a council, cross-legged in circles of ten or twenty; Riley asked to be ransomed in Morocco but was told this was 'a great distance, and nothing for camels to eat on the way'. The negro slaves made fun of the prisoners, the women spat at them, hitting them with sticks and stones if they tried to lie in the shade of the tents, though one did grease a seaman's burns: 'His legs and thighs . . . hung in strips of torn and chafed flesh – the blood was trickling down the sides of the camel'. Riley's dreams alternated between hell and deliverance.

Next the camel pasture ran out, milk then became short, the nomads poured the last water on the ground as a rain-invocation to Allah. The least of wild plants was eaten, snails were roasted, the camels were watched for their urine, which was caught and drunk. The seamen were so hungry that they began to bite the flesh off their arms and Riley tied one man's behind his back. Just in time, he caught two others, behind a tent, about to dash out the brains of a four-year-old child . . . a last, a good meal. The nadir had been reached.

Mercy came disguised as a travelling cloth-salesman, Hamet, who, weeping at Riley's story – the captain had been diligently learning Arabic – bought him for two blankets, a blue cotton covering and a bundle of ostrich feathers. After many fist and scimitar disputes, the nomads also sold Savage, the near-death Clark and Riley's 'son', Horace the apprentice. Though of course intending to make a profit out of their ransom, Hamet was a humane person. The ransoms were to be $200 each for Riley and Horace, $100 each for the others, together with a double-barrelled gun. To keep his bargains alive, Hamet bought an old camel: killed whilst tied in a crouched position, the blood from its neck vein was boiled for them, in a big copper kettle, until thick. The nomads thrust their heads into the camel's side to drink the paunch juices, using a part for cooking up the meat. The seaman Burns was acquired by Hamet, but Hogan, after changing hands, was returned when the seller demanded further payment. The nomads stole half the camel, Hamet countering by stealing a check shirt for Riley – resplendent in this and a pair of camel-skin sandals, the captain of the *Commerce* left with the others on the walk to Mogador, some 1,300 km away.

Desert and dry riverbed succeeded each other, the nomads smelling the sand to tell the way. They passed a man with Riley's telescope and, further north, another with 'Mr Savage's kerseymere pantaloons'. In an area of great dunes blown by the trades, probably around C. Bojador, they stole the belongings of a sleeping traveller: barley, opium, short hollow sticks filled with gold-dust and some roots which, smoked through a hollow bone, gave protection against the evil eye. Vegetation, animals, humans, all now increased. The band forcibly exchanged a dying camel for some goats. A woman described Lanzarote to them, having been there to collect a ransom for captives from a Spanish shipwreck; it was well known that there were a hundred Canary boats of fifteen to fifty tons fishing the coast, with hardly a year without a wreck and a crew to massacre or enslave. Hamet's band now took great precautions against robbery, from a tribe said to throw six to eight pound stones so as to kill a man at fifty yards; fires could not be lit, they slept with the camels in a circle around them. A putrid goat was declared delicious.

At last the first stone houses and ploughed strips of the Nun were reached – it was 19 October, not two months since the shipwreck. William Willshire sent their ransom, now totalling $920 and two guns. So weak as to keep falling off their camels and, later, donkeys, the seamen entered Mogador, their state 'absolutely too shocking for description'. Riley, staying at Willshire's house, was told later that he was 'continually bathed in tears . . . shuddering at the sight of every human being, fearing I should again be carried into slavery. I had slunk into the darkest of my room . . .'; in the night he would find himself trying to get out through a grating. Normally weighing 240 lb, he was now down to 90 lb, with some of the other four down below 40 lb. In the course of 1816 – with Scott ransomed that August too – Willshire redeemed two more of the crew. He wrote to Riley that two others had reached the Sus, two had died and there was news of the twelfth and last. By then the master of the wrecked brig was working on his book, the first ethnography of the western Sahara: his detailed observations will be used in the chapters on the tribes, together with the information given to Riley, before they parted, by his great friend Hamet.

# Chapter 7

# Invasion and Colonisation, 1850–1940

In this chapter begins the sequence of events which has led to the present confrontations. Spain took over the littoral desert in the hope of improving its trade, especially necessary after the loss of the American territories, and of enhancing its international prestige. Also, it was simply fashionable to have colonies, even such apparently valueless ones as the coastal Sahara.

*'Close to Sta Cruz de Mar Pequeña . . .'*
In 1860, following two decades of renewed Spanish reconnaissance of the coast opposite the Canaries, the Spanish victory over Morocco led to the Tetuan treaty, the Sultan engaging 'to cède for ever . . . on the coast . . . close to Sta Cruz de Mar Pequeña, ground . . . sufficient for the formation . . . of a fishing establishment, similar to that which Spain possessed there in ancient times'. The Arabic version confusingly said 'close to Agadir' but in any case the Spaniards could not place Sta Cruz themselves. The Sultan had long had no power over the *bilad as-siba* and in fact the 'unfriendly country' even declared itself independent in 1861. The monarch said he would have to buy the land off the tribes, but he was, in fact, relying on a policy of procrastination to avoid the treaty altogether.

In 1864 a Spanish doctor, Joaquin Gatell, was officially asked to make a secret reconnaissance of this dangerous coast. Disguised as the 'Caid Ismail', he made three determined journeys, their furthest point being C. Juby. Here the Skarna tribe, accepting him as an important Moslem, made him their guest; however, the guide then told them that Gatell was a Christian and they decided to kill him once he was no longer their guest . . . but he escaped in time.

In 1878 the still-frustrated Spanish sent the *Blasco de Garay* to look for Sta Cruz, the expedition deciding on a ruin at the mouth of the R. Assaka; the local chiefs agreed to the construction of a fishing port. So, in 1882, a Spanish force was ready to leave from the Canaries and take over, but the Sultan's diplomatic manoeuvres resulted in a new commission instead. Stating next that Sta Cruz had in fact been at Puerto Cansado, he agreed to the proposed fishing base at Ifni, the Assaka mouth, but outside the treaty . . . but had anyway still no intention of letting the Spaniards into south Morocco. In this same year he attempted to assert his authority over the southern tribes, including those of the coastal zone under discussion – and, as will be described next, over a Scottish trader – by marching down with an army of 20,000 men. However, the campaign failed, 6,000 soldiers apparently dying of thirst and hunger. As to the fishing base, this was still over half a century away for the out-manoeuvred Spaniards.

## *The Scottish Trading Counter at C. Juby, 1875–95*

Donald MacKenzie has gone down in history for two schemes. The first, the idea of flooding the Sahara, by means of a canal from the Atlantic through Wadi Chebica, would make the desert fertile and allow steamers to sail direct from Southampton to Timbuctoo. Simpler, and in fact successful, was his trade-post of Port Victoria, installed on the coast within a few kilometres of the ruins of Hilsborough and, doubtless, of those of Sta Cruz.

Equally unwilling to co-operate with him, the Moroccan Sultan produced the same excuse as to the Spanish: he did not control below the Draa. Not perturbed, MacKenzie chartered a Canary schooner, the *Rosario*, and surveyed the coast. By 1878–9, with European territorial aspirations developing, the Madrid authorities had instructed the Canary Islanders to be less helpful. The Sultan now offered MacKenzie money to go away, cheaper than losing the royal ten per cent on those Sudanese and Saharan goods which, he feared, would no longer reach Morocco; he was also afraid of arms getting to the untameable south. MacKenzie began trading from a prefabricated wooden house, taking it away in his ship when his goods were all bartered; aboard went gold-dust, ostrich feathers and other local products. The slave caravans, however, did not come nearer the coast than Tindouf – not only were there no buyers, slavery having been illegal in Europe since the beginning of the century, being replaced by colonialism – but MacKenzie was a Special Commissioner for the British and Foreign Anti-Slavery Society. Times had changed since Herrera's day.

In 1880 the Sultan sent an expedition to harass the new counter, causing only minor damage. In fact, MacKenzie was already considering expanding. He now explored the 'Rio de Oro' bay, being well received by the local people since they knew of his post at C. Juby; he opened trade negotiations with the emir of the Mauritanian Adrar. Two years later came the Sultan's unsuccessful attempt to intimidate the Sus and expel the Scot, for whom a reward was offered. And, although the Sultan preached a 'holy war' against the Christians, trade at the fort continued at capacity.

The year 1883 saw MacKenzie prospecting the coast to the north of C. Juby and then going some distance up the Saguiet-el-Hamra. On the way, a Moslem holy man said to him: 'You are the only Christian who could stand here and live.' Returning, he stopped amidst the grain-fields of Daora, the nearest settlement to his own post, and stayed in one of the two clay-walled forts, built in 1878, of the Izarguien tribe; he described it as square, the loop-holed sides 45 m long and 8 m tall, with a 12 m tower at each corner, the building having underground grain-cellars.

In 1884, hearing that MacKenzie was about to set up a counter in 'Rio de Oro', the Spaniards at last became active on the Sahara coast – as will be described next – and simultaneously made difficulties at MacKenzie's Canary base, this eventually left alone after intervention by the British government. The Sultan too continued his offensives, leading in 1888 to the murder of the C. Juby manager; Morocco was forced by the British to pay £5,000 compensation. For long there was intermittent fighting between MacKenzie's allies, primarily the Izarguien, and the Sultan's men.

On the shore a small walled settlement was built for the Africans . . . simultaneously a battery was added to the island fort. MacKenzie sent out various missions, kept trading rivals at bay, ransomed captured Europeans. A Belgian official mission arrived offering £50,000 for a share in the outpost, with the particular aim of building a sanatorium for the Congo Free State – MacKenzie refused. The French worried that arms for use against them were being imported at C. Juby.

The last decade of the century saw the British government trying to obtain C. Juby 'in independence' from the Sultan, presumably to free the trading post from his attentions. This attempt failing, in 1895 the enterprise was sold to the Sultan for £50,000, in theory to be a free port. In 1910 the outpost was occupied by Izarguien tribesmen, these trading with the Canaries. Though nothing further was heard of the Southampton–Timbuctoo steamship line, the C. Juby settlement was only temporarily in Saharaui hands.

*Spain Protects the Nomads*
Heralding serious Spanish interest in the territory was the formation

in Madrid, between 1876–84, of five organisations oriented towards Africa, their aims in order of appearance being exploration, geography, fishing, colonisation and commerce. The year of action in the field was 1884. In January the 'Soc. Española de Africanistas y Colonistas' was apparently ceded the Rio de Oro peninsula by a treaty signed in Lanzarote by Saharaui chiefs . . . but the government refused to take it over. In February the 'Co. Mercantil Hispano–Africana' anchored trading-schooners at Rio de Oro and C. Blanc. In November, aboard the warship *Ceres*, the local tribes agreed with the Spaniards' leader, Emilio Bonelli, that shore-stations should be established; they came under Canary jurisdiction. These ports were to be called after Spanish Africanists: Villa Cisneros, Medina Gatell and, a third, at Angra da Cintra, to be Puerto Badía. In December, under desperate pressure from the colonial society, intent on protecting Spanish fishing and potential trade along the Sahara coast against the various other European nations active in north-west Africa, and against the looming MacKenzie in particular, Spain's ambassadors declared internationally that 'Considering the importance of the Spanish installations . . . and in view of the documents signed by the independent tribes . . . who have on various occasions asked for and obtained the protection of the Spanish . . . the King has decided . . . to take under his protection the territories . . . between Bahia del Oeste [now La Guera] and C. Bojador.' According to a modern Spanish writer, this was done 'simply to protect the region's nomads, bereft of all material and spiritual aid'.

Bonelli, in charge both of trade and the military – the garrison was strengthened after an onslaught by the local tribes in 1885 – had only contempt for the Africans. Those on the coast, naked or in skin capes, lived either in caves or inside roofless wind-breaks, the walls 50 cm high and made of dried seaweed stalks; he is referring here to the tributary fishermen. The desert nomads were lazy long-haired slavers, notably the Sba. The 30-year-old Captain Bonelli, always pictured in his bemedalled uniform, noted that the Africans could be sold Spain's poorest cottons, worst tools, old guns and, for use in these, blasting powder.

A trading fort was soon built at Villa Cisneros, with the aid of Canary workmen. It was entered by two doors, one from the bay to the east, a warship below, the other the Moors' Gate, facing up the promontory with, pointing towards it in the courtyard, an 8 cm Krupps field-gun. The trading building formed one corner, a defensive tower manned by twenty-five soldiers another. Goods brought from the Canaries were, in 1884, the popular blue cloth and other fabrics, with flint-lock guns, powder, tools, candles, blocks of sugar and general food. The Africans traded sheep and goats – which the Spaniards had trouble keeping alive until the boats arrived – and ostrich feathers, wild animal skins and, occasionally, gum and gold-dust. The Spanish agreed to dig a line of wells across to the Adrar, to help transit, but the real problem which kept the big caravans away was that the Europeans would not buy the slaves.

In 1886 the 'Soc. de Geografía Comercial' sent two expeditions into the desert, with state finance. The Saguiet-el-Hamra region was explored by Alvarez and, although he took an Izarguien tribesman to Lanzarote to sign a treaty of 'commerce and protection' – the pattern of Spanish manoeuvres becomes gradually clear – the government refused to take over the R. Draa–C. Bojador territory on this pretext.

The second expedition was by Cervera, a captain in the engineers, Quiroga, a professor of natural history, and Rizzo, experienced in Spanish–African affairs and as interpreter; with them went two Rif riflemen. The party was well-equipped, carrying not only the explorer's stock set of gifts but also Arabic and Spanish editions of the geography by El Edrisi, another good Spaniard of the Middle Ages – the work was presumably to give the Saharauis a sense of Arab–Iberian fraternity, but in the event they would not look at it – and several Korans. The aim was 'treaties to gain commercial advantages for Spain'.

With the five northerners went two important Sba, a Delim chief and two guides requested in advance from the Emir of the Mauritanian Adrar, this the goal of the journey. In turn, as their territories were crossed or their tribes were at hand, the Africans demanded tributes – to be sent from Villa Cisneros – and tried to kill the expeditionaries and take their belongings. At the Bou Hofra well the Europeans had to make a redoubt around their tent, out of boxes and bales, and by demonstrating their Winchesters dissuaded the 130-strong camp, in fact led by the Emir's guides, from their imminent attack. The women, more fanatical than the men, threatened to cut the explorers' throats if not given their belongings. Scientific work was hampered because the nomads became enraged at the sight of note-taking, specimen-collecting and the use of instruments; Cervera said the nomads lived as in the time of Mohammed. The heat dried the eye-balls, the rock-surfaces reaching 65°C, and three Africans got sunstroke. Quiroga was very ill. An attempt was made to throw Cervera down a well but somehow his uniform – always worn, of course – saved him. The *irifi* blew as they crossed the Tiris.

At last, on 10 July, they marched over the Ijil salt-pan. On the further side not only were they apparently received by the chiefs of all the many tribes of the C. Bojador–C. Blanc–Ijil zone, irreconcilable enemies, but these at once signed their territories over to the Spanish: there took place in Quiroga's words: '*El acta de toma de posesión para España*'. The expedition proudly unfurled the Spanish flag. The Adrar Emir, Aidda, now appeared; the Spaniards always upgraded him to 'sultan' since otherwise he, and thus the planned treaty, would be subject to the Sultan of Morocco, at least in diplomatic circles. The Emir's influence reached from the Saguiet-el-Hamra to Timbuctoo. Now he placed his own territory, notably the Adrar, under Spanish 'protection' . . . as soon as his back was turned, his subjects threw themselves like wolves on the explorers, just about able to protect themselves. The return over the 400 km, by much the same route in spite of the Europeans' attempt at exploration, was marked by the same incidents as on the way out.

Cervera and the others nevertheless saw the nomads more as human beings than did Bonelli. They felt the local name of Ed-Dakhla, the Indent, should not be replaced by Villa Cisneros. Of the fishing people, the women and children hung about the trading post begging biscuits – *galletas*, hence the present Spanish nickname for all Saharaui children, *goyetes* – in exchange for an 'obscene and immoral dance' or 'a handful of rice for favours more . . . punishable'. The resident Spanish did nothing to educate the local people to be of 'great use in future enterprises'. Less submissive were the prowling Delim, making it dangerous to leave the military camp, a situation that in fact lasted until after the Civil War. The explorers noted that the nomads respected the Moroccan Sultan as a descendant of the Prophet but 'the Desert Arab has no other chiefs than Allah and Mohammed'. One of the most important of these proud nomads stole Quiroga's handkerchief out of his pocket and, made to return it, was not in the least embarrassed. As for the expedition's treaties, the Spanish government refused to be involved, saying they were only an affair of the Society.

So, lacking official support and in the face of local hostility – inevitable, given the two sides' approach to trade – and of French and Moroccan manoeuvres, the coastal outposts languished. As usual, the fishing industry was the most workable project as it involved least contact between the two peoples.

### '*Seeing the Desert*', Camille Douls, 1887

Badly beaten, his front teeth knocked out with the flat of a knife, robbed of his possessions and then almost thrown in the sea – all immediately on landing – Douls might fairly be called the territory's first tourist. His overt reason for crossing in a fishing boat from

Lanzarote to Garnet Bay, between the Scottish and the most
northerly Spanish trading counters, was 'to see the desert', an attempt
to do so two years earlier, through the Sus, having failed. Probably
he was on a similar mission to that of Gatell two decades earlier, this
time a French reconnaissance.

Disguised as a shipwrecked Algerian, the young Frenchman hope-
fully greeted the first nomads he met, a long-haired quartet in skins
and armed with guns and knives. He was automatically set upon.
Saved from drowning by a woman, he was told: 'A Moslem does not
come by sea'. Handcuffed, he found he would have to prove he was
not a Christian. The women prodded him, the men tried to strangle
him, but, after he had prayed as a Moslem, the local chief decided to
support him.

A holy man next suggested that he should be taken to Ma el Ainin.
This man has been the most important figure in the territory's history.
As will be described next, he combined the qualities of 'mystic' and
warrior to the extent needed to build a new north-west African
dynasty comparable to that of the Almoravides – but had to contend
with the peak of European colonialism and its superior military
organisation and armaments. After three days, Douls reached Ma el
Ainin's camp, 'a multitude of tents . . . on a vast plain, around a
larger, splendid one of European construction . . . The great
sheriff was reclining at the door surrounded by his secretaries . . . a
voluminous turban . . . a sky-blue *haik*, Mulainin stood out . . .
by his pious bearing: he looked at me in silence . . . whilst the
nomad crowd passed in front to kiss his hand . . . and asked for
remedies for their ailments, which usually consisted of some sand-
grains on which he had breathed'. Douls was accepted after reciting
from the Koran. Nevertheless his captors took him on to a wise
man, who pronounced him a Turk, and then to be cleared by a
council of the most learned men. Douls had then only to explain
that his compass was for fixing the prayer hours to be finally above
suspicion and, freed, was invested with a goat-skin.

Douls lived with the tribe for five months. A main journey was up
the Saguiet-el-Hamra and on to Tindouf, founded in the eighteen-
fifties and, said the Frenchman, by now a fine walled town of several
hundred mud-built houses. Tindouf's famed slave-market was then
absorbing three-quarters of the negroes brought up from the south,
the rest going straight through to Morocco; the main 1887 caravan
brought 520 slaves to Tindouf. With the midsummer heat imminent,
Douls perhaps felt he had seen enough of the desert: an agreement to
marry a skinny, bronzed dark-eyed 12-year-old called Eliaziz, in
exchange for seven camels, meant he had to go off to his own lands

for his possessions. However, the marriage feast was held first, one of the tribe's wisest men giving the address: 'God had put his eyes into me, for not only had he freed me from death but he had recompensed me by causing me to pass my life in the happy company of the enchanting Eliaziz, and amongst flocks of dromedaries'.

Douls' would-be father-in-law accompanied him to Goulimine; the Frenchman noted that though the Sultan's domain reached to the Draa, the Wadi Nun area was effectively independent. Then – thin, sunburnt, in skins, his hair shaved but for a tuft – Douls crossed the Sus, not surprisingly escaping notice, and was free again. The following year, this time in the desert north-west of the Ahoggar, he was killed by the nomads.

## Ma el Ainin and the French

To understand the evolution of the Spanish Sahara over the last century or so, it is necessary to keep in mind that of the adjacent territories, with their own development from feuding tribes through French colonialism to a comparatively unified independence as individual states. Throughout the first half of the period, into the nineteen-thirties, the Spanish watched cautiously, too weak to imitate France's gradual military control of the whole of its territories – then, choosing the moment when the French were finishing the 'pacification' of the Sus, Atlas and Tindouf areas, thus completing their cosy encirclement of Spanish Sahara, the Spaniards both extended into the littoral desert from their three coastal bases and at the seventh attempt managed to annex the minute Ifni. The year was 1934. Now – since 1956, as will be described later – the departure of the sheltering French has allowed in a chilly wind off the desert, the *bilad as-siba* is all around.

Though the Arguin trading post had declined in importance – to take up the French action at the point reached in Chapter 6 – in the early nineteenth century France was still manoeuvring on the C. Blanc–Senegal coast. Following conflict with both its black and white Africans, in mid-century pacts were signed with the powerful Trarza and Brakna emirs, their tribes effectively then within 'protectorates'. From this date the French were actively considering the rest of the western desert. Three examples: in 1860 Captain Vincent explored the Adrar Soutouf; a negro, Bou el Mogddad, was commissioned to cross the whole of the present Spanish Sahara in the following year; in 1879, in Algeria, Mecca-bound pilgrims from the Mauritanian Adrar were questioned by the French. Discussions were held with the Spanish, in 1885, over the B. du Levrier. About 1890 the French began to spread into the interior of the present Mauritania.

Their opponent was Ma el Ainin. He was born in either 1831 or 1838 in the Hodh, now south-east Mauritania; though his parents are said to have been Lemtuna Berbers, he claimed that his father, a noted *morabite* or professional holy man, was descended from Moulay Idriss of Fez, thus bringing Ma el Ainin into the *chorfa* class by line-age, the maximum in religious status. Named Mohammed Mustafa, he became called Ma el Ainin, or 'Water of the Eyes', as a result of his mother's tears of joy or from a reference to him in verse by his father – or because he had an eye disease which affected the lachry-mose gland. At seven he knew the Koran by heart. By 1854, the year of his pilgrimage to Mecca, this nomad was becoming famous in north-west Africa, until by his death in 1910 he was known every-where for his religious zeal, with miracles such as rain-bringing; for his healing powers; for his erudition in theology, law, astronomy, astrology, and literature, on which he wrote over 300 works, together with panegyrics on himself. Coupled with these qualities went the essential austerity and stamina, valued in the desert, though he did not lead his troops into battle but commanded from headquarters. His immediate progeny – sixty-eight children by twenty-six women, the most important a Berebich from the Hodh – were to form a tribe in themselves, the present Ma el Ainin.

After living a while in Chinguetti, the young Ma el Ainin centred himself and his growing band of disciples upon Bir Nazaran, 100 km east of Ed-Dakhla; these morabites became known as the Berik Al-lah, 'those of God's blessing'. An early exchange with the Euro-peans came about 1883, when Ma el Ainin is said to have told a Spanish trading ship to leave Rio de Oro unless it had permission from the Moroccan Sultan – or so a pro-Moroccan grandson of Ma el Ainin affirmed to the present writer's companion in 1974. In 1886 Ma el Ainin had a hand in disturbing Cervera's expedition, preaching that it was 'defiling the desert'. In 1887 the new Sultan, Hassan I, gave the nomad leader guns and the title of his Caliph in the desert – in fact, monarch after monarch was to hope to extend his power into the Sahara through Ma el Ainin. As for the Spanish, forced to deal with him, they had nothing but mistrust, finding him an opportunist; in 1893 his insistence that he was returning the crew of the *Icod* with-out a ransom demand – but he should be sent a specified 'present' – showed deviousness-cum-hypocrisy too.

Coming now to the French advance in 1890, this caused a great part of the nomads to group around Ma el Ainin and, announcing a holy war, about 1895 he began to move his base to a strategic point high up the Saguiet-el-Hamra. A patch of rushes, *smara*, showed him there was water – he began to build a *ribat*, a religious cultural and economic centre, fortified, very similar in conception to that from which had diffused the Almoravide puritanism, conquerors and dynasty. Only the political aspect of Smara needs be noted here: the funds, with other aid such as arms, came from the Sultan, now a boy, Abdelaziz, over whom the charismatic nomad had much influence. MacKenzie's old post at C. Juby was handed over to Ma el Ainin. There is no record of his having asked the territory's Spanish 'protectors' for permission to found Smara, rather more trouble being given by the rising Reguibat tribe.

In 1903 the territory of the Trarza, now divided amongst themselves, was officially declared a French Protectorate, under the astute Coppolani; the future Mauritania was becoming separate from the Senegal. The intermittently-independent Trarza people – whose emir had from time to time been invested by the Sultan – now appealed to Morocco for help, but the forthcoming expeditionaries were defeated in 1906. During this period the *insoumis* of the Mauritanian Adrar asked Ma el Ainin to send them a son as regional leader. Hassenna came, taking over their resistance. The Adrar Emir whom the Spanish had met in 1886 having been expelled for fraternisation with the Europeans, his replacement was nominated . . . from Smara. The nomads had some success against the French at Akjoujt and in the Tagant; Coppolani was killed at Tidjikda in 1905, possibly to a plan by Ma el Ainin.

Nevertheless, the invasion continued in its north-easterly direction, its command strengthened from 1907 by the hand of Gouraud. For, though Ma el Ainin was pre-eminent, he could not unify the nomads: the perennially-feuding tribes would not combine, others found it to their advantage to fight with the French. No less a handicap were the nomads' poor equipment and unsuitable tactics – the massed attack of men and cavalry, with shouts and flying standards, were met by French machine-guns and artillery.

In 1907, Ma el Ainin and his appointed emir went personally to Morocco for more help. This was the moment when the country split between the unpopular Abdelaziz, collaborator with the French, and his brother Abdelhafid, the Pretender and hope of the indomitable south. Ma el Ainin changed allegiance and the direction of his journey, on his inevitably-impressive entry into Marrakesh being humbly received by Abdelhafid. Seating himself on the throne, with the future Sultan and his own eldest son at his feet, the nomad refused to drink the proferred tea, presumably for fear of poison; he transmitted his *baraka* or holy essence by dipping his finger in the tea, then drunk by the grateful Abdelhafid. In exchange came guns, otherwise no longer so easy to get from Morocco: there was criticism

7 Two arches of the unfinished mosque of the Smara *ribat* and, left foreground, variably-ruined domed rooms showing the mud-brick construction.
All the white buildings are barracks.

Main square and mosque, Smara.

Nomad tents on the outskirts of Smara.

8    Drawing water at Hassi el Aouej, near Ijil; a well with radiating troughs.

Dead camels at Sebaiera well, central interior.

Zebu cattle foraging in rubbish bins, Nouadhibou. A naval post behind.

of the nomads' lack of success, that they were undisciplined and even simply sold the arms.

It has been said that during this journey Ma el Ainin helped to bring about the Casablanca riots, allowing the French landings and the fall of Abdelaziz. It must have been clear to him that the French would soon be on the northern horizon of the desert too. Published in Paris that year, 1907, a dictionary of the southern Morocco Berber dialect of Tamazir't held a section called 'With a traveller; a spy; a prisoner'. Its useful phrases, all in the second person, used to an inferior, gave an idea of what the nomads could expect: 'You are a spy . . . I will have you shot . . . I will let you live . . . where is your army . . . where are your silos . . . you lie . . . they will be well treated . . . they will keep their possessions . . . we will work together . . . for everybody's benefit . . . we will protect the good . . . we will punish the bad . . . we will teach your children . . . they will have the same jobs as us . . . because we are powerful . . . useless to let us destroy your *ksar* [a fortified settlement] . . . with our artillery . . . give yourselves up today'. But the nomads went on fighting.

In 1908, with freshly-equipped hope, bands of Smara disciples – the most determined of all the nomad fighters, usually with one of Ma el Ainin's sons as head – were effective in leading the more southerly desert-people against the French and their local supporters and Senegalese troops. This brought about Gouraud's Adrar column, on the march on 6 December; the French were supported by the southern desert's leading holy man, Sidia of the Biri tribe, the only African whose influence could possibly be matched against that of Ma el Ainin. Hassenna defended the entry to Atar, the Adrar's main town, but his men fled. Relentlessly, Gouraud now entrenched himself in the capital, appointing his own emir. The defeated force, many dispirited, were now in conflict amongst themselves, and so split up, the southerly Gailan tribe submitting to the French, Hassenna with the Reguibat going north. Long-awaited reinforcements from Morocco were attacked after an arduous desert crossing and defeated by Gouraud. He, provisioned again by mid-1909, then led 500 riflemen and two machine-gunners up to the Aouej well on the edge of the Ijil pan, the end of his campaign. It would be twenty-five years before the French would 'pacify' the desert to the north and link up with their compatriots in Morocco.

Ma el Ainin now left Smara, still unfinished, and made a base at Tiznit, in the as-yet unconquered south Morocco. The pliable Abdelhafid, now Moulay Hafid, then promised the French he would suppress the desert *jihad*-preacher. In May 1910 Ma el Ainin countered by declaring himself a *mahdi*. Presumably his final discouragement came when, on 23 June, General Moinier defeated a combined force of 6,000 Moroccan and Adrar *insoumis* on the Tadla plain. Saint or fanatic, gifted politician or horse-dealer, according to the nationality of the observer, the old nomad, the first 'blue sultan' of the desert, died at Tiznit on 23 October 1910.

### France 'Pacifies' the Nomads, 1910–34

Still watching from the coastline, the Spaniards must have been pleased to see the territory's military spirit being crushed for them by the French, the latter also taking on the conquest's legacy of direct hatred. Cautiously, whilst the nomads' failing strength was elsewhere, during the period 1916–20 the Spanish did annex a little more of the coast.

In the desert, Ma el Ainin's role was taken over, in 1910, by his son El Heiba: a man of thirty-four, of average build, long hair and blue dress, he was pious, lettered and courageous, but not an original thinker like his father. In 1912, after the signing of the protectorate treaty in Morocco, the south grouped itself around El Heiba in Tiznit, proclaiming him *mahdi* and Sultan. His brothers took Agadir and Tarudant; to the south, El Heiba's power extended over 'Spanish' Sahara and the rest of the western desert to the north of the Adrar. In August the second Blue Sultan made a triumphant entry into Marrakesh at the head of 5,000–15,000 men. It is said that the delights of the city then softened the spirit of the rough southerners . . . with the decisive battle approaching, El Heiba forecast that the cannon of Col Mangin would simply sing the praises of Allah or jet water, the rifles would fire beetles. At Sidi Othmane the massed charges learned the truth. The citizens of Marrakesh, glad to be rid of the nomad troops, referred to the fleeing El Heiba as 'the impostor' in their speech of welcome to the French army.

Still, the Blue Sultan had lost little ground, so in 1913 the invaders began to move south against him. At this point the Adrar-entrenched French sent a flying column under Col Mouret to assault the unprotected Smara, their first notable action in the Spanish-claimed territory. When the enraged nomads returned from their defence of southern Morocco, they found that the 400 French soldiers and local collaborators, together with 200 men of the Mauritanian Gailan tribe, had blown up the dome of the main building, damaged the library and gone. The *ribat* never recovered from this desecration. It became instead a symbol, a permanent stimulus to hatred of the Europeans.

To avenge this attack, 1,400 nomads of the Reguibat Sahel,

Lahsen, Yagut, Izarguien, Musa Ali and Usa – the tribes will be analysed in the next chapter – led by Agdaf, another of Ma el Ainin's sons, attacked and killed forty French in the south. Experts in the divide-and-rule strategy, the Europeans now sent the Gailan of Chinguetti against the northerners. At this point a Spanish estimate was that their territory could muster 6,000 guns, apart from the long Moorish muskets. Thus it seems clear that the nomads failed for lack of unison – notably, the war-loving Delim, already taking up their present role of Spanish supporters, did not usually fight beside the other desert people. Feud-raids continued alongside and were interwoven with the resistance to the French.

The first world war saw the nomads practising politics. Agdaf encouraged the Spanish occupation of C. Juby in 1916, to prevent this being done by the French, advancing down the 'unfriendly country' of the Sus. The nomads operated from and retreated to the Spanish-claimed territory, the French frequently demanding either the right to cross the frontier in pursuit or that the Spanish should take punitive action. In 1916 the nomads saw an even more fish-like ship than the medieval Portuguese caravels: after a month underwater, from Heligoland, a German submarine surfaced off the desert coast. With Turkish Moslem influence, it was bringing arms and funds to El Heiba – but, with little of the cargo ashore, a blunder led to the seizure of the crew by the Spanish at C. Juby. In the last year of the war, El Heiba died.

Merebbi Rebbu, his brother and appointed lieutenant, now took over the resistance. Then aged about forty, he is known for his poetry, such as that on the first aeroplane to fly over the desert and on the Alhambra. El Heiba had been forced to retrench to the Anti-Atlas and from here too the third and last Blue Sultan fought on, until about 1926. The extensive Reguibat tribe now headed the attacks, for example in a three-day battle against the French and their Adrar *soumis* in 1925. By this point the Sus people had been defeated, the French turning onto the Rif's tribesmen, finishing the ineffective Spaniards' war there.

About 1929, with the French net drawing tighter around the coastal desert, a new character appeared, Mohammed el Mamun, son of a cousin of Ma el Ainin. Aged fifty, he was a widely-travelled intellectual, a poet and teacher. Around 1918 he had agreed to act as German agent in stimulating the people of north Morocco in a rising against the French . . . the complexity of the task plus his scholarly bent led him to take on a safe post in the mosque at Taza in the south . . . and he was decorated by the French. Nevertheless, in 1929 he went back to the desert and, preaching the *jihad*, effectively took over from the despairing sons of Ma el Ainin. In 1931–2 he made various successful attacks on the French in Mauritania, at Umm Tunsi using a combined Reguibat–Delim force; the current Adrar Emir was shot by the French whilst on his way to join El Mamun.

In September 1933, with the end approaching, the Spanish post at C. Juby was making the usual notes on Saharaui movements round-about: 'Know of intention to make up a raid . . . chiefs acting suspiciously . . . road to the north closed so market has no goods, much hunger . . . have put a double guard on the flour store'. El Mamun's arms were certainly landed in the Spanish territory, causing tension with the French.

The last stage was reached in 1934. French motorised units from south Morocco 'pacified' the Reguibat, taking their base of Tindouf, and linked up with the occupying forces in the Adrar; for various reasons, Col Trinquet was careful to have no Moroccan troops in his column. The French were in command of their territories at last.

Reassured, the Spanish now ventured to occupy the interior of their Protectorate and also Ifni. Before describing these events, it is necessary to run through life on the Spanish coast since 1900.

## Spain Watches and Waits, 1900–25

The 1900 Paris treaty was the first of the many attempts by the French and Spanish to share out the desert, then nevertheless still uncon-quered. Spain's territorial pronouncement of 1884 had been met with reserve by the French and, following the latter's 1900 mission to study the minerals, the present zigzagging boundary line was drawn up through the western desert, at least on French maps. The northern frontier then ran from C. Bojador to the Zemmour angle. In the south it began at the tip of C. Blanc, dividing the promontory down the middle, the Spanish retaining the right to fish in the B. du Levrier.

The cliffs of the Adrar massif formed the south-east corner, the curve above designed to keep twenty kilometres from the valued Ijil pan, its salt however to be duty free on export to Spain. Thus taking a paper hold on the Adrar, reached by Cervera's party in 1886, the French had justified this by the claim that they themselves had actually occupied it in 1890, nineteen years before they in fact did so, as has been seen. The indignant but impotent Spanish alleged this was a quite different Adrar, the Algerian Tuat, and quaintly pointed out that the Mauritanian Adrar was peopled by descendants of the Moors who had 'left' Granada in the fifteenth century and, retaining their door-keys and traditions, were still good Spaniards. The Spanish negotiator later shot himself rather than face his disgrace on return to the peninsula. Spain refused to delineate the Ijil curve on maps or on the ground until, in 1956, a chance for revenge made it expedient to do so.

In 1902 a project for a second treaty extended the Spanish northern frontier east to Bir el Abbas and then, through Tindouf, right up to C. Guir, above Agadir, potentially more than doubling their holding. And, had they in fact acquired the 'unfriendly land', infinitely multiplying their problems. However, the 1904 agreement only added the present north-east right-angle together with the territory up to the R. Messa. But no effective action had been taken over the 'unpacified' Sus when, in 1912, a third treaty fixed the boundaries for almost half a century: the area below Punta Stafford, two kilometres south of C. Juby, became a Spanish possession – El Heiba was not at the conference table, though – whilst, above this, there was to be a Spanish 'protectorate', though only as far as the Draa. To shrill protests from peninsular colonialists, Lyautey now set about the conquest of the south.

Turning to the existing Spanish coastal posts, their history after 1886 was one of stagnation and abandonment, initially due to their lack of success in attracting the desert caravans and, subsequently, to the French invasion of the desert, trade lines moving east as always. In 1900 only Villa Cisneros remained, surviving as a fishing port rented to the private 'Cía. Trasatlántica'; based in an anchored hulk, the fish brought in by its few boats were sold, primitively dried, to undemanding markets in Senegal and Guinea. The port suffered a further trade decline when, following the Mission Gruvel in 1905, the French decided to found their own fishing station in the B. du Levrier: the present Nouadhibou, appropriately meaning 'Desired of the Fox', in 1906 this began as 'Port Etienne', after the French Colonial Minister.

However, some new life had been instilled into the Spanish outpost, in 1903, by the appointment of Capt. Francisco Bens, aged forty, as 'political-military' governor, under Canary supervision. During the period to 1925 he practised towards the nomads what is still contemptuously referred to as 'the sugar-lump policy': friendliness, paternalism, appeasement. In the words of a modern Spaniard 'the order that not a shot be fired was given by feeble governments without insight into Africa'.

Bens began at Villa Cisneros by holding a great feast for the local Delim, Sba and Arosien tribes, importing 200 sheep as food. A year later, also according to Lodwick (1956), he took many local chiefs on the steamer to Grand Canary, to meet King Alfonso XIII, even their camels going to take part in a day of pageantry. In the years of

French incursion into the Adrar, from 1907, Bens made expeditions to the interior, in co-operation with the resistance movement and in spite of the pro-French tribes; during this period a line of forts was stretched across the Villa Cisneros peninsula.

In 1911 Bens took an expedition to meet a Moroccan delegation at Ifni, with a view to its immediate occupation – this both came within the 1904 treaty and, as described, had been agreed to by the Sultan in 1882, as a substitute for Sta Cruz. But now French manoeuvres led the Sultan to withhold his envoys, with his usual excuse of lack of regional power, and also to Bens' recall by the Spanish authorities. The fighting in south Morocco of course made it impossible for the militarily-weak Spanish to act without the approval of all parties.

In 1913, the Spaniards sent out Enrique D'Almonte to examine their new if still nominal acquisitions under the 1900–12 treaties. Upon eventual occupation, he counselled, the nomads' leadership should be shared amongst two chiefs to allow manipulation of one against the other; the Spanish should wear local dress to avoid long-distance sniping; the nomads should only be called traitors if the Spanish could prove it, punish . . . and escape. Many other useful practical hints (D'Almonte 1913) show he would have made a successful colonial governor.

In 1914 Bens decided to act on his own initiative; he put his soldiers in a ship and set off to take MacKenzie's old post at C. Juby. However, the boat was at once told by the Admiralty to return. Not dissuaded, Bens marched overland in seventeen days, only to be received by a Spanish cruiser with a message from above: 'Kindly go aboard with all personnel and return to Rio de Oro'. In 1916 Bens did take over C. Juby, with three dozen nomad troops; El Heiba and the Saharauis preferred him to the advancing French, the French preferred Bens to the openly-hostile Saharauis, so there was no opposition. With little trade now and, for lack of fish, not worth a curing station, this outpost was unimportant.

In 1919 Bens tried to occupy Ifni, the fourth attempt, but again the French diplomats had him recalled by the Spanish government. However, in 1920, Bens was officially told to take over La Guera for a fishing station. Backed by three officers and fifty soldiers of the 66th Infantry, Bens and the representative of the Marcotegui fishing company went ashore from the gun-boat *Santa Isabel* and, to the accompaniment of salvos from the ship, raised the flag: 'The Saharauis, dumbfounded, and imitating . . . Bens, raised their hands to their foreheads . . . and the radio gave Spain . . . the news of peace for the Saharauis of good will'. However, a poor anchorage, La Guera has always been dominated by Port Etienne.

Thus, in the year of Bens' departure, 1925, there were three ports again; at this point the nomads' leader, Merebbi Rebbu, offered the Spanish a calm take-over of Ifni, but the French, knowing it would then become one of the resisters' last refuges, forced the Spanish to turn down this tempting offer. Villa Cisneros was then still only a fort, curing station and jetty; inside the fort was Bens' Sevillian-style house. The more co-operative locals had been given minute houses; about 800 Saharauis were now camped around the settlement. The Cía. Trasatlántica employed some of the tributary-class Imraguen as fishermen, cheaper than Canary labour; they were now to some extent proof against tribute-extortion by the nomads, with a few leaving for the Canaries and even S America, their frugality an advantage.

From 1925, with a military dictatorship in Madrid, control of the two southern settlements passed increasingly from the fish companies to the army, already holding the third post, C. Juby. The next decade saw the strengthening of the Spanish military forces, prior to the expansion which, in the event, took place in 1934.

*1925–30, the First Aviators*

The nomads were thrown into a ferment, not only poetical, by the appearance of the first aeroplane. Nevertheless, in 1925 the Toulouse–Dakar service of the 'Co. Générale Aéropostale', later romanticised by St Exupery, was landing in Spanish Sahara; air-strips were cleared at C. Juby and Villa Cisneros and, of course, at Port Etienne. Partially for flight security, partially as a result of Primo de Rivera's military philosophy and of the problems caused by his deportation to the desert of quantities of political prisoners, the garrisons were strengthened. In 1928 the Saharan Police Troops came into being, one corps on foot, one on camels, and a six-plane squadron for reconnaissance and communication was established in Villa Cisneros.

In 1930, a British aviator, Findlay, flew a three-seater cabin plane from Agadir to C. Juby in two and a half hours. Below Tiznit, an emergency landing would have meant either death or ransom, no matter whether in the French or Spanish zone; women could never be carried. Just before his own flight, a pilot had had to land in the Draa bed, an accompanying plane following down and helping him mend the machine in time for both to take off again as the nomads were on the horizon.

It appears that Findlay found C. Juby much as the last Britisher had left it in 1895, apart from a hangar and a caterpillar Citroën car. The officers, now no less than twenty and under a lieutenant-colonel, were gloomy: there had just been an air crash with their comrades captured. The soldiers wore tattered uniforms, with rags bound around their feet instead of boots, their sullen faces reminding Findlay that the bases were also military penitentiaries; this has continued to the present, Spain's best-known conscientious objector starting two years in a disciplinary battalion at El Aaiún in 1972. Findlay was told that many became unbalanced by the heat and the desert; the men mutinied against the officers, the officers plotted against the King. From time to time the Saharauis attacked, to be dissuaded by force or by food offerings, left outside the walls. Whilst Findlay was getting the sand out of his engine, the CGA plane came in . . . crouched in the back was an African, always carried to explain to the tribesmen that ransom would pay them better than murder.

*The Last Explorer, 1930*

The last of the desert romantics to set out on foot – St Exupery still had to fly across – was a 26-year-old Frenchman. Michel Vieuchange left Tiznit in September 1930, disguised as a local woman, his aim Smara, dramatically introduced by him as 'the Forbidden City'. The narrative of his two months is the sad story of a physically-weak, un-prepared, self-important intellectual in a Quixote-like quest for glory, in his own words 'to be the last of the great explorers'.

Cheated by his bodyguards, forced to pay tributes to all the chiefs on his route, he limped along, taking his pulse, doctoring him-self . . . perhaps he has typhoid now, or is it anthrax . . . no, it's malaria, rapidly dealt with by a dose of quinine. His moment of triumph comes when he manages to eat most of a tin of cherries before his guide notices. The Frenchman's attitude to this man: 'I am willing even to go so far as to put myself out if he asks me to fetch something . . . act as servant to an Arab. But the time will come. . .'

At length the little band, passing through the tents of 3,000 Reguibat and 2,000 'disciples' – presumably Berik Al-lah or similar – who were then camped around Smara, entered the deserted and partially-ruined *ribat*. The florid prose does not disguise that 'Smara is a dead city' and something of an anti-climax. Vieuchange buried a note for posterity in a corner and left.

True to his self-inflicted brief, he died, dysentery killing him at the end of the return journey. Adding little to knowledge of the region, his march rather mapped his own mind, to which Paul Claudel even added a key. Though this may always have been a subconscious aim of the explorer since Hanno, yet – by the articulate emphasis on him-self – Vieuchange should perhaps be treated as one of the first of a modern type of expeditionary, clearly exploring himself.

*The Spanish Take Advantage of the French Pacification, 1934*
Reassured by the success of the French campaigns, the Spaniards
decided to move. Further landings in Ifni, in 1932 and 1933, had
failed but now – at the seventh attempt – they succeeded in taking the
diminutive territory. Why it had been so difficult is not clear if, as in
modern articles: 'Col Capaz took over . . . amidst the tribes' en-
thusiastic ovations, paralleling those at Herrera's occupation'. The
French had co-operated in the 1934 landing, now that the nomads
had been pushed back to the Draa River. The 1912 treaty had turned
Ifni into an enclave again, awkwardly for the Spanish; with its inland
boundary twenty-five kilometres from the sea, it covered about 2,500
sq km.

Stimulated by this, in the desert, in May, the Camel Corps
advanced on Daora, just north of the future capital, and in June
entered Smara, deserted; they came across Vieuchange's note. The
Camel Corps was put to patrol the tracks, other Police Troops commanded various key watering points: at Tan-Tan and Tisguiremz,
both just below the Draa and, respectively, coastwards and in the
mountains; at El Aaiún, 'the eyes' or springs; the important 'guelta'
in the Zemmour massif; at Tichla in the Tiris; and others.

Spain's two territories were now grouped under a Governor-
General at Villa Cisneros, with delegates at C. Juby and Ifni. Development had however to be delayed since, once the period of self-
congratulation was past, the Civil War had begun in the Peninsula.

*The Ripples of Peace and War, 1930–40*
Primo de Rivera's exiles were replaced by those of the changing
governments of the nineteen-thirties: the leaders of the Oviedo
miners, difficult priests, trade unionists. In 1932 there arrived some
twelve dozen officers who had backed Gen Sanjurjo in his rising
against Azaña's Liberal government. One of these exiles, Martín
Alonso, soon escaped; four years later he was leading the Nationalists
in La Coruña. A violent break-out of political prisoners from Villa
Cisneros occurred in March 1937. In 1974, after 'Thirty-five Years of
Peace', a few muttering Republicans, more or less in exile, live on in
the towns of Spanish Sahara.

Upon the outbreak of the Civil War in 1936, the military play-
ground, 'Spanish West Africa', soon settled into Nationalist control,
after some initial resistance to the rebellion; the Nationalist ranks
recruited Saharauis as soldiers. As a part of the price of German aid
to Franco, in 1937 Hitler demanded bases in Spanish Sahara. In 1940,
with their own internal strife officially over, the Spanish were tempted
by the sight of the Axis powers' ascendancy into territorial acquisitive-

ness. As a result, on 8 August, Baron von Stohrer told Berlin, in the Memorandum called 'Operation Gibraltar', that the Spanish would enter the second world war 'in exchange for Gibraltar, French Morocco, that part of Algeria colonised . . . by Spaniards [Oran] and . . . the enlargement of Rio de Oro and the Colonies in the Gulf of Guinea'. But Hitler needed Petain's co-operation to avoid the French territories joining the British and so could not offend France in favour of Spain.

In 1940 the territory's government was still called 'political-military' as in Bens' day. Plans were begun for reconnaissance of the desert's various aspects. The official magazine *Africa* opened its covers to suitable contributions. Now was the moment for the new Spain to catch up with the rest of colonial Europe which, in the words of one article, had in the last century 'seen with pity that Africa had fallen into anarchy and misery, separated by an impassable wall from the culture and well-being of its friend across the water . . . and had had the idea of raising the level of life . . . dedicating to this its soldiers, money, engineers and doctors . . . against a panorama of syphilis, leprosy, immorality, analphabetism, brutality, slavery, plagues, sterility and hunger'. Before considering the Spaniards' actions in the field, three chapters will be devoted to the nomads of the twentieth century.

# Chapter 8

# Nomad Society

Studies of the physical and social anthropology of the Saharauis have to be read against the background of international politics and internal policy. The influence of these varies in result from the obvious distortions of the apprehensive colonialist to the subtle effect on the subconscious of the anthropologist. Thus, current external propaganda tries to show that the territory's nomads differ from the people of the neighbouring states so that it would be 'natural' that the Saharauis should have the Spaniards to protect them or, a grudging second, be independent; it has even been claimed that there are no Arabs in the territory. Internally, however, some tribes are less the 'real' Saharauis than others, the latter notably the Delim – in fact of course Arabs who only arrived about 1400 – chosen because of their enrolment on the Spanish side. Thirdly, population statistics are manipulated, both by the Spanish and their opponents, with the intermittently-imminent referendum in mind; for the same reason the authorities physically keep out or entice in one or another group, though the extent of this seems beyond determination. Even without these factors, a nomad society presents many natural difficulties to the student.

*Census*
Population statistics are, then, of limited value. Some of the wild fluctuations will have been due to inefficient census technique. Groups of nomads may genuinely have changed from one side of the boundary to the other between censuses, for non-political reasons, temporarily or permanently . . . the argument as to which state should count them underlines the artificiality of the frontier lines. Apart from these problems, the figures can hardly include both the Spanish military, about 15,000 strong since 1970, and the large number of Spanish workers in the mining, construction and other industries which have been developing since early in the nineteen-sixties.

| | Official Figures | Saharauis | | Spanish | |
|---|---|---|---|---|---|
| | | Men | Women | Men | Women |
| 1950 | 13,627 | 6,615 | 5,672 | 951 | 389 |
| 1960 | 23,793 | 8,983 | 9,506 | 4,087 | 1,217 |
| 1970 | 76,425 | 32,742 | 27,035 | 11,239 | 5,409 |

These 1950 and 1960 statistics include only the more sedentary Saharauis; the 1970 figure reflects not only a wider count but also the drought, bringing the nomads more or less permanently into the settlements. However, Morocco and Mauritania put forward a 1970 figure of 75,000 nomads alone, by including the anti-Spanish members of the Reguibat, whose pastures straddle the interior border. The resistance movement in favour of independence, MOREHOB, claims that no less than 600,000 refugees from the Spanish territory are now in the surrounding countries. Chapters 13–15 will describe the internal and international political and military conflicts.

Long-term trends appear beyond discovery; though a Civil Register of births, deaths and marriages was begun in 1956, registration was optional for the Saharauis, whilst the Spanish often leave the territory for these events. The number of tribes is much the same as it was at the beginning of the last century, according to Caro Baroja (1955), with the addition of the Ma el Ainin people. The high birth-rate, in line with a need for security and of many to pray for a father after his death, was until recently to be balanced against those who died in battle and in the desert. The relaxation of the rule of marriage within the tribe may now increase fertility. Food hand-outs during famines, free medical care and other help from the Spanish, together with increased wealth, can be expected to help towards population increase. In spite of the 1960 figures, it is thought there are at present more adult men than women. Finally, it seems that in age distribution through their society the nomads are comparatively young.

*Physique*
Riley gave full details of his typical captor: about 5ft 7in tall, well-made and lean, of dark-olive complexion, with high cheek-bones, rather prominent aquiline nose, lank cheeks, thin lips, round chin, black eyes, coarse thick black hair, cut so as to stick out six inches all around, and long beard. The ferocious women were short and meagre, their features harder and more ugly; then, relenting, Riley described their long black hair, braided and bunched on their heads, and their eyes 'round, black, very expressive, and extremely beautiful, particularly in the young women, who are generally plump and lascivious'.

A Spanish anthropologist, Alcobé (1947), studied 270 men, these nomads then being in the Saguiet-el-Hamra latitude. His average subject was 165 cm tall, with few outside 161–8 cm, and was of light build; long-headed, the cephalic index being 74, with two-thirds under 76; face a narrow oval, with high forehead and marked tapering to the chin; some occipital prominence; nose thin, most commonly straight but a third convex; the lips sometimes thickish but not bulky, with only 8% near negroid; eyes black or dark brown; skin brown with a yellow tint; hair black and curly, beard sparse. Alcobé noted a second group, differentiated by its tendency towards features of 'Cro-Magnon' or, in north Africa, 'Mechta-Afalou' type. Each group held possible evidence of crossing with negro people; Alcobé's study deliberately did not include any of the ubiquitous negro slaves, whilst he also noted that the lower the caste the greater the negro element. Attempts have not been made to separate the Saharauis into 'Berber' and 'Arab' physiques; due to inter-breeding, this would be difficult to do, though one would expect the remaining Berber-speakers, the Tekna confederation in the very north, to retain the most from the earlier physique and the Delim most from that immigrant during the Middle Ages.

On the same expedition, Alcobé (1945) produced blood-group statistics for 260 of his subjects which, in fact, placed them closer to the southerly negroes than to the north African Berbers and Arabs: O group 45%, A 24%, B 23%, AB 8%. There is thus some discrepancy between the negroid element shown by the physiques and that shown by the blood groups.

### Social Groups

In way of life, the inhabitants of the coastal desert abut, in the north, against the sedentary cultivators of the Anti-Atlas; to the south, as the Senegal is approached, the sedentary negroes and their culture appear; eastwards spreads the empty desert, with some contact through the south-east, in the Hodh and at places like Timbuctoo, with the related Touareg and their similar society. Linguistically, the northern Tekna, semi-sedentary, are to be associated with the contiguous Anti-Atlas peasants since both speak Berber; the territory's Arabic speakers, the great majority, share their tongue with a large part of Mauritania, without geographical break; Mauritania does retain enclaves of Berber-speakers and the Touareg also speak Berber, the rest of Africa's Berber dialects being of course found in the countries of the Maghreb.

Spanish Sahara's 'sons of the clouds', or *ulad el mizna*, live in a caste-bound society, now forced to relax in many of its practical aspects. The four main classes, interlinked, are those of warrior, religionary, tribute-payer and slave; the craftsman and the musician form independent low-caste groups. False claims, disputed, are made to membership of the first two classes. Throughout the last centuries, various tribes have in turn become dominant.

The warriors, or 'sons of the gun', are the Reguibat and Delim tribes, both of which will be described in separate sections, and the Tekna tribes of Lahsen, Usa, Yagut, Musa Ali and Izarguien. The claim to the desirable status of 'Hassan descendant', or to be Maquil Arabs, can only be substantiated by the Delim, the northerners of the Arab 'locusts' who settled on the region of the present Mauritania in late medieval times, then subjugating the indigenous Berbers and confirming their superior strength by winning the thirty-year war of the late seventeenth century.

The tribes calling themselves *chorfa*, the plural of *sherif*, claim to be descended from the Prophet Mohammed and thus should only be Arabs. However, the leading groups are the Reguibat – vigorous claimants of the double status – followed by the Arosien, Filala, Taubalet, Sba, Berik Al-lah and Ma el Ainin. The *chorfa* grouping has become intertwined in practice – and sometimes confused by modern writers – with the Mauritania-centred *marabout* or *zaouia* division. This holds 'the people of the books' – teachers of the Koran and dispensers of the traditional justice – of which only a part claim to be Arab and descended from the Prophet, the rest being Berbers therefore. In the middle of the last century the Berik Al-lah were a Mauritanian *marabout* tribe but, rising to prominence as Ma el Ainin's chosen people and moving northwards, they then called themselves *chorfa* also; most are once again in French-speaking territories, as are many of Ma el Ainin's own descendant tribe. The Filala and Taubalet also call themselves *marabout* and *chorfa*. In Spanish Sahara, the nomads' religion is centred on the *chorfa* tribes.

The tributary tribes of Fuicat, Imraguen, Lamiar, Menasir, Meyat and Tidrarin are called the *zenaga*; one of the ancient variations on the name Sanhaja, the title seems most likely to reflect the greater social status, from about 1400, resulting from calling oneself Arab. Defeat in battle was a way of dropping to *zenaga* status. The Tidrarin Berbers were accepted as *chorfa* until, reaching a low state in the late eighteenth century, they became subject to the Delim; however, the religious prestige of their Taleb Ali fraction, said to have been exempt from the tribute, did keep the Tidrarin from maximum social degradation. Most tributaries fish the coast – a habitat and way of life despised by the nomads as the last resort of the fallen – and accept into their midst the defeated and also those expelled from the interior, upper-class tribes. The Tidrarin are exceptions, living in the desert as herdsmen and retaining their tribal homogeneity. The tributary tribes have a greater negroid element than have the first two classes. The alternative name is *lakhme* or 'flesh without bone', whilst *zenaga* is also a general term of abuse.

The slaves have always been negroes, in immediate or distant origin from the south; they are scattered throughout the tribes making up the preceding social groups. Also classed below the *zenaga* are the *malemin* or artisans, said to be of Jewish origin and feared for their occult powers, and the Mauritania-centred *iggauen*, itinerant musicians and poets, both groups described later. Although it is said 'Better the negroes than the *malemin*, better the *malemin* than the *iggauen*', these two groups do in fact command some respect at the side of the slaves. Recently a new social group has appeared, the carving and jewellery sellers from the Senegal; prosperous, poised and friendly, these negroes trade from the pavements with the Spaniards but are rarely seen in contact with the Saharauis.

The normal geographical range of the tribes is shown in Fig. 10; it has changed little since Scott's day, 1810–16. An idea of the relative size of each tribe was obtained in 1954 by counting the 6,300 tents then in the territory: Reguibat 2,500, Delim 650, Izarguien 500, Tidrarin 500, Arosien 350, Yagut 350, Musa Ali 350, Ma el Ainin 200, Lahsen 200, Sba 100, Usa 100, the rest about 50 each. At about five persons to a tent, this gave a total of 31,500 people. The numbers in each class of society depend on where the Reguibat and Tekna are placed but it is safe to say that three-quarters claim warrior status and, in spite of being Arabised Berbers, most of these also claim to be descended from the Prophet and thus *chorfa*; a further eighth are Delim, warriors but not *chorfa*, though they are at least of Arab origin and the only ones who could thus even begin to make such a claim; the remaining eighth are mixed-origin tributaries and negro slaves. In October 1966 a petition 'to remain indissolubly linked to the Spanish State' was sent to the UN, signed by 14,637 of the 16,433 males, aged over eighteen, to whom the Spanish gave votes. The eligible voters were divided up: Reguibat Sahel's eight fractions 4,900, Reguibat Leguacem's nine fractions 3,286, Delim's five fractions 1,964, Izarguien 1,444, Tidrarin 1,101, Arosien 515, Yagut 139, Musa Ali 213, Ma el Ainin 429, Lahsen 709, Sba 56; although not directly comparable to the figures just given for the number of tents in 1954, it is noticeable that the order of size of tribal presence is no longer the same. The 1966 petition gave the voters for most of the other tribes in the territory: Berik Al-lah 311, Taubalet 106, Meyat 102, Filala 95, Aita 93, Foicat 81, Skarna 49, miscellaneous 840; this last must include the Usa. The differences over the twelve

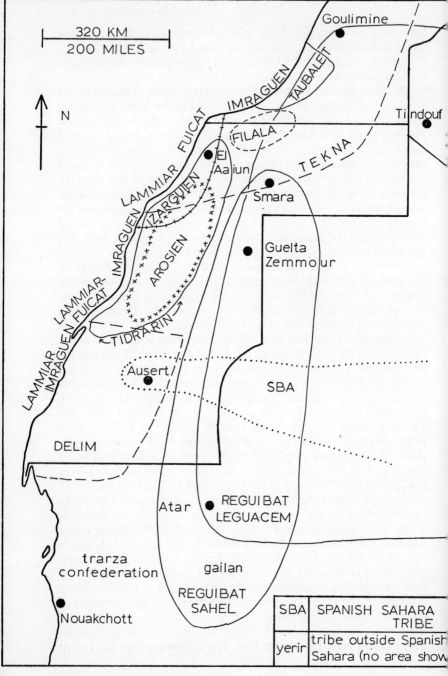

Fig. 10. Recent Distribution of Tribes

9   Two slaves quarrying salt, a third cording the bars, Ijil pan. Note the long-handled chisel. Below, their dwellings.

10 Dawn over the phosphate pier and, background, the terminal, on the beach, Aaiún Playa.

Amphibian bringing cargo ashore from anchored freighters, beside the unusable jetty, Aaiún Playa.

Shepherd and flock, across a creek in the El Aaiún lagoon. Sand covers Saguiet-el-Hamra north wall.

years will be partially due to the 1957–8 fighting with the Spanish and French, described later, since this led to population movements, especially of the anti-European Tekna and Reguibat. Also, much of the Tekna territory – Spanish Southern Morocco, with some 6,000 inhabitants – was returned to Morocco in 1958.

## The Interaction of Masters, Tributaries and Slaves

The Spanish have claimed to have abolished the tribute but according to the territory's leading anthropologist (Caro Baroja 1966), the system was still alive recently. The *horma* usually began as an agreement made by a tribe under duress, exchanging goods or services – with specific individuals – for, say, protection by the recipients' tribe. Or if, after a murder, the offending tribe could not provide immediate compensation, it might be forced into perpetual tribute. Once begun, the *horma* usually escalated to the point of total despoliation and servitude, the superiors simply helping themselves to the inferiors' possessions, occupying their tents when desirable, putting the men to work and taking over the women. The tributaries were not allowed to bear arms. The right to the *horma* is, or was, saleable.

The extortions of the Delim – partisans of the system in general – led the Tidrarin to rebel in 1875, backed by the Reguibat; but, these withdrawing, the *horma* continued. The Izarguien, perhaps the most 'civilised' tribe – though with the Lamiar as tributaries – continued to treat the Tidrarin as *chorfa*. In fact some nomad sages say the *horma* is a sin, though the reactionaries claim it to be well within orthodox belief and that 'protected' tribes got good bargains; the 'protectorate' was not limited to Europeans. The *chorfa* and *marabout* tribes exploited the *zenaga* as much as any. In spite of Caro Baroja's information, the tributaries do now wear a more jaunty air, some goading their cast-off masters by saying: 'We're all *zenaga* now!', referring to the Spanish domination.

Two rather more voluntary pacts are the *gafer* and the *asaba*. The former means, at least in the north, a simple contract between two tribes, such as to pay a transit 'protection' fee in terms of camels; *gafer* to mean a *horma*-like tribute received *en bloc* by one tribe from another was probably only current in the south, the Delim always preferring force to agreement. The *asaba* is a pact in which a tribe takes into it one or more members of another tribe, perhaps because it has expelled them or has gone away permanently to another region; the vestiges of a whole tribe, perhaps decimated in battle or by a natural catastrophe, might be thus absorbed. The incomers are called *tarien* or *dahlins*. It is said that nine out of ten of the large Reguibat tribe are the result of *asaba* entrance.

Finally, the master-slave relationship, also still current in effect if not in name; as recently as 1955 the slave-caravans were still going through Smara, recorded Lodwick, though usually keeping east of the Spanish territory. Riley, a century and a half ago, described the slave's life. The rich nomad had perhaps three *abd*, treating them as children, without serious punishment; they did all the menial work, could only marry other slaves and only then with the owner's consent. Long meritorious service might lead to their being freed, when they apparently held full rights, including to marry Arab women. However, other travellers have said the slaves were very badly treated in day-to-day life, adding that the women did no work at all; Riley, conversely, thought the women had much the worse role, the head of the family treating them with contempt and like animals. Clearly there has been much variation.

Recent students have distinguished two classes of slave. The *na'ma*, born in the master's tent, was never sold and might well one day be freed or allowed to buy himself out; the mother might also feed the master's children, making both sets of off-spring milk relatives, though it would be rare that the master's wife would suckle a slave's child. The second group were those bought, exchanged for salt in the south or caught in raids; these *terbia* slaves lived in separate tents. Slavery is justified by legend: the patriarch Noah was laughed at by his black sons. Great holiness or the death of the master might also bring freedom. The slaves were despised for their degradation and feared for their 'evil eye'. Negro equals goat, say the nomads.

The Spanish claim to have brought freedom to 2,000 slaves in the territory, with subsequent protection. Tactfully, the authorities point to the merit gained, according to the Koran, from freeing a slave. However, the new *hartani*, freed slave, then usually out of work, normally signs an *asaba* with his old master, remaining 'associated'. Of the tribes covered by Caro Baroja's study, the highest proportion of slaves was in fact found amongst the Tidrarin: of 150 families visited, 23 had slaves, these being 32 men and 44 women out of the totals of 439 men and 383 women. These slaves were usually in pairs of parent and child; women were preferred as they produced children, these automatically slaves too.

## Structures within the Tribe

Each tribe takes its origin from a real or imaginary common ancestor, usually a person of both natural and supernatural abilities. Subsequent history, memorised by the wisest, is, of course, as favourable as possible to the tribe. Each member must know the names of at least his seven immediate forefathers.

Each tribe may or may not form part of a confederation. A tribe is divided into fractions and these perhaps into sub-fractions. Below one or the other of these comes the tent as a division, corresponding to a family of five to nine individuals. Four specific tribes can be summarised.

## Ulad Delim, a History of Rapine

Leo and Marmol, in the sixteenth century, saw the Delim as 'Poor Robbers . . . Strangers to Gallantry' and this appears to be the general opinion on them from their arrival in the fourteenth century until their enrolment in the Spanish service from the eighteen-eighties; they came in the meantime to dominate other tribes such as the Tidrarin, Arosien and Imraguen. Raiding and extortion were justified as a livelihood by the unproductive environment, said the Delim.

An example of their preference for blood came as late as 1932. Two French policemen, Trarzas, were killed by two Sba, these pretending they were Delim. Other Trarzas amongst the colonial police thereupon killed a few Delim. The French authorities at Port Etienne offered material compensation – mainly guns and money – but the Delim were determined on revenge on the Trarza as a tribe. In the event their force clashed with French negro troops, not Trarza, and, killing up to two dozen, claimed a satisfying victory. Pacification in 1934 brought loss of livelihood to many but an outlet was found in 1936, the Delim joining the Ifni-Sahara battalion of the Nationalists. According to the Spanish they volunteered to chase out the 'invaders' of 1957 and, in June 1958, held a mass demonstration of loyalty to Franco, doubtless encouraged, if not actually organised, by the administration. The Delim have always been in the majority in the locally-employed Saharaui police-cum-military units.

Within the tribe there are families with traditional functions. The Ahel Esber are raid-organisers and water-point guardians. The Ali uld Sueied keep a drum, made of the skin of a pure Arab horse, used as a call to council meetings and to war, it then being carried as the tribe's battle insignia. Now *zenaga* to the Spanish, they are looked down upon for their early willing co-operation – the sight of a vulture may bring the joke: 'Here come the Delim'. Nevertheless they have continued their old arrogance: at their zenith they, like the Reguibat, decided to ignore the custom of dismounting at a distance from a strange tent, and to the side or behind – a privacy measure, also observed by the country people of Fuerteventura when calling at a house. The Delim now find this arrogance less easily accepted. They had no brand-marks for their animals . . . they said all were potentially in their possession. The Delim were said to have been the most primitive of the territory's tribes, at least by others, for example still using skins when carpets were normal. Originally limited to the coastwards half of the south, they are now widely spread.

### The Reguibat, Warring Pastoralists of the Interior

The pious Ahmed Reguibi is said to have founded the tribe in 1503, as agriculturalists centred on Wadi Chebika; according to Rumeu this watercourse held Sta Cruz de Mar Pequeña, the year 1503 being in the middle of the Spanish activity at the tower. Their claim to *chorfa* status is denied by other *chorfa*, asserting that the Reguibat are a mixture of Berber and Yemen Arab. The many *asaba* pacts can be expected to have produced a very mixed people. So it is interesting to compare Alcobé's blood groups for the Reguibat and Izarguien, both claiming Arab ancestry: Reguibat O 39%, A 21%, B 31%, AB 9%; Izarguien O 53%, A 25%, B 18%, AB 9%. Not only are these far apart but the Izarguien are very similar in blood group to the Touareg upper caste, presumed the purest remnant of the desert's original Berber stock. As opposed to the Reguibat *asaba* frequency, the Izarguien have not let in other people and have doubtless kept to the general rule of endogamy, at least in the past. Within the Reguibat tribe, a hierarchy developed in which the founder's descendants were followed by incomers by *asaba* and their descendants, importance within the second group being in order of adoption.

Over the centuries the tribe gradually became more mobile, first moving to sheep-rearing in the Gaada, Saguiet-el-Hamra and Zemmour and then on to full desert-nomadism as camel herdsmen; crops were gradually reduced, finally to the occasional sowing of patches of the Zemmour. The Reguibat have long been divided into two groups, overlapping territorially. The Sahel or westerners traditionally graze an area with the Zemmour–Tagant line as its long axis, the Leguacem or Cherg reach from the Djebel Bani in south Morocco down to the Adrar. In 1954 the territory's 1,000 tents of the former and 1,500 tents of the latter represented about a third of the population; however, these tents only held from a quarter to a fifth of this extensive tribe, its members nomadising in all the adjacent countries as well.

The size of the Reguibat led them to supremacy about 1907, the year in which they defeated their last contestants, the Sba. In 1934 some officially chose Spanish domination, others stayed in the French zones. This pacification led to various changes. The necessity to keep together for defence, awkward in a land where the scanty pasture is quickly exhausted if only a limited area is grazed, was replaced by freedom to range at will, in the most viable units of four or five tents, a small *friq*. On the other hand this brought about a disintegration of tradition and command, leading to schisms within the Reguibat.

The Zemmour massif is perhaps the base most used by the tribe: they spend the lean summer months there, moving out rapidly to any rain-awakened zone of the desert and returning once it has been stripped. Tindouf is their town, to become important whenever the iron ore of the nearby Gara Djebilet is exploited by Algeria. Bisson (1961) felt the Reguibat had not been much affected by the oil developments nor, apart from the temporary halting of their trade with the north, by the conflict in south Morocco in the nineteen-fifties; the 'blue men', outnumbered by tourists, sell their camels in the Saturday market at Goulimine, though they only do so in quantity if there is drought. However, the 1957–8 war in Spanish Sahara saw many Reguibat fighting against the Spaniards and leaving the territory at the end of the clash. In 1966 about half the Reguibat on the voters' role for the petition to the UN did not sign, the only way to dissent. According to the press releases of the surrounding states and liberation movements, many Reguibat are still living as refugees outside Spanish Sahara; however, their camps are not conspicuous to the traveller, not at least in proportion to the huge published figures.

## *Sba, 'the Sons of He of the Lions'*

Amer uld Hamel came to Marrakesh from the Oran region. His flock being one day on the point of being stolen, he successfully prayed for his animals to be changed into lions, though they were not to bite the thieves, only to roar at them. His descendants claim *chorfa* status.

The tribe at length rebelled against the Sultan, probably in the eighteenth century. Half went north-east, returning on being pardoned; they can be found near Marrakesh at present. The others drove their flocks to the lower Saguiet-el-Hamra and attempted a settlement, sowing crops, digging wells and building. A second attempt was made at the Dumus well, on the tropic in the Tiris, and here the Sba did prosper as traders and animal dealers. A battle brought them the good crop-lands of the Imiricli, just below C. Bojador.

Then there appeared on the horizon a Wadan man called Ahmed el Cunti: leading a horde from the Adrar and the Hodh, he titled himself 'Sultan' and claimed submission from all tribes. The Sba sent thirty lettered men to meet him at Gleibat Mosdat: they would give him a large present but their only Sultan was that of Morocco. The ensuing hostilities forced the Sba to join forces with the Reguibat in the Zemmour. In the decisive battle, in 1887, Cunti, who claimed invulnerability, was killed by a charm-stone fired from a gun.

However, the period of turmoil was then at its height and the Sba, some now in the Nun, were involved in fight after fight. At first, armed with their advanced guns – the French 1874 model, probably obtained in the Senegal – they were on top, but then a Reguibat fraction wiped out the desert Sba in 1910. The few survivors and the Sba of the Nun returned to full-time trading, establishing themselves in the territory again in 1917.

Subsequently they have become dispersed, some running caravans, others dealing in livestock, the rest becoming sedentary merchants. In 1969 they had some 400 tents in west Mauritania and the south of Spanish Sahara. Though no longer important, they were the first to attempt to make a settlement in the coastal desert.

## The Imraguen Fishermen

The resort of the defeated, the shore probably received many of the 'black Bafots', conquered by the Berbers, and then in turn a part of the Berbers themselves, subjugated by the Arabs. During the life of Arguin and Portendic as slave-counters, some of the negroes were put to fish to provide food both for those in transit and for their masters – a number of them would have become part of life on the coast. The fishing tribes' physique is a mixture of black and white.

Valentim Fernandes described the *schirmeyro* or 'fishing' Sanhaja in 1507. In seventy dwellings on Arguin they lived off baked turtle, very occasionally a little camel meat. *Zenaga* to the Portuguese, these received a fifth of their catch in exchange for protection against the usual extortions of the nomads and, also, for water.

The name 'Imraguen' for the best-known of the coastal tributaries – about 500 people in the late nineteen-sixties – was first recorded in 1858, its meaning being 'collectors' of food, rather than hunters. By then the Saharan coast was divided into sections, named after the masters of the tribes who fished the shores; the fish brought by this parasitic relationship was important to the nomads, these extracting additional income such as the Berik Al-lah's purchase of slaves in the Sudan with shells collected by their Imraguen vassals. The Ahel Laghzel of the B. du Levrier were unusual in that they both fished and bore arms. The first Spanish colonials on the Villa Cisneros peninsula described its sixty fishing people. Anthonioz (1968), studying the fishermen just south of C. Blanc, noted that any Saharans could join them, though initially at least they would have less rights than those already established. The fishing techniques have been well studied in recent years and will be described in Chapter 10, on daily life.

## Inter-tribal Conflict

Fighting, to rob or revenge, has been more than a mere cultural characteristic, such as those to be described in the next chapter: it and nomadism, interwoven, have formed the central strands in the way of life. Fighting used up the belicose tribes' superfluous men, now in the Spanish Army. Robbery was often the only way to survive a drought, a plague – or another robbery. In semi-agricultural southern Morocco the tribes sowed in October, lived peacefully until the harvest in spring, then raided through the summer heat, making treaties in October so as to be able to sow again. In the desert, without the obstacle of regular crops, there was never a close season for raiding.

The *gazi*, raid, had its traditional methods – D'Almonte referred to the 'irreproachable technique' – with a complex code of behaviour, inter-group politics and peace settlements. Each expedition had its appointed leader, the *demin*, not usually the tribe's chief; a luck-bringer might be included in the party. The *demin* called a nightly meeting with the words 'Come and hear the news'. If water and food became short then these were put in the hands of particular members of the band. Sentinels were appointed each night; if it was thought that the party was being watched, the nomads would circle their camp smelling the sand; binoculars came to be used. The gear might be hired in exchange for shares in the raider's personal loot: a third for a camel or a gun, a sixth for a supply of cartridges. Great care was taken not to tire the camels, both for the approaching raid and for emergencies. Guns were usually few and poor in the desert, so that a tribe obtaining the latest weapons usually enjoyed a period of dominance. A speciality was the speed at which action was taken.

The *demin* was the first to saddle his camel for the actual attack. This usually took place by surprise, at night and in silence, the men naked other than for the camouflaging dust. The band would probably attack as a level front of three groups, together with a rearguard. The loot of a successful raid went in large shares to the leader, the guide and any distinguished fighters, with smaller portions to the rest, including any associated holy man. Death in battle gave no share, unlike death afterwards.

The raids were in fact usually expected, with sentinels around the defenders' camp: the first to spot the attackers would later receive an animal from each tent. Assuming an initially-successful raid, then, if the attackers were pursued and the loot recovered before they reached their own camp, the possessions were returned to their owners; but if a return *gazi* were needed, then recouped property was shared as after a first raid.

Peace was by negotiation. Verses were read from the Koran. The last cartridges were fired into the air.

Many of the important conflicts have been mentioned. One of the longest feuds was begun in 1820 between the Reguibat and the Tajakant, both claimants to religious status: in 1895, following endless raids, a thousand of the former laid siege to Tindouf, founded by the Tajakant in the eighteen-fifties, and after eleven days burned the town and killed most of the opposition's warriors. In 1863 there had been war between the two Reguibat divisions; from 1877–91 there was the Delim–Reguibat struggle with the Tidrarin in the middle. The appearance of the French led many tribes to ally with them, in intention temporarily no doubt, as an excuse to settle local vendettas; this was of course within the plans of the colonialists. Thus in 1900 the Gailan were set against the Reguibat; the former stuck an opponent's heart on a bush, to which one of the latter countered by tossing captive infants in the air and impaling them on his knife as they fell. In 1903 the Sba, terrorising the territory, sent the Arosien in flight to south Morocco, though not before they had tied a captive to four camels and had them pull him, in different directions, to pieces. In 1905 the Yerir of the Moroccan Tafilalet, site of the ruined Sijilmassa, were provoked by the Delim and launched a campaign against the coastal tribes: these did unite and, in 1909, drove the Yerir back again.

To give a final example, the last large-scale battle took place in 1934 under the walls of the Spanish fort at C. Juby, its occupants watching from the ramparts. The Izarguien, Tabaulet and other local tribes were under attack from a marauding force, but this fled when the mail plane appeared, fearing it had been called in to bomb them. The women of the Izarguien – MacKenzie's associates half a century earlier and, some have said, the most civilised of the territory's people – tore out the eyes of the tribe's dead opponents.

In spite of the permanent fighting, the nomads of course considered themselves good people: 'Northerners have clean clothes and dirty hearts, here it is the reverse'. The young men told Bens: 'Possessions belong to the strongest, the weakest are good for nothing . . . if the camel were the stronger, he'd eat us', though a few others did say that 'the bravest are those who don't raid'. In Riley's words: 'Such is the wandering Arab of the great African Desert: his hand is against every man, and consequently every man's hand is against him'.

*Chapter 9*

# The Culture
# of the Nomads

Saharaui culture, like the desert people's work – detailed in the next chapter – has been strongly affected by the Spanish presence. Inevitably, by the mere sight of European ways; and politically, by deliberate policy on the part of the colonial administration. There is also the usual belief, by the Europeans, that their own culture is superior and thus should be openly or covertly implanted in the nomads' tents: 'The Saharaui woman, due to conservatism, climate and, often, sheer lack of interest, hasn't the least idea of how to run a family . . . no knowledge of child hygiene, cooking, dress-making, ironing, cleaning, and is even inadequate in personal cleanliness', the article going on to describe the action taken by the 'Feminine Section' of the Falange. An officer's wife told Lodwick in 1956 that it was difficult to turn a Saharaui woman into a domestic. In short, the changes are due to imitation on the nomads' side, to policy, from a mixture of 'mission' and self-interest, on the Spaniards' side.

Some aspects of the desert culture continue with only light interference; notably Islam, of course, though there are now free jets to Mecca. Others, such as the ancient legal system, run parallel to a Spanish counterpart – the law thus an uneasy yoking of camel and ass. A third group of traits are disappearing totally, as when the nomads dismantle their tents and take up residence in the tiny houses of 'Calle Erquibat' – an alternative spelling of 'Reguibat' – and 'Calle Ulad Delim' in Villa Cisneros. The Spanish-imported culture will be left until Chapter 12, together with the important subject of the old and new forms of government.

*Language*
A quarter of the Maghreb and a third of Morocco speak in Berber dialects, the rest in Arabic. Of eastern origin, ultimately through

south-west Asia and then north-east Africa, the Berber language may
have been the tongue of the Oranians or Capsians, respectively in the
Maghreb from at least 14,000 and 10,000 years ago; Libyan, the
written alphabet current by 200 BC in the Maghreb, expanded into
the desert *tifinagh*, only to contract again – with the advent of Arabic
– to its present restricted use amongst the Touareg of the central
Sahara. The earliest main immigrations into the Canaries, probably
soon after the time of Christ, were of people of Oranian and Capsian
physiques, that is Mechta–Afalou and Early Mediterranean: then in
isolation for a thousand years, in the fifteenth century their tongue was
found to be based upon Berber. As noted, in Spanish Sahara only
the Tekna tribes now speak Berber, the Tamazir't dialect; to the
south the nearest Berber is spoken by the Duaish, below the Tiris.
The tribal names will often be seen prefixed by *ait*, 'sons of', as in Ait
Lahsen.

'Their language is the ancient Arabic; is spoken with great fluency
. . . powerful emphasis and elegant cadence. When they converse
peaceably,' went on Riley, 'it thrills . . . like the breathings of soft
wind-music, and excites in the soul the most soothing sensations . . .
in anger, it sounds as hoarse as the roarings of irritated lions'.
Arabic of course spread from the east; the local dialect is *hassaniya*,
after the ancestor of the Maquils, immigrants around 1400.

In 1445 João Fernandes found the region's Arabic different from
that of the Mediterranean Maghreb. Since then it has evolved little,
remaining near to classical speech; it is easily enough understood by
other Arabic-speakers. It includes words of Berber and Sudanese
origin, notably for local features such as the topography, animals and
plants. A noticeable characteristic is its short vowels. There are
differences, such as in grammatical accuracy and in accent, between
tribes and between castes: the southerners, notably the Delim and the
Berik Al-lah, speak the best, the Reguibat Leguacem are said to be
poor – more evidence over the Arab origin of one or another tribe.
Tribal names often include *ulad*, 'sons of', as Ulad Delim.

The origins of the place names can be summarised here. The basic
elements, the Berber and the Arabic, have not yet been studied in
Spanish Sahara; many names beginning with *T* or *Ch* on the Spanish
map will be Berber, whilst some Arab origins are obvious, for example the Maatallah well, near Gleibat Mosdat. The place names
refer to natural features, water sources, important people, battles
and so on. From the late Middle Ages, Europeans have imposed their
own names on the topography, beginning perhaps with 'Riu de l'Or'.
The Portuguese named a few bays, *angras*, after their dead, their
horses, the red mullet. The succeeding European tenants of Arguin

made up names for that area. Africans caught by the Canary raiders around 1500 transferred their home-land place-names to the islands, for example 'Tarfaya' in Fuerteventura. Glas, 1760, and the officers of the *Magpie*, about 1820, added the English flavour to the charts. MacKenzie, 1875, was the first to attempt to re-name the Tarfaya anchorage, with 'Port Victoria'. From 1884 the Spanish were naming the coastal features, the only part over which they ventured; in fact, all inland posts and water-points still use the Saharaui names. Bahia del Oeste, West Bay, was early on given up in favour of La Guera, from Aguera, in turn derived from the Aguerguer, the region of hummocky topography. Along the frontier, the French set up Port Etienne, Fort Gouraud and Fort Trinquet, now respectively Nouadhibou, F'Derick and Bir Moghrein. The last Spanish attempt at renaming, a pastime dear to undemocratic governments everywhere, was to call Tarfaya 'Villa Bens', on the general's death at eighty-two in 1949; the name left with the Spaniards when in 1958 the Protectorate passed into Moroccan hands. With the evacuation of Spanish Sahara imminent, the map-makers of the mid-nineteen-seventies will do best to await developments.

## Belief

Daily life in the desert, a hostile, lonely, mind-affecting environment, goes on in the midst of a myriad of supernatural forces, the bad seemingly outnumbering the good and the cause of endless precautions, invocations and exorcisms. This animism, the 'primitive Berber' religion, is still effectively the most important, in day to day life, of the three groupings of Saharaui beliefs.

The spirits, *yenun*, of good disposition, rather rare, reside in such valued objects as trees and wells; these may be decorated and receive offerings such as the sacrifice of animals and birds – *yenun* liking blood – and in exchange find lost or stolen goods or buried treasure and give news of distant relatives. People who can contact these spirits are called *emhaden yunun*.

The evil *yenun* fall into two groups, sedentary and nomadic. The first reside in all kinds of natural features, such as the Leyuaf hills in the Tiris; its *djinn* are provided with only one arm and one leg each. Taking many forms and with extraordinary powers, the spirits' existence appears to be confirmed by the Koran; they were 'created of pure fire'. It will be seen that the desert's animism also draws on the numen of the Moslem religion.

The evil *yenun* have many practical effects. Able to move at great speed, they can be seen approaching the camp as whirling dust-columns. As hyaenas, for example, they eat the traveller or turn him into an animal. Once in the camp they take many forms, the nomad men aware they can appear not only as animals but also as women and, in particular, as negroes. A spirit may get into the tent at night in the shape of an animal, perhaps to suck blood: the creature wounded, a negro is found similarly hurt the next day, the extreme consequences once being, in Atar, death by burning.

At this point the *yenun* appear to merge with all the humans who are thought to be or in fact are trying to bring harm on other people: their methods, indirect, are the 'evil eye', universally feared and practised. The blurring results from the impossibility of deciding whether a misfortune is due to a spirit or to the evil eye. Important effects of one or the other include causing illness or death, spoiling crops and distracting from prayer.

Moving on, now, to the evil eye in its application, this is found to take many forms. To kill there are three degrees: thinking or shouting formulas, perhaps in a propitious place or before a suitable object; this together with putting unpleasant matter in the person's food, such as tomb soil; these two and a potentially-lethal action. Then there are two sexual conjurations: love-concoctions by the women, usually of burnt pieces of the human body and especially of hyaena corpses, so that the men refuse food of unknown provenance and also burn all dead hyaenas; secondly, the sex-obstructing spell, in which verses of the Koran are written on a knife or scissors together with 'May God send impotence to X in front of the sexual organs of Y'. Many common north African curses are current, for example 'Fatima's hand' or 'five in your eye', this said to oneself with the right hand stretched out, fingers extended, towards the victim.

Further, and worse, evil eye powers can be acquired involuntarily, either by being the subject of the powers of another, or by mere contagion, or even for no apparent reason. This grades into the belief that some people bring bad luck.

Threatened at all times, precautions are essential; most of the activities covered in this and the next chapter call for them. Newborn children are especially vulnerable, especially handsome ones, so they are not left alone for forty days, are hidden from strangers, kept dirty, their names a secret; it is always unwise to appear proud of one's children. Sterile women or those with deformed infants are very dangerous. A child's age must only be mentioned in lucky numbers; for example, under five, over five, three times five, with uneven numbers best, especially 1-3-5-7, as God is one. The child must be kept hidden whilst eating, as evil enters more easily with food; the use of the veil may partially or wholly derive from this belief. Necklaces are hung on the children, of red, yellow and white beads, with a blue bead especially good; the inclusion of a little bag of sand will also slow down the devil's work, since it will have first to count each grain.

Adults take endless precautions too. A general prophylactic is a herb potion drunk whilst walking round the hearth, taken twice daily with a prayer; the favoured plants are *drinn* (*Aristida pungens*), *nsi* (*A. plumosa*) and *had* (*Cornulaca monacantha*), with *guetaf* (*Atriplex halimus*) and *damran* (*Tragonum nudatum*). To avoid the first glance of a traveller falling on one's flock, distractions such as camel bones and big soot-daubed pots are hung up conspicuously; it is worse if the stranger speaks simultaneously. Before praising anyone or anything, one must say 'God bless'. A person's shadow is to be avoided. Certain times of day, especially noon, are dangerous. To drive off a hovering devil the fingers are bitten, much as in 'touching wood'. Blue-eyed people are bad – usually Europeans, by coincidence – and female ones the worst, with old women the worst of all.

The universal protection is the amulet, made by the *fokaha*; a camel or two goats might be given for a good one. The typical small squarish amulets, *yedauil*, have to be made of layers of leather, cloth and metal and contain ashes, bones, spiders' webs . . . and verses from the Koran. The *fokaha* knows the herb to be burnt during its preparation, the number of folds for the paper, the right ink; for the latter, pitch, henna, blood and indigo are best. Also a drawing of one or two eyes, perhaps just as squares – remnant of the eye-goddess cult, probably. The amulets are hung round the neck or on an ailing part. Other charms are sulphur stones, holed shells and, particularly valued, the little black 'bezoar' stones found in antelopes' stomachs. Tattooed charms, more common in Morocco, are permanent protection. Tables of magic symbols are kept. Animals are protected by such evil-absorbers as stones placed in their drinking troughs.

If, in spite of this defensive network, a spirit or the evil eye penetrates, there are exorcisms and antidotes. These divide into household remedies and those prescribed in serious cases by the holy and wise men and their magic books, by witch-like crones for the women, and for some ills by the barbers. For example, to neutralise the effects of a blood-sucker, *sal-lala*, get a little blood from their mouths and burn it, with ashes, in a cloth: the smoke will take the form of a lamb whose throat must be cut by a member of the victim's family. The blood of a black unmated chicken is daubed on affected parts of the body; salt is good too. One might seek out the person cursed and suddenly shout his name; if they just look at one, or answer in a single word, the evil eye is lifted.

To drive out an evil spirit, surprise is best: an egg suddenly smashed in a person's face is often effective, or hair unexpectedly pulled from the nape of the neck and burned. A piece of sulphur and a few drops of sap from various plants will be thrown on the fire. As a last resort, the sufferer might be publicly paraded wearing an ass's head, as a Spanish-army soldier once did at El Aaiún.

Advance information on the actions of the spirits and the evil-eyed comes from the passively-received omen and from divination. The houbara bustard is good, a crow on the road bad, though two of these are good; to be hailed when starting a march is a bad sign. To divine a devil's intentions, a *kefif* is held: the people recite formulas whilst in a circle, then melt some lead, with aromatic herbs, in a spoon, pouring this in water and knowing that, if it solidifies with a smooth surface, all will be well. The ink-mirror is another method, a skilled person being able to interpret blots made on various parts of the body.

Finally, amongst the most primitive beliefs, the rain ceremonies; the Leyuaf engraving will have been part of one of these. If it is in fact about to rain, the clouds must not be upset: they must only be looked at with kohl-encircled eyes, must not be talked about, certain games must not be played, the sieve must be put out of sight of everybody. When it does rain, the water pots must not be got out, let alone the rain collected, until the downpour is over. Drought calls for special rituals, these drawing on the second group of beliefs, described next, the cult around dead and living holy men. The first recourse is to sacrifice an animal for the benefit of one of these, asking for intercession. This failing, the people might seize a live sage, strip him to the waist, tie his hands behind his back to his feet and put him in the sun until he agrees to send rain. Thirdly, a delegation will go to a really eminent holy man, such as Ma el Ainin: he will write a suitable verse of the Koran on a tablet and this will be hung on a tree, its power going out in all directions as it turns in the wind. Of more immediate value than any of these is the children's action: carrying the *talghenkha*, a weaving stick dressed as a woman, they drag a container around the camp, each tent contributing a handful of barley to be shared amongst those worst affected by the drought, the grains being counted out one by one like the beads of a rosary.

The original form of the second or 'advanced Berber' grouping of Saharaui beliefs exists in the Sus and the High Atlas (Gellner 1969): the veneration of past and present holy men, *igurramen*, who are intermediaries between man and god. This deity, Sidi Erbbi, is more paternal and life less fatalistic than in the Moslem religion; animism survives alongside. The live *igurramen* lead prayers. The shrines and tombs of those dead are the objects of pilgrimages, *almuggar*; these holy places have curative properties; the offerings go to charity.

In Spanish Sahara, the 'saint-cult' appears to be practised by all the nomads, no matter their origins or that they are nominally Moslems or, even, *chorfa* too, the very descendants of the founder of Islam. There are dozens of shrines, including those of the originators of the tribes; a circular enclosure has been built near some to receive the offerings of passing caravans; round stones, *kura*, lie nearby and (presumably absorbing the good, as those in the animal troughs absorb the evil) are applied to ailing organs. This goodness is called *baraka*, primarily transmitted by the holy men. Ma el Ainin's endless outpouring fell, amongst many, upon his disciple Haddara, his hair never whitening, unlike his beard, after his master had passed his hand over it; Haddara lived many years with an ostrich flock, coming to walk and eat like the birds, devouring all objects in his path. *Baraka* allows its holder to work miracles, such as healing; it sometimes gives rights, such as to sow or shoot first. One of the most recent shrines is the tomb of Merebbi Rebbu, buried in 1942 at Tafudart on the Saguiet-el-Hamra. Many living men of the Boihat fraction of the Reguibat are holders of *baraka*.

Islam is the third belief grouping; as animism and the saint-cults draw upon it, so it has incorporated parts of its predecessors. The arrival of the Moslem religion over a thousand years ago has been described, together with its various reformations by the Almoravides, the Maquil and Granada Arabs and, recently, by Ma el Ainin. The nomads practise the orthodox Malekite ritual. Prayer is preceded by washing in sand or, upon the Zouerate-Nouadhibou train, with a stone; the prayers themselves, according to Riley, include requests for rain, camel pasture and enrichment by the looting of an enemy. The concept of sin exists, since drought may be due to this – the tribe stops raiding, prays more. The Mecca pilgrimage has been helped by the special boats and aeroplanes laid on by the Spaniards; the returning *hadj* is greeted at the airport with ululations from his womenfolk, clapping and drums. Observation of the Ramadan fast is not strict; perennially short of food, such abstinence would not be easily accepted by the nomad organism. Alms are given, usually as animals.

The cry of the owl in the night comes from a soul in pain for non-fulfilment of religious duties in life. Local belief is that the soul leaves the body as a fly or bee, hovering for three days near the house and for forty days around the tomb; these insects must not be harmed during this period. Then the soul goes to heaven, *barzak*, a sort of beehive. It may however return to the tomb as a bird, a creature never killed near a cemetery.

The most important feast is the Aid el Adhia, the Aid el Kebir of

Morocco. The sacrifice, by throat-cutting and bleeding, is by yearly turn of lamb, goat, cow, if any, and camel; these must be perfect, the ear must cover the eye if folded forwards. This full-dress feast lasts three days, with readings from the Koran, rites such as circumcisions, formal reconciliations, the distribution of the charity 'tenth'. In El Aaiún the boys run about in the skins of sacrificed animals.

Moslem belief is in the hands of the religious tribes and fraternities, each led by a holy man or sage; these run religion-centred schools for members of all tribes and casts, with initiation rituals such as prayer recitation; many remain as adherents throughout their lives. Individual devotions take place either in the open air – wherever the nomad finds himself at prayer-time – or in the shelter of one of the desert's many small scattered crescentic prayer-walls, or in a tribe's dedicated tent. Ma el Ainin's mosque at Smara was never finished; otherwise the northern tribes of Izarguien, Filala, Yagut and Reguibat have built their own mosques, respectively at Daora, Hagunia, Tilemson and Wadi Chebika. However, between 1955 and 1969 the Spaniards have built mosques at Villa Cisneros, El Aaiún and Smara.

A fourth stream, Catholicism, has been available to the nomads since 1954, year of the arrival of the Oblate Fathers of Mary the Immaculate, an arm of the Congregation for the Propagation of the Faith. Until then there had been a few military chaplains and Franciscan friars, focused on the Spanish population and under the control of the army. The Oblates came in the face of the hostility of the Saharauis to Christianity, but as their children were entering the Spanish schools 'through this channel it is possible to introduce Catholicism to the mass of the Mahometans', though caution was advocated. Agreements were made with the Saharauis that there would be no preaching as 'to be sure, their religion is, after Christianity, one of the most perfect', though it does make 'certain concessions to the flesh'. However, Mohammed 'could not help but see the flaws in his religion' and so forbade all discussion, unlike Catholicism. Orders from Rome were not to accept any conversions, usually done from self-interest. So the missionaries were to limit themselves – on the active side – to good works such as giving out charity. In the hospitals, the Saharauis have long been in contact with nursing nuns, Salesians from Murcia. At Christmas the Wise Men distribute gifts to the Spanish children and then, with many prayers to Jesus, 'even more miraculous . . . there are toys for the *goyetes* too . . . the Magi know their names as well'. One wonders what the *goyetes* made of the Three Wise Men's preference for the Spaniards, given their origins.

11   Route discussion north of Miyec, central interior.

A lorry with a puncture, part of a convoy between Tah and Tan-Tan.

The track from Tah to Tan-Tan turning the head of a ravine, from the top of a lorry.

12   El Aaiún, across the watercourse and the tarmac road from the north.

Goats hunting through rubbish, El Aaiún lagoon. One of the original fortlets on right.

The fortress-like *parador*, El Aaiún. The secondary school can be seen, right background. Shell-conglomerate in right foreground.

*Birth*

Pregnancy is thought to last not only nine months but, if the child is asleep in the womb, one, two or three years. A boy is greeted by the women with cries of joy; for a girl there is only silence. Once born, the infant gets its special amulet of sugar, salt, sulphur and other substances. Apart from the many other precautions against evil eye, there are many essential customs. The umbilical cord is buried. A neighbouring woman makes three cuts in each of the child's temples, the blood thrown in its eyes to ensure good sight. If available, somebody with *baraka* should chew some dates and their juice be given to the infant, to pass on the quality. Tightly swaddled in black cloth, the child is through the first rituals.

It is named at seven or eight days, the bigger ceremony for a boy. The two parents and maternal grandmother each name a stick, two being drawn by a fourth person and the remaining stick's name being given to the child. Or, using three or seven named sticks, the women draw these, the first name to come up three times being used. Another possibility is to give the child a name dreamed up by somebody, preferably somebody important. There may also be hereditary nicknames. Boys take their father's surname, girls that of the mother's family.

The first words taught to a child are from the Koran. Circumcision is carried out on the boys at two to three, five, or seven to eight years of age, according to tribe. Often on a Moslem feast day, the ceremony is in the hands of a medicine expert armed with ritual phrases and equipment. The *salaha* plant is the traditional antiseptic and hot dry camel-dung is good against haemorrhage, since it consists of a mixture of all plants. Riley was told circumcision was done to prevent disease but its immediate practical consequence is that the child enters a more adult category for the nomads.

He now wears clothes; these are first put on by the girls at about eight years. The boy is now taught to ride and fight by his father. He also takes up the obligations of a Moslem, learning to pray and to sacrifice. At seventeen he makes his first Ramadan fast and is then adult and can marry; for girls the proper age for these is fifteen.

*Marriage*

Fatness has always been much admired but bride-stuffing is not current; common amongst the Tuat, at least until recently, it probably once occurred over the whole Berber zone, having been common in the pre-conquest Canaries. The Spanish expedition of 1886 noted vestiges of the tradition in the drinking of milk, night and morning, by the women, to fatten themselves. Before coming to marriage, a girl has to go through evil-eye purification.

Endogamy is as strictly enforced as possible, to the maximum in the Ma el Ainin tribe. The aims of this are social exclusiveness and the avoidance of divorce, easier if husband and wife are from different tribes. Children may be betrothed at birth, though they can repudiate the agreement. Kinship may be very close, as cousin–cousin and uncle–niece, in spite of the prohibition of second-degree marriages. Milk relatives, the impotent or incurable are also forbidden to marry. Marriage to Europeans, rare, incurs maximum disapproval; one of the territory's main *kif*-sellers, a young man from the family of a sedentarised nomad, married a Glasgow woman and went to live on the Costa Brava. There is prostitution to the comparatively-rich Spanish soldiers.

If the man and the woman are young, then the former's family will negotiate with the latter's, especially as to bride-price, highest for youth. The Ma el Ainin will demand a hundred camels, an ankle bracelet, a ring and a set of clothes for one of their daughters; the Reguibat once priced them at half as many camels, a Lebel carbine and a rug; the poorest will ask only a camel or two and some cloth. A part will be handed over at the wedding feast, the rest perhaps never – showing that it is a matter of honour, the setting of a high price. In fact, the rich will give the bride-price to the poorer castes, so it is said. The bride brings some possessions too. Sometimes the disputes lead the Saharauis to ask the Spanish 'Office of Native Affairs' to intervene.

Once oral, the contract is now drawn up in writing before an official scribe, to the accompaniment of shouts from the women and shots and drumming by the men. The wedding may follow at once or a month or two later. The feast tent, richly adorned, is pitched opposite the aligned camp. Special singers are hired; there is a traditional wedding-song, the *maruru-iagi*. Festivities will last seven days, or three only if one or other has already been married.

The groom sits at one end of the tent, with his knife and a decorated flail of leather thongs. The bride's family present themselves. The girl is brought from hiding by her friends, to refuse the groom's caresses with scratches and blows; her honesty is shown by her reluctance. The groom chases her with blows of his flail. At length they are left alone, sometimes not until the last night of the feast, to the accompaniment of jokes, showers of sand, the pulling out of the carpets and of the tent poles. If the girl is a virgin then the man appears with his slipper-backs up over his heels; if not he paints one eye, leaves a slipper outside the tent, and perhaps claims damages, including the return of the bride-price. Normally the bride's friends will be able to spread that 'Fatima is going to nomadise with Mohammed'.

If both parties have been married before, then the contract is drawn up in private before a scribe and two witnesses. This is followed by a short feast.

Polygamy is statistically limited to a few rich men, but there is a practice of taking a second wife for a short period and then repudiating her under a pretext, possible three times with the same woman; the women must wait three months before marrying again. A Spanish Sahara missionary, in an article, suggested that the local monogamy was due to poverty. Divorce, common, is at will for the man, but the woman has to show cruelty or impotence; the bride-price may be returned. Some tribes say the many children belong to the mother only until weaned, others until adolescence, when they pass to the father; this a subject of much litigation.

## Death

Defeated at length, the nomad dies. Resigned, for he has gone to a higher place, his male relatives wash and perfume his body, placing aromatic herbs in the ears and nose, then wrap him in a white cloth, tie this round with strings and envelop the whole in a white shroud; a sage directs them. Carried on a wooden bier, the body is taken by the men to the cemetery; the graves have been described. The men eat a funeral meal. The sage advises on the distribution of the deceased's belongings, or the men decide for themselves. For three days the family is visited by friends and relatives, bringing presents. The tent is dismantled and put up on a new site.

The women must mourn for four months and four to ten days. They rarely leave the tent, do not change their clothes, paint their faces or wear jewellery, and remain veiled, the only mourning dress. The tomb is visited, with prayers and sacrifices, these being given to the poor.

## Education

Aged seven, and circumcised, the Saharaui boy of any caste goes off to school, leaving his sister behind in the tent. He takes his own equipment: Riley first described the acacia-wood board, often very old and held together with iron clamps, up to 24 by 18 inches in area, with a pointed reed as a pen, home-made black ink, and sand as an eraser. The school may be a tent or a mere windbreak of dead bushes. Education lasts three to seven years, during which the boy learns to read, write and recite the Koran, studying this seven times through; in Riley's day, each family kept a parchment copy, together perhaps with some poems. The Filala tribe teachers instruct in various sciences. The masters, often from other tribes and especially from the Adrar – Chinguetti has had many sages – receive from the parents a maximum of a camel a year for each child; their food is provided by the tribe, for example the milk of one camel each day together with three measures of barley a month and meat whenever an animal is killed. The teacher may play many parts, such as prayer-leader and funeral director. Some send their children to live with a learned Mauritanian tribe, or even to Marrakesh.

The standard of adult literacy is unrecorded but a preliminary document to the UN petition of 1966 was signed, by the General Assembly of Spanish Sahara, half in writing and half by thumb-prints. A 1970 declaration of loyalty to Franco was written by a local hand in *hassaniya*, the Assembly's signatures this time all written and varying from educated to near-illiterate. The nomads admire the educated person, revering the memory of Mohammed el Mami, a Tiris poet, mystic, jurist and mathematician who died in 1865, of the scholar Hamet el Arosi, founder of the Arosien tribe, and, of course, of Ma el Ainin, their leading intellectual. But nomad society does not foster intellectual curiosity.

*Medicine*

Since all misfortunes are thought to be due to spirits or the evil eye, cures for physical ailments are often a blend of the magical and the practical, with recourse to either the holy sages or the medicine men. The former might prescribe verses from the Koran on a tablet, this to be washed clean and the liquid drunk. The latter, once incurring a blood-debt if his patient died, is paid by results: there is often an effective element in his remedies.

Riley noted that the nomads were extremely fit, ascribing this to their regular habits and unvarying diet, to the dry climate and to the nomads' adequate exercise without overwork; Riley's saviour, Hamet, put it down to the milk diet. The American noted examples of great age, these old people being hairless, their flesh wasted away, eyes extinguished, without the use of a single limb or of any sense, 'so that when their breath should be spent and their entrails extracted, they would . . . be perfect mummies . . . a sight of such beings . . . might have given the ancient Egyptians their first idea of drying and preserving the dead bodies'. The death rate is higher amongst children, women and negroes than amongst adult men, in keeping with the male dominance.

Spanish doctors note that syphilis at all stages, and particularly tertiary, is the most common complaint, together with its associated conjunctivitis, not connected by the nomads: they use the colocynth gourd to treat syphilis. Tuberculosis, not as widespread as was once thought, is treated by a concoction of herbs, honey and egg-yolk. Appendicitis is considered incurable, but the sterile eat various roots. Scabies, caused by the most widespread of the many external parasites, the acarus mite, is common, and ascribed to dirt or mosquitoes: children and the aged are cured by rubbing with sand wetted with camel urine, adults by a pitch lotion or an unction of fat mixed with sulphur or gunpowder. Ear-ache, also common: drops of goat-fat and garlic. The regular outbreaks of smallpox are understood to be passed by contagion, the tents being isolated. The infant mortality is the result of diet, rickets and hereditary syphilis. Popular cure-alls are cauterisations with hot wood or iron and anointing with fish-liver oil.

Some illnesses are grouped by type or organ, with a single all-embracing cure. Thus, those related to 'cold' are all treated by standing the heavily-dressed patient in the midst of hot stones on which water is poured; further sweating results when the sufferer is put to bed under thick covers; finally he is greased with ostrich fat and, hung by his feet, his calves are massaged. Respiratory diseases are treated by a dose of very hot camel-fat; ostrich eggs are used for asthma; the patient is thought contagious and his eating pots isolated. Headaches are treated with perfumes, since their origins lie in bad smells. Eye surgery is practised; an ulcer is dealt with by putting a fine metallic powder or minute husked seeds under the lid.

Three plants have special uses, recorded Lodwick. *Euphorbia granulata* cures snake-bite. The colocynth is good against urine-retention – the penis is pushed through a hole in a heated leaf. A henbane, *Hyoscyamus muticus*, is given in small doses to fatten women and animals rapidly; men are merely made thirsty. There must be many more plants in use, some with medicinal value, but the knowledge will be lost unless studied soon.

## Justice

Three authorities are available to dispense justice: the tribal assembly or *yemaa*, the Koranic judge or *cadi*, the Spanish legal system, described in Chapter 12. The authority invoked depends on the circumstances – on the nationalities, place and nature of the affair, as examples.

The tribal assembly administers its own unwritten custom-law, the *orf*. Once demanding an eye for an eye, it is now based on a scale of compensations. Murder equals 50–150 camels; the murderer usually flees, then his family sacrifice a camel in front of the victim's family, followed by discussion of the penalty by the *yemaa*; a hundred witnesses are needed to support an alibi; collective responsibility may be assumed for the compensation. A thief must pay a camel and five goats, or ten if he entered a tent; or he might be fined four times the value of his theft, also returning the stolen object; if claiming innocence and the object is found in his tent, then he may need fifty people to swear that he is guiltless. Wounding with a stone leads to a fine of three camels, breaking a tooth five camels. Adultery brings severe sentences. If the penalties are not accepted, the *yemaa* may decree the burning of the person's tent or his expulsion from the tribe. Where the case affects two tribes, the two *yemaas* will sit together.

The Koranic judge is trained to administer justice on the basis of the Malikite laws; these cover civil, criminal and religious matters. Training is for six years, in science as well as law. However, the judge is also versed in the *orf* of each tribe and would be called in by the *yemaa* over difficult cases.

Finally, although the Spanish are theoretically ostracised, they may be invited to resolve disputes: robbery, debt, agricultural-land disagreements, divorce, escaped slaves. Naturally, the petitioner has in mind that the Spanish law will benefit him: if, in a fight, one man loses a tooth and the other breaks a rib, the local law awards the latter two two-year-old camels . . . the Spanish sentence is ten days jail and 100 pesetas fine each.

## Social Conscience

A run of good years, in terms of pasture, bring riches to many nomads. Caro Baroja's study of the leading Tidrarin fraction, the Taleb Ali, gives an idea of this wealth; these tributaries were then prospering simply by keeping their property for themselves. The richest man, Emhammed uld Emboirik uld Mohammed, had 300 camels, 150 sheep, 100 goats and three negro slaves, with the leading twelve owners totalling 1,810 camels, 840 sheep, 700 goats, 33 negroes; this was 1945–51. The charity to be given is based on a person's camel holding, on a detailed scale. The owner of 25 camels gives a one-year female; 91 beasts incurs a donation of two three-year-olds, with a further such *hegga* for each succeeding 50 camels. There is also the *meniha*: a rich man lends milking or breeding animals to a poor man, this shading into payment in kind for shepherding services.

Old people are treated with respect; they are not abandoned as in some nomad societies. Riley described the care taken of the old 'mummies': given the first milk, and more even than the chief if it was short, carefully placed in a woman's *howdah*-like camel seat, with a child on each side for support, equally kindly installed first in the newly-pitched tent at the end of the march. The *tuiza* is a day, say, of communal aid to a neighbour who is in difficulties due to age, illness and so on. Typical work would be to dig a well, make a tent, sow or harvest, shear animals. It is a festive occasion, with meals in common, provided by the host if possible.

Reconciliation after a dispute involves a ceremony. Husband and wife make up a quarrel at a meal, the *erzaa*, the man sacrificing an animal before the woman and a few invited elders of the tribe.

The traveller is welcome at any tent, custom prescribing three days stay, in practice a limit often ignored in the territory. Getting off his camel twenty-five metres from the tent, the visitor waits; the head of the family appears, welcomes him, carries his saddle and gun inside. They start by drinking tea, the traveller answering questions about his movements, the rain, the pasture. An important visitor will be offered a *targuiba*, a gift or sacrifice to make a bond of friendship. Outside, the camel grazes with the tent's own animals.

*Personal Appearance*

Dress has evolved since Riley wrote, in 1817, that the poorer men wore only a goatskin or a strip of camel-hair cloth, covering themselves from the waist almost to the knees, and their women a neck-to-knee tunic of the coarse weaving; the latter garment, stitched down the sides, left the arms and bosom bare, with a fold at the back for a child, this being able to feed on the march due to the length of the women's breasts. Riley does not say whether these were still being deliberately deformed; he does mention that the canine teeth were made to project forwards, an attribute of beauty. The few rich men were then wearing blue shirts, linen or cotton sleeveless tunics comparable to the general female dress and, sometimes, the *haik* on top, this a woollen strip four yards long and four feet wide. Children went naked until puberty. All were barefooted. In 1876, MacKenzie's reconnaissance opposite Fuerteventura gave a similar picture of the women.

The dress of the rich of the last century has now become that of the ordinary Saharaui, due to increased purchasing power and the cheapness of the industrial-era cottons; cloth had in fact been available, through traders, for many centuries. Men now wear a shorts-like cloth, the *serrual*, said to be seven and a half metres long; over this, and covering the whole body, two layers of cloth, sky-blue over white, each of these *derraa* also seven and a half metres long. In the towns, baggy shorts are worn under the cool and simpler manufactured *boubou*: a sleeveless loose-fitting smock with embroidered pocket on the chest, its colour is also sky-blue or white. The woollen *jellaba*, a hooded and voluminous smock, usually in animal colours, is worn for travelling and in cold weather. The black face-veil may be the *nikab*, from below the eyes, or the *litham*, from below the nose. The blue dress and face-veil is seen from Agadir southwards. A black or white turban and leather sandals complete the men's dress. Until recently a bandolier holding cartridge pouches and knife overlay the toga-like *serrual*, being accompanied by the musket. A sage will wear only white.

The women nowadays wrap themselves in three layers of unsewn cloth, the *lemlahef*, darkest on the outside, for example black-blue-white, and each again seven and a half metres long; they wear slippers. The outer cloth, draped over the head – and over a pad of false hair, there to increase the woman's height – is held across the face as a veil by many, though not as strictly as in Moroccan towns, say. The climate and the dust anyway encourage the use of the veil. In the south some women will use a bunch of keys, a status symbol, as a weight for the head cloth. Cervera admired 'the richness of forms and elegance' of the women's dress, still fair comment. Children now wear a single *derraa* cloth, three metres long, a boy a white one and a girl a black one – hers only from chest to knees – until they go into adult dress at about fourteen.

Hair-style is important in women and children, the men of most tribes having always let theirs grow long. A girl's hair is first cut at eight days, a boy's either at seven days or when a year old. The styles, adopted at once, have both aesthetic and magical-religious significance and, no less important, indicate tribe and caste. The main styles for boys, in relief by shaving, are combinations of the central strip of hair from the forehead to the nape of the neck, a strip across the forehead, a tuft at the back, a tuft at each side; the hair is left to grow as it pleases after puberty or the first fast, though the Delim could only give up the childish style once they had killed a man in a raid.

Girls' hair is more complicated. Until twelve, it is limited by shaving to stringy plaits at front and back. After this they become more intricate, perhaps with shell fastenings, and without shaving; in the Reguibat a tress frames the face. Once married, or perhaps at eighteen, a nomad woman may take three hours each normal day to do her hair, helped by old women, needles and fish oil, such is the complexity of the rolls, tresses, shells and small jewels; the ornaments are omitted if her husband is away. Riley described how the long black braided hair was kept on top of the head with the aid of thorns. Freed slaves will adopt a higher caste hair-style; incomers into a tribe will adopt that of their new group.

The women paint their faces, especially the eyes – MacKenzie mentioned also the upper cheeks – and their hands and feet, including the nails. The dark-tan henna is used on the palms and the feet; ochre, collected from the coast's Tertiary sandstones, has been used too as a face-paint. The men paint around their eyes, said to be good for them. The women file their teeth to make themselves look younger; brushes made of a chewed splinter of wood, preferably palm, are used for cleaning the teeth. Aromatic herbs from Mauritania were made into perfumes. Early travellers all deplored the women's smelliness.

Riley described the strings of beads around the women's necks, white circular three-inch bones in the hair, more beads around the wrists and ankles. Nowadays, apart from cheap imported trinkets, one sees the Berber-style necklace of real or fake amber and metal balls, fertility symbols. Some men wear rosaries. Occasionally a west African 'trading bead' may be seen on a child; eagerly sought by young north American and European speculators for sale to the fashionable shops of their capitals, the shipment northwards of these coloured-glass tokens reverses the earlier flow southwards of cowrie shells. The most common adornment is the permanent coating of most women's skins, including their faces, with the blue-black dye from their *lemlahef*, many refusing to buy fast-coloured cloth; these women can rarely or ever wash, and perhaps even deliberately tint their faces with squeezed-out dye, coming to acquire an ashy-blue complexion which can lead to the first impression that they belong to a different human group from that of their menfolk.

*Architecture*
The rare fort or attempted settlement of the nomads having been described, only Smara remains for discussion. Begun in the eighteen-nineties, it was built by Moroccan workers with materials regularly brought by Moroccan and Spanish steamers to MacKenzie's recently-relinquished port. From here it took 1,200 camels some five days to haul the wood, cement and other materials to the patch of rushes high up the Saguiet-el-Hamra; a cart drawn by mules was once tried.

Ma el Ainin's architects were from Morocco and Mauritania and in fact the style is a rustic Hispano-Mauresque with Adrar additions. This blend no doubt helped Smara's intended role as a link between the two lands above and below the desert; the nomads of the western sands used it as a base. As one would expect, construction was as far as possible in dry-stone style, of single flat or double and chevron courses; there was much pisé work. Fifty wells were dug, 200 palms brought from the Draa and the Adrar.

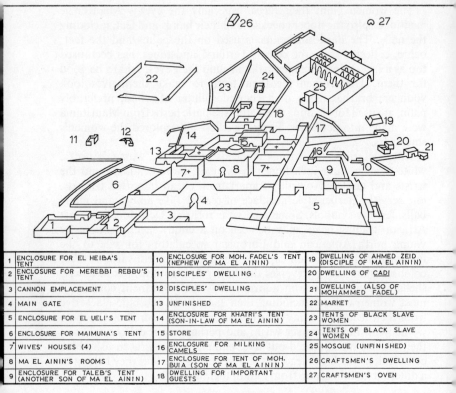

| | | | | | | |
|---|---|---|---|---|---|---|
| 1 | ENCLOSURE FOR EL HEIBA'S TENT | 10 | ENCLOSURE FOR MOH. FADEL'S TENT (NEPHEW OF MA EL AININ) | 19 | DWELLING OF AHMED ZEID (DISCIPLE OF MA EL AININ) |
| 2 | ENCLOSURE FOR MEREBBI REBBU'S TENT | 11 | DISCIPLES' DWELLING | 20 | DWELLING OF CADI |
| 3 | CANNON EMPLACEMENT | 12 | DISCIPLES' DWELLING | 21 | DWELLING (ALSO OF MOHAMMED FADEL) |
| 4 | MAIN GATE | 13 | UNFINISHED | 22 | MARKET |
| 5 | ENCLOSURE FOR EL UELI'S TENT | 14 | ENCLOSURE FOR KHATRI'S TENT (SON-IN-LAW OF MA EL AININ) | 23 | TENTS OF BLACK SLAVE WOMEN |
| 6 | ENCLOSURE FOR MAIMUNA'S TENT | 15 | STORE | 24 | TENTS OF BLACK SLAVE WOMEN |
| 7 | WIVES' HOUSES (4) | 16 | ENCLOSURE FOR MILKING CAMELS | 25 | MOSQUE (UNFINISHED) |
| 8 | MA EL AININ'S ROOMS | 17 | ENCLOSURE FOR TENT OF MOH. BUIA (SON OF MA EL AININ) | 26 | CRAFTSMEN'S DWELLING |
| 9 | ENCLOSURE FOR TALEB'S TENT (ANOTHER SON OF MA EL AININ) | 18 | DWELLING FOR IMPORTANT GUESTS | 27 | CRAFTSMEN'S OVEN |

Fig. 11. Ma el Ainin's Settlement at Smara

The partially-fortified settlement, on a bank of Wadi Seluan, straggles over a few hundred metres of brown earth. The low simple buildings are of dark brown stone, the domes and other parts washed in white or ochre. The main complex is a walled square some fifty-seven metres along each side. Having obtained permission from the Territorial Police – for the Foreign Legion's imitative domes and Costa Brava boundary wall is overlooked from the parapets of the crumbling *ribat* – the visitor enters by the Bab Heyen. Large enough to take a laden camel, the arched entrance bears an inscription: 'In the name of God the Merciful.' Beyond the blind entrance, and also in view of the empty look-out posts in the corners, there is a courtyard. Under a cupola against the front wall, the chief bathed. Opposite, in the centre of the complex, stands the council hall where Ma el Ainin carried out his multiple functions, including that of *khalifa* or lieutenant of the Sultan of Morocco: arched, with private rooms to each side, the chamber is surmounted by a decorated flattened dome . . . the construction has been criticised by architectural purists . . . yet, as a feat of building in an otherwise empty desert, as a centre of religious revival, of resistance to the European invader and, most important perhaps, as the focus of a people's attempt to weld themselves into a social and cultural unity . . . for all this it transcends the details of its architecture.

The side rooms served the chief as library, housing his own 300 works, and as treasury, office and sleeping quarters. In pairs to each side of the main building are the houses of Ma el Ainin's four legal wives. All five structures have parapets. The floors were paved, lines in the flags connecting the doorways. Windows were few, the minute vents which opened on to the courtyards having carved wooden shutters. Within the main wall, at the back, there are also a corral, a patio and a store. Scattered around this focal complex are many other structures: the houses of the old nomad's leading sons and of his disciples, the stores for perfumes and water-skins, a travellers' lodging-house, a small market, the craftsmen's dwellings, an oven, pens for slaves and animals, even a special one for those wild beasts which were to be given to Moroccan dignitaries. The mother of his best-known sons, the Berebich tribeswoman Maimuna, preferred to live in a tent in a special enclosure.

Religion had two important buildings. For general use, a mosque; this was designed with nine rows of nine arches each, but it was only half-finished. Ma el Ainin also had a small round domed sanctuary, derived from Berber architecture, built on the opposite side of the water-course; this was for his own retreat on Fridays.

The fighting with the approaching French having halted the work, a step backwards was taken when, in 1913, Col Mouret blew up the dome of the council hall and damaged the library. Ma el Ainin by now dead, the attacked nomads had neither resources nor spare energy for repairing the damage and continuing the work. In 1954 the Spaniards restored the dome. In 1974 the settlement was empty and clearly long unused. Beyond the legionaries lies the Spanish-built village, with mosque, inhabited by a mixture of variably-sedentary Saharauis, the police and the barracks' over-spill; on the outskirts, further nomads live in tents. In the wastes round about, the guerrillas fight with the Spanish patrols; in Smara itself, both sides have the *ribat*'s past very much in mind.

## The Calendar and History

Society's past is divided into three phases: legends, dealt with next in the forms of stories, poems and songs; then, very important, events occurring comparatively recently but before living memory – for example the founding of a tribe, or an epic battle; finally those occurrences within the lives of the present people.

The events of this final period, of about seventy years, recited by the old people, act as a calendar for reference to the immediate past. Each year is thus known by its most important event; if a year has no universally-significant occurrence, then each tribe will have its own event-cum-name for it. The name-worthy events include the astronomical, as the passing of a comet, or great rain or bad drought; the death of an important person; an epidemic or locust plague; a battle or a political event, inter-tribal or involving Europeans. The year is quartered into four seasons – different from the weather divisions – with spring beginning on 15 February and the others following at three-monthly intervals.

The social calendar applies to individual lives too, a man thinking of himself not as born in the Moslem year 1324 of the Hegira but during the best-known year for camel-pasture in the Tiris. Subsequently his life will be divided into nine phases: until he walks, until he talks, then until his first Ramadan, next until twenty, then until thirty, subsequently as a mature man, then the period following his first grey hairs, next his decline, finally his old age.

The Moslem calendar is also known, with printed copies in the territory; its months are called by local names except for Ramadan. There is some use of astronomy for dating within the year as well as for desert navigation.

## Stories and Poems

These help to transmit the tribe's past, to add to their solidarity, to form the characters and attitudes of the young. Though told at any time, they are an important part of the entertainment at a feast.

The stories and poems may be devotional, battle-proud, about love, humorous, genealogical. Their legendary subjects include the conquered Bafots, the Hilalian Arabs and the Europeans. In spite of the Maquil-ancestry claim, the Hilalians are described as heathens with supernatural powers; the size of tombs said to be Hilalian show they were also giants. The Iberians get the same whippings as do the Moors in present peninsular mythology. Otherwise, there are always the myriad *yenun* for the sinister roles. Speeches at council meetings can reach to oratory, with much reference to history.

As an example of a belligerent poem, here is a verse from one from the last century, a Tidrarin inciting his fellows to rise against their masters:

> 'Though weak and without arms,
> When there are twenty together
> Though perhaps not feared
> At least they can be free.
> And the more so if eight hundred
> When the Delim number only three hundred,
> Vultures who, year after year
> Have us by the ears.
> A Tidrarin's above this!'

The tribes actually took their poets into battle, to recall their exploits and describe the enemy's feebleness; composing as they went along, these bards also played on bamboo flutes.

A Saharaui love poem can be translated:

> 'I love myself when you love me,
> I hate myself when you hate me.
> When you are sad
> I am sad too.
> When I see you the memory of my poor past happiness vanishes
> To leave the way open to the happiness I feel when I am beside you.'

Lighter stories are told around a Chaplinesque figure who suffers in all situations and also about the traditional idiocy of negroes. Children listen to tales of magic. All nomads enjoy the many stories about animals, with the hedgehog, *ganfud*, a popular figure who comes out on top by his astuteness or, as some might feel, crookedness; the usual losers are the jackal, fox and ostrich. Another type of story explains the behaviour of the lark: he rises up to see if any part of the world is better than his own, then sinks back contented onto his own bush.

The nomadic mind draws satisfaction from the proverb, shortest of stories. Easterners are irreligious; southern women never work, above the Draa they live like slaves. Other tribes have proverbial attributes. Nearness is equated with goodness, the remote is evil, especially if black or Christian.

## Song

There are two classes of professional singers. The *iggauen* are comparable to wandering minstrels; they never join a tribe and, whilst considered good company, are both feared and held in awe for their independence of spirit. They chant or sing of the same subjects as the stories, accompanying themselves on the drum or, less commonly, on the harp or the laud; their wives may sing and play too. The musician performs seated, eyes perhaps closed, swaying his head or whole torso to the feeling of the song; the women often contribute short vibrant shouts, the whole audience will sing the refrains. The *iggauen* are hired by the richer people, being well-paid so that they will sing their patrons' praises in other parts of the desert; underpaid, their verses become satirical. Though the skill is handed from one generation to the next, the performances are in great part improvised:

> 'At the little well of Atila we lack nothing,
> At Bacor camp tea and sugar are very scarce'

The second group are the *lailas*, travelling troupes of female singers, also hired by the important families. Their speciality was composition around each tribe's war exploits and the songs were monotonous and melancholy; in fact these are the most common characteristics of Saharaui music-making. It seems likely that the transistor radio will have a serious effect on both classes of itinerant musicians; the Spanish-installed Radio Sahara tries to keep the nomads happy by putting out a non-stop rondo of their favourite few dozen tunes.

The Saharauis also sing spontaneously, of course – perhaps an impromptu gathering between the tents, with a drum, or when all is going well on a march across the desert. Here is a cradle song, to a girl: 'Quiet, don't cry – When you're bigger – I'll buy you a fine necklace – and have them make you a pair of pretty bracelets – and I'll marry you to a brave man, young and handsome – and I'll give you a great fortune – and you'll be in a good family'.

*Music*

There are half-a-dozen instruments. The ancient war-drum, *tobal*, with its West African flavour; the *malemin* make these from big pots, *tazua*, covering the mouths with skin. A small drum played with sticks, *guidra*. The third instrument played by the men is the guitar-like *tidinit*, sometimes described as a four-string laud. The women specialise in the *ardin*, a harp of nine to twelve strings that run down a wooden rod and into a calabash-shaped sounding box encased in a tight skin decorated with charms. The tambourine, *igarbel*, completes the orchestra. A flute, *guesba*, traditionally made of a tree-root, used to be the amusement of the shepherd; it too was heard, together with the drum, before and during battle. Playing is highly interpretative, individualistic.

The music does not seem to be evolving. Its origins, little studied in the territory, include West African rhythms and the Koranic plain-chant, and it is likely that the sad, monotonous element stems from the primitive Berber population; the songs, music and dances of the pre-conquest Canary Islands were similar. And it is this kind of music which most delights the Saharaui still.

*Mime and Dance*

If there is to be miming and dancing too, the spectators sit back under the tent walls. The best-known act is the *guedra*, a sensual mime: the woman begins sitting or kneeling, motionless, then very slowly begins to paint her face, prepare her hair, put on her necklaces. At first lethargic and repetitive, the tempo of her hand, arm, shoulder and head movements becomes rapid, her limbs undulate, the audience claps and sings to her rhythm, her dress falls from her shoulders, her hip movements increase to a frenzy . . . at length she is naked, and finally falls sweating and exhausted to the ground.

The women also dance in groups, the men may then mime a parody of the women. The Spanish Army's nomad troops like to mime war epics to the sound of a drum. The negro men and women have their own dances, and songs too, accompanying themselves on big drums, beaten with round-ended sticks, and with the castanet-like metallic *carcabat*; the rich and varied colours of their West African dress are a characteristic of the spectacle.

*Games*

An evening's entertainment might include a contest by two men, armed with sticks, between two lines of singing women. Outdoors, the Saharauis will play *aarag*: a group of men in a circle will try to hit one in the middle whilst he, arms held up defensively, attempts to kick an assailant, the unlucky man taking the first's place in the middle.

The most popular seated game is a form of draughts. The square board is drawn, between the squatting players, in the sand; each position is a little pit, nine rows of nine in each direction. The pieces are, on one side, camel-dung pellets and, on the other, small sticks. The game follows the same course as in draughts except that there is no reward of a 'crown' on reaching the back line opposite – an obvious reason being that the pieces will not balance on each other. A popular variety makes the distance of each move dependent upon a previous throw of a complicated set of dice-sticks, the game then called *sig*; the eight pieces of wood, 15–30 cm long and 1–2 cm wide, are flat and blackish on the *felua* face but rounded, patterned and multi-coloured on the *lebraga* side. A throwing game is played with antelope bones. The Saharauis have many pastimes to enliven desert life.

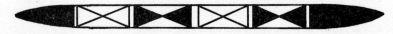

Fig. 12. *Sig* stick, used as dice (half life)

Now, as in all aspects of society, European influences are appearing. Thus, the camel races at a 1964 feast were timed, introducing a new concept; the winner, Beidun, his jockey Hassan uld Hamadi of the Nomad Troops, covered the eleven kilometres in forty minutes. By 1974 it was upon glossy motorcycles that the sons of the richer sedentary Saharauis were racing each other across the dunes around El Aaiún.

13 Domed houses at El Aaiún with, beyond, the watercourse, old fortlet and new barracks.

Nissen-style houses and local women, El Aaiún.

Flats under construction and, background, completed Civil Service *residencia*.

14 First Spanish fort and, beyond the blue man and Land-Rover, the church, Villa Cisneros.

The main square, Villa Cisneros, with the fort, church and, beyond the sandstone pillar with ancient inscription, modern wind-shields for dwellings behind.

Road named after Reguibat tribe, in Villa Cisneros, with airport control tower behind.

*Chapter 10*

# Daily Life and Work

The nomad lives out his days, then, against a background of magic and religion, of group ceremony and entertainment, these last, with their insistence on the tribe's glorious past and demonstration of its present solidarity, being his support against the adversities and uncertainties of his immediate daily life. For, armed with a minimum of technology – though this does usually allow maximum exploitation of his environment – he must extract his food and other essentials from one of the least productive zones in the world. Recently, the nomad has found these material wants becoming more easily satisfied . . . at the price of his culture and independence. In this chapter, the long-established way of life and work will be described, together with those Spanish additions and substitutes already established in the nomad's tent; Chapters 11 and 12 will cover the less-assimilated European importations.

*In the Tent*

The traveller will see the first tents as he goes south from Agadir. Out in the desert, the small camp of a few tents, the *friq*, is the rule; large camps, *makhsar*, cause long daily marches to the pasturage, though a feud could mean as many as 250 tents grouped together for safety. Members of different tribes will camp near each other if there are marriage ties. Caro Baroja (1955) studied a Tidrarin fraction's camp, in a line 700 m long: ten tents, with two small ones, sheltering 47 people, with 158 camels, 70 goats and 75 sheep roundabout. Tents are pitched so as to give privacy and to avoid muddling up the flocks.

The tent itself, *khaima*, is a rectangle rather broader than it is deep; the average width is 4–8 m, with 11 m thought enormous. It is made of 6–12 strips of woven goat or camel hair cloth, *fliy*, the lengths running across the tent; stripes are common. Each strip takes a woman seven days to make. Riley often watched the nomads pitching camp: the tent was pegged out first, using a hammerstone, always carried, then the family got under and, putting a domed block into the apex, to take the main pole, lifted the tent on this, manoeuvring the lower end into a hole previously made in the ground. There were ten guy-bands, of skin or woven camel hair, the latter the current material. The apex of the tent is towards the back; the roof is in fact supported by several more poles, variously angled so as to take the wind from any direction. The front, facing the sun or the cooler Atlantic according to the weather, is kept up during the day by supports; coolness is increased in the summer by the tent's sides not reaching the ground, the gap being filled in winter or at night by hanging cloths. A second tent, *benia*, is usually put up inside – some would be inhabitable alone, others are just strips of cloth – to give privacy and to demarcate the women's domestic zone, usually the left when looking inwards. A tent, with a life of four years, is worth a camel or 18 bales of cloth.

The nomad family sleeps on skins, esparto mats and small carpets, on the ground, covered with blankets; Riley noted that 'their long bushy hair . . . resembling a thrum mop, serves them instead of a pillow'. Carpets, *faro*, are hung up as signals, for example of quarantine. The more sedentary have long possessed wardrobes and chests of drawers. Otherwise clothes are stored in a wooden box or, the most common, in a leather sack, *tazufra*. The women have a personal bag for make-up and jewellery; the men have pipes and ornate tobacco pouches.

The most important daily task is the milking. Camels are milked by the men into the *aders*, a broad wooden bowl with incised decoration, and goats by the women into a tall narrow wooden pot, the *mehelab*; the milk is stored in the huge *tazua*, up to 25 litres in capacity. There is a special milk ladle and a pouring funnel. The animals are given water in a skin shaped by a wooden frame, the *hauz*, a smaller version being used to pull up water at the well. Each family has a small goatskin to carry 6–7 litres of milk when on the march. For water there are the 25–40 litre *guerbas*, kept on a rack made of wooden sticks.

The women spend much of the day making household objects, preparing and cooking foods. Each woman has a set of craft equipment. A widow's tent is a favourite place for meeting and working in common. Grinding is done in a conical rotary quern, seemingly always with only one handle. There is a mortar, often of palm-wood. Butter is churned in a skin hanging on a wooden tripod. Cooking is carried out over an open fire, usually in front of the women's side of the tent; Riley said camel dung was used as tinder and, recently, some nomads were still rubbing sticks together or using flints as strike-a-lights. If starting a fire from someone else's, this must be done by lighting new sticks – not by taking out burning wood – and these must not be held aloft when carried away, in each case to avoid the evil eye on the children and animals. The cooking pot is suspended over the fire from an iron tripod.

The men eat before the women and children. The food is eaten directly off a communal tray, large, decorated and wooden – made in Mauritania, the trees there big enough – and from bowls of wood and esparto. Wooden spoons are common. The tea ceremony, a nineteenth-century import through the Sba of the Nun, involves the most ornate vessels: a tiny metal teapot, *magray*, a brazier or *maymar*, a brass tray, glasses from a special container, a metal sugar-hammer. Household objects are decorated with chevrons, lozenges and simpler designs, those of leather being often coloured black, yellow, red and green.

In the evening, the light from an oil lamp, a shallow dish, reveals a few further possessions in the corners of the tent. Perhaps some farming tools and sacks of grain, possibly a large rectangular padlock for a granary. Camel saddles. A Koran and the musical instruments, one or the other now brought out. Perhaps a gun, illegal and kept for hunting and for the day of uprising against the Spanish. These have introduced new household goods, at first through the Canary fishermen and by barter at the coastal bases, now through the mail-order catalogue and the many new shops, these mushrooming during the turning-over of the land in search of minerals in the nineteen-sixties. As examples, in 1955 Lodwick saw the DDT spray and the pressure cooker in the tents; he noted shiny goods were popular.

If the tea and sugar ceremony is the more elegant, the milk distribution is the more essential. Riley described how the father, and none other, gave out bowls of fresh and sour milk to each of the family, according to their importance, adding water if the amount did not give a good drink. This ceremony is even carried on, messily, on the Zouerate-Nouadhibou frontier train, a vehicle notorious for its irregular camel-like motion. The milk may be heated by placing hot stones in it. Water will be drunk even if bad and tasting of the skin and of the pitch used to caulk this. The nomads will drink straight from a churned-up water-hole in the animals' wake. They can smell water in the ground, will follow a bird to its drinking place.

Meat is rarely eaten. In 1886 the Spanish expedition noted that it might be devoured raw and also bad. For preference it was roasted in holes in the ground, a fire on top, the cooked viands beaten with the camel-driving stick to remove the sand. Camels were only usually killed for feasts. The bones are broken to get at the marrow. Fat from ostriches and camel-humps is eaten; goat-cheese and butter have become common. Gazelle meat is the greatest of delicacies. It is not thought correct to eat predators such as the hyaena. Fish, once caught only by the tributaries but partially consumed by the nomads, is now available from both Spanish and Saharaui fishermen, these of all castes. After a locust plague, the *yerada* are eaten roasted, the dried surplus forming future meals, perhaps as flour in a soup: the locust is 67% protein, with vitamins A and D and also phosphorus, calcium and potash.

Bread, of barley or wheat, is kneaded in a pot, then baked for fifteen minutes in cinders or heated stones, then eaten hot. Alternatively the grain will be roasted and then ground into *bulegoma*, similar to the Canary pre-conquest *gofio*; it is then heated with hot water. Ground barley may also be dissolved and drunk with sugar as lightly-fermented 'barley water'. Using a flour of wheat and rice, a *cus-cus* is made, served with meat. Fruit is limited to dates, eaten in quantity in the Adrar harvest festival.

Famine brings in the wild foods of last resort. Acacia gum. Roots. Tea substitutes. Seeds of numerous plants, eaten raw or treated like barley: *anafis* (*Salicornia* sp.), *agamis* (*Nitraria retusa*), *afzu* (*Aizoon theurkauffii*). Lizards and skinks are hunted for food. The ailing camels are eaten one by one. As a last resort, starving tribes will go up to the Sus-Nun zone and live off cheap foods such as prickly pears, as did occur in 1956–61.

With raiding not at present practised, it is the pasture which determines the length of stay at a camp, about eight days being usual on the normally poor vegetation. Camp is broken before dawn; the household goods go on the camels. The men walk or ride, the leader often scouting on ahead. The women and children travel in enclosed seats. The march may involve tracking and star-navigation. Sometimes the nomads are on their way to market, to sell surplus produce and buy or barter for oil, tea, candles, cartridges, grain, salt, cloth and tools, but usually it is a move to new grazing. The new camp will probably be pitched at about four in the afternoon.

*Domesticated Animals*
Once upon a time a Reguibat fell ill whilst in the Anti-Atlas. The local medicine-sage offered to cure him, in exchange for the nomad's camel. 'What!' exclaimed the Reguibat. 'But I only want to get better in order to enjoy my camel a while longer.' And, raising a finger in the air to proclaim the unity of Allah, he died. The camel, *jmel*, or *naga* if female, provides most of the nomad's needs – if the pasture is there. Though branded, the mark called *elama*, the camels will be recognised by their owners even if in a flock of a thousand. A unit of

Table 4: *Domesticated animals, 1952–71*

|  | 1952 | 1953 | 1954 | 1955 | 1956 | 1957 | 1958 | 1959 | 1960 | 1961 |
|---|---|---|---|---|---|---|---|---|---|---|
| Camels | 72,000 | 74,000 | 48,000 | 51,000 | 52,000 | 51,000 | 44,000 | 44,000 | 50,000 | 24,000 |
| Goats | 101,000 | 101,000 | 81,000 | 89,000 | 62,000 | 50,000 | 39,000 | 22,000 | 49,000 | 35,000 |
| Sheep | 46,000 | 45,000 | 37,000 | 39,000 | 23,000 | 23,000 | 29,000 | 14,000 | 26,000 | 7,000 |
| Asses | 550 | 580 | 360 | 600 | 590 | 480 | 360 | 320 | 880 | 870 |
| Horses and Mules | 10 | — | — | 20 | 20 | 10 | 10 | 10 | 10 | — |
| Miscellaneous | 80 | — | 50 | 30 | 40 | 60 | 30 | 10 | 130 | 60 |
| Totals | 220,000 | 221,000 | 166,000 | 180,000 | 138,000 | 125,000 | 112,000 | 80,000 | 126,000 | 67,000 |

|  | 1962 | 1963 | 1964 | 1965 | 1966 | 1967 | 1968 | 1969 | 1970 | 1971 |
|---|---|---|---|---|---|---|---|---|---|---|
| Camels | 24,000 | 24,000 | 25,000 | 37,000 | 38,000 | 32,000 | 56,000 | 58,000 | 58,000 | 60,000 |
| Goats | 35,000 | 35,000 | 24,000 | 52,000 | 54,000 | 48,000 | 141,000 | 145,000 | 145,000 | 146,000 |
| Sheep | 7,000 | 6,000 | 6,000 | 8,000 | 9,000 | 10,000 | 18,000 | 18,000 | 18,000 | 17,000 |
| Pigs | — | — | — | 80 | 160 | 140 | — | 200 | 260 | 320 |
| Zebus | — | — | — | — | — | 70 | — | 400 | 100 | 40 |
| Asses | 830 | 790 | 520 | 380 | 440 | 320 | 2,140 | 2,400 | 2,400 | 2,120 |
| Miscellaneous | 40 | 140 | 90 | 140 | 190 | 180 | — | 3,200 | 5,200 | 5,500 |
| Totals | 67,000 | 66,000 | 56,000 | 98,000 | 102,000 | 91,000 | 217,000 | 227,000 | 229,000 | 231,000 |

measurement is the distance at which a camel can be seen clearly, about two kilometres; a goat equals a kilometre. Nomad veterinary science is limited to applications of fire and oil.

Table 4 gives an idea of the territory's stock; the drop in the middle years reflects deaths due to drought, nomadisation to other countries in search of pasture and for political reasons, and the 1958 loss of the Protectorate. In 1950 the largest herd was Reguibat, 14,000, with the old tributaries, the Tidrarin, in second place with 5,000 camels, causing much head-shaking at the passing of tradition; their masters, the Delim, had only 3,000, as had the Arosien, Yagut and Izarguien. A poor family will have 4–6 camels; the middle classes have about fifteen each, divided into a mating male and three carriers, five females with young and six being milked; above this come the rich, with up to a few hundred.

Mating is between November and April, gestation lasting a year. The females breed from four years old and can reproduce up to 18 times until the age of thirty, though 7–8 offspring is normal. The male is mature at seven years, at his peak at 10–13 and getting old at twenty; in the market his worn teeth will be noted, for woody plants then become inedible, reducing his chances of survival. Some males are castrated when two years old, to resist the conditions better. Once the females have reared 3–4 young, feeding these for six months at a time, they go over to milk production, their offspring then suckled for a year each; in both cases, pregnancy follows soon afterwards.

Camels are milked beside the tent, the goats just behind, the sheep behind and further away. The animals are often fettered, with their udders netted to keep the young to their rations. A camel gives 5–7 litres a day, milked morning and night, with 15 litres the maximum; this is reached six months after giving birth. Riley saw some camels drink 'two barrels' of water each – others have guessed at 200 litres – and then go twenty days without drinking again. The temperature and the available fodder affect the camel's water needs.

A camel's favourite foods are *askaf* (*Nucularia perrini*), *ansil* (*Aristida plumosa*), *sbot* (*A. pungens*), *markuba* (*Panicum turgidum*), *sdar* (*Rhus oxyacantha*) and the acacia trees. Rain means fodder within a week. As soon as grazing becomes short, the camel begins to draw on the fat in his hump, another aspect examined in the market. As the drought goes on the nomad will usually eat his camels, particularly this store of fat and the water, now greenish, though the author saw two dozen corpses at the Sebaiera well in 1974, apparently left to die. One of the last services of a camel has been to be used, opened up, as a shelter from the sun.

The men ride on a saddle of camel-skin over wood and iron; it is placed in front of the hump, the man's feet crossed on the animal's neck. There is an art in getting up on a camel's back. The seat for the women, children and aged is either a squarish roofed structure made of a light wooden frame, covered with cloth if conditions demand it, or a broad saddle with highly-carved corner posts linked by low walls of cloth; Riley referred to a leather basket some 4 ft wide. There is also a pack saddle; weights of 150–200 kilos seem normal, or four water-skins of 40 litres each. A camel will walk at 5 kph, go into its 'lesser trot' at 9 kph and 'greater trot' at 12 kph, with the riding camel able to gallop above this speed. On an average day, before dawn to mid-afternoon, 11–14 hours, a camel will cover 70 km; the Spaniards recall a patrol which crossed the Tiris from Tichla to Villa Cisneros, 500 km, in four days, the temperature reaching 50°C.

Riley said good camels had understanding and obeyed orders. One man, armed with a stick, can control up to seventy; a hired shepherd may be paid in milk. Camels do remember ill-treatment and will suddenly savage the person responsible; the males are especially dangerous in the mating season; the only way to escape if chased is by sudden change of direction. Cutting and pulling off of the hair, for cloth-making, takes place in the *tifiski* season, in advance of the summer's heat; it is neighbourly work. The camels of Spanish Sahara are usually brown or grey, occasionally white.

The other animals are not held in such esteem. The goat usually has a short dark smooth coat, though the hair can be long. The sheep is white, the wool of varied length; it is most common in the cooler north. Both the 'blacks' and the 'whites' give milk, meat, wool and skins. A camel is worth 10–12 goats or 5–8 sheep. There are a few donkeys and horses.

Around Bir Gandus, just north of La Guera, the tribes of Berik Al-lah and Ma el Ainin have reared zebu, humped cattle, two species distinguished by horns of different lengths. Needing to drink every other day, they are good milkers, 6–7 litres every twenty-four hours, and are also appreciated for their meat and as riding and pack animals.

*The Crops*
'Where the plough enters, shame and slavery follow', say the nomads. But it has long been the slavery of the black people which has cultivated the Sahara's few cropped plots, though members of the warrior caste can now be seen working the land. Crops can only be grown, and then in favourable years, in the *grara* bowls of the coast and up the Saguiet-el-Hamra. Notable are the Spaniards' grain-fields at Daora, the vegetable plots at El Aaiún, Meseyed and Smara, the

Table 5: *Area planted and crops, 1950–72*

| | 1950 | 1951 | 1952 | 1953 | 1954 | 1955 | 1956 | 1957 | 1958–65 | 1966–8 | 1969 | 1970 | 1971 | 1972 |
|---|---|---|---|---|---|---|---|---|---|---|---|---|---|---|
| Barley– Hectares | 965 | 668 | 450 | 364 | 432 | 279 | 280 | 320 | Drought | — | 20 | 666 | 145 | 300 |
| Barley–Metric Quarters | 4,680 | 22,064 | 1,265 | 898 | 17,573 | 4,615 | 2,437 | 12,240 | Drought | — | 9 | 333 | 127 | 1,500 |
| Lucerne– Hectares | 8 | 1 | 130 | 7 | 7 | — | 6 | 5 | Drought | — | 10 | 10 | 12 | 14 |
| Lucerne– Metric Quarters | 85 | 145 | 3,588 | 120 | 152 | — | 40 | 58 | Drought | — | 250 | 150 | 178 | 210 |

intermittent cultivations in the Zemmour and at Imiricli, this just south of C. Bojador; there are occasional sowings near Villa Cisneros and in the Bir Gandus area. The return of the Protectorate meant the loss of some of the best agricultural land. Table 5 gives statistics for 1950–72.

Crop-growing is handicapped by dryness and also by the saltiness of such water as does exist, including that from the new and prolific borings – 1·6 grams a litre has been put forward as average – with the irrigable plots often poorly drained. There are very strong winds. The day-night temperature variation is too high. There is little soil; pale brown, formed mainly from chemical weathering of the rock, with some mechanical disintegration, the soil lacks humus, this decomposing faster than it forms at above 25°C. There is of course a lack of farming understanding, difficult for a nomad to acquire.

With the cry 'In the name of Allah!', the master furrow is begun. The first tribe to have ploughed a plot will have precedence each year, close to the concept of ownership. The land is marked out with stones; measurement is in *habel*, cords whose length varies from 30–60 cubits, about 15–30 m, with 900 sq cubits a *telatin*. Plots are usually under ten hectares. There are thick protective hedges. The land is normally burnt before cultivation. From the master furrow, the plough and its grumbling camel work up and down at right angles, then turn the ground a second time by ploughing across these furrows. The Roman plough, *maharaza*, has come from the north and is unknown in Mauritania. Sowing for grain-crops is broadcast. Small fertile irrigated plots, giving two crops a year, will be worked with a Mediterranean hoe, with blade and pick ends; the soil is divided by earth baulks into strips about three metres long, flooded as often as the water-supply allows, a system paralleled in Fuerteventura.

Planted about October, the barley will be ready, with good fortune, in between four and six months; the nomads will be away in the interval. The barley is a dwarf rapid-cycle type. Normal yield will vary from complete failure to four times that sown; during 1945–50 the yields were ×22, ×9, ×7, ×$\frac{1}{2}$, ×5, ×11, the drought worst in 1948; it is said that in 1923 Imiricli gave 23 times its seed. Lesser crops are wheat, lucerne and a Mauritanian small-grain maize. If there has been rain, the Saharauis will try another sowing in March.

Harvesting is communal work, either using toothed sickles or, if the stalks are short, pulling them up. Camels are used for threshing, with negroes doing the hardest tasks. Measures are the handful, the amount held in two hands together or *hafne*, the *fatra* of 3$\frac{1}{2}$ kilos, the *saa* of 7 kilos or of 20 *hafne*; the word *grara* also means 210 kilos. A five-person tent will eat 3$\frac{1}{2}$–10 *graras* of barley a year, according to the milk supply. In the north the grain and perhaps the heavy plough will be stored under the protection of a saint, for example at the shrine of Hamet el Arosi in the Saguiet-el-Hamra. Artificial caves, taking perhaps two tons of grain, are dug in soft rock, as in Marrakesh and the pre-conquest Canaries; there is usually a paid guardian.

Fruit trees are extremely rare. There are palms at El Aaiún, Daora and Smara. The irrigated plots bear a scattering of figs and a few olive trees.

The Saharauis list nine plagues, by air, land and underground. One of the most tangible is the locusts, the red and yellow bodies obscuring the sun, in Ca da Mosto's fifteenth-century description; the plague then occurred every three or four years. The insects usually appear from Mauritania, coming from the Niger bend and flying in a north-westerly direction; now certainly able to appear in successive years, as in 1954–6, they devour the crops, throw planes into difficulties. The 1954 grey-brown horde took an hour and a half to cross Smara, from north-east to south. The Spanish have had an anti-locust team in the territory since the nineteen-fifties; it is now modernised and a part of the African international network. Combat has usually taken the form of poisoned bait strewn on the plague's route, this forecastable. To the opponents of colonialism, the Spanish effort – four million pesetas in 1955 – is aimed at keeping the locusts from reaching the Canaries, rather than for the Saharauis' benefit.

The Spaniards have installed several experimental farms. In 1959 Daora was taken over by the Count of Belalcázar. Buildings were put up, with seventy Saharauis taken on as workers, and wheat and barley grown, using tractor-ploughing and a combine harvester; a camel-breeding unit was opened. No information seems available on the farm's subsequent life: certainly, such a scheme could seem to be colonialism.

Next, beginning in 1965, three model farms were laid out around the Villa Cisneros bight, taking advantage of the vast newly-discovered water-table, tapped by 400 m borings. Just outside the town, half a hectare of shelly limestone was divided into three plots, with a protecting 3 m wall. One plot received a 40 cm layer of grit, drainage in the second was ensured by borings, the third was left without drainage; a half-metre soil covering was then spread over each plot, being mixed with peat and phosphates. First crops were encouraging at 50 tons of tomatoes and 25 tons of potatoes the hectare; grain and other vegetables grew well enough. Bigger farms were set up at Tauarta, towards the back of the peninsula, and near the Argub post, opposite Villa Cisneros; each had soil already.

Between them the farms were put to produce grain, vegetables and, in particular, fodder, with a view to raising zebu and, possibly, Charolais cattle, the stock to be 200 cows and 400 calves; there was a passing mention of providing camel-food during the droughts. The territory's few tractors will belong to these Spanish concerns. It is interesting that two Spanish varieties of barley gave 700 and 900 kilos the hectare but the Saharaui type yielded 1,100 kilos.

All the farms have to cope with up to 1·8 grams of salt to a litre of ground water; it has to be cooled from its initial temperature of 37°C and the gases allowed to escape. By 1970, twenty-six hectares had been made irrigable at Argub. Nothing more has been heard of the Bilbao experimenter who, about 1960, was to filter sea-water by pumping it through deep galleries.

*Crafts*

A woman's daily work includes the spinning and weaving of blankets and of the tent, the making of rush and esparto mats and the curing of skins, these the raw material for many household objects. Spinning has always been by simple spindle, Riley describing the plied yarn as the thickness of a goose quill; at present iron-toothed cards are in use for the wool's initial preparation. There is a custom, the *zerga*, that if a rich person passes in front of a spinning party, the women throw a ball of wool at him – he has to give them a present. Weaving is slow and primitive, much as in Riley's time. The front and back of the loom each consist of a pair of posts sunk in the ground; the width of the warp averages 65 cm; the common shedding device is to have two leash sticks, one above the warp and one below. Woven strips will be stitched together with special needles; in an emergency, Riley noted, thorns would hold pieces of cloth together. Small measurements, as in weaving, also use limb spans, for example the *fum el kelb*, the gap between the thumb and index finger when spread to the maximum.

Coming to skin-curing and the manufacture and decoration of leather goods, though the woman will work at these, they are a speciality of the *malemin*, the artisans. They are perhaps the most distinctive products of the west Sahara. The range is endless: bags and cushions, saddles and sheaths, cattle bowls and reins, sandals and amulets, musical instruments and tobacco pouches, these last sometimes of lizard skin. The nomads delight in the fringes which border most; colours, with red, green and yellow favoured, are now from Mauritania and the Canaries, being applied to an incised decoration of lozenges and other geometric forms. Tools are few: the *maalem* has a working board, knives, reed pens for the colours, these kept in sea-shells, and a polishing stone, this sometimes a Neolithic axe.

The most essential and most common work is the making of the goat-skin *guerba*, the water-carrier used at least from the time of the Neolithic pastoralists. Scott described how, the animal's head cut off, the nomad pushed his hand down through the neck and right round the warm body until he could extract the flesh and bones from the complete uncut skin. To cure it, the main ingredient is now acacia bark. The skin is first salted for a night, then treated with a paste of powdered bark and by scraping with a sea-shell; next it is filled for a week with a solution of acacia powder and water. Washed out, it is daubed with a mixture of two parts of oil to one of pitch, being then ready for use. Other curing is on these lines, with delicate skins tanned with 2 : 1 of acacia leaves and bark; *Rhus oxyacantha* is also used.

Coming to the *malemin* themselves, they are essential to the nomads, with whom they travel, yet despised for their hard work and mixed origins. Often similar in appearance to the Jews of the Moroccan *mellahs* but sometimes with negroid traits, roughly comparable in way of life to the ancient gypsies of Europe, the *malemin* are part of a fraternity – aside from their links with the tribes with which they travel – though it has not been studied. These craftsmen are also feared, for their skilful hands and independent minds. Riley watched one making charcoal for emergency use on a long march; this *maalem* travelled with a foot-long pointed anvil, easily driven into the ground, and a pair of alternating skin bellows, *hanut*, for use with a hole in the ground, perhaps clay-lined, as a furnace. Thus equipped he could repair a saddle, make an axe, braise up a hole in an old gun-barrel – most of these salt-eaten as they had come from shipwrecks, as Riley well knew. A couple of small boys often helped the *maalem*, a black one working the bellows. Other tools were a metal crucible and a wood-working adze. The *maalem*'s wife helped, mainly with the tanning, engraving, colouring and stitching of leather goods.

The nomads' recent increase in wealth brought an initial surge in metal-working by the *malemin* – in iron, copper and, particularly, silver. The craftsmen's physiques are in line with their designs, part Jewish and part Sudanese, the southerners said to have spread into the desert after the breaking-up of the Songhai empire in the sixteenth century. The main metal products have been knives, sugar hammers, boxes, trays, cigarette holders and pipes, talismans and bangles. Intricate workmanship goes into the long rectangular brass padlocks for the *tazufra* bags. Silver is used for the wrist and ankle bracelets, some penannular with knobbed terminals.

Wood is used for normal household objects, including for teapots – copies of the metal vessels – decorated in red and black. Much craft goes into the rosaries of *Rhus* wood. Horn of oryx and gazelle is worked into personal ornaments.

The Spanish have recognised the value of the local craftsmen and have taken steps to try to halt the degeneration in standards and to avoid their disappearance in the future. The causes of these threats are the nomads' increasing preference for European goods – or, as bad, their imitation by the local craftsmen – and the gathering wealth of the *malemin*, often leading them to go over to trading or herding. The administration therefore built in 1968 a group of workshops, at Villa Cisneros, for the *majorreros*, as the Spanish call them; materials and equipment are available. Work must be in the traditional styles.

## Traders

Slavery is now outlawed, the ostriches all gone and the gum arabic, down to 3,000 tons a year, is sent out direct from Mauritania, the chief source a species of acacia in the south of the country. The nomads' exports are now all but limited to livestock: the animals go to the ports, up to south Morocco, down to Nouadhibou and Atar, with camels and donkeys bought by the eastern Canaries too. Often the nomads themselves will take a caravan of surplus animals to market, this chosen according both to the prevailing prices for the beasts and for sugar; otherwise they will sell to travelling middlemen. A few other products do leave the desert: skins, of both domesticated and wild animals, butter, tent-cloth.

Money circulated little until recently, the nomads bartering amongst themselves, with passing caravans and in the markets. The chief unit, really approaching a currency, was the 15 m bale of blue French cloth and the $22\frac{1}{2}$ m bale of white Spanish fabric, in the nineteen-fifties worth five sugar cones or 125 pesetas. Since that time, the trend towards European-style goods has brought about the proliferation of small general stores, with the 'supermarket' since 1965, run by Spaniards and sedentarised nomads, the latter setting up in Smara too; hygienic *souks* have been built by the administration.

Smuggling, long a major occupation, flourishes on the same wave of material prosperity. Cargoes about to enter Morocco and Mauritania illegally, such as cigarettes and luxury goods, are organised quite openly in Spanish Sahara. A few nomads have become very rich on trading and smuggling.

## Employment

With the described increase in consumption, markedly European in flavour, has come the wider spread of the concept of regular work for a fixed wage paid in cash. Diminishing parallel are the numbers of slaves and 'self-employed' nomads.

Wage-earning began in 1884, when Saharauis first joined the crews of the Canary fishing boats. The earliest enrolments in the Nomad Troops and Police took place half a century ago. Agreements between Saharauis began when the settlement of rich nomads in the ports led them to pay shepherds, in pesetas, to look after their flocks, these being sold to the Spanish. The surveys and prospections from the nineteen-fifties, described in the next chapter, brought employment to many Saharauis, including in their favourite role of 'protectors' or guards. In 1958 the labour laws of the peninsula were extended to cover Spanish Sahara.

In 1967 the administration published figures for the Saharauis with employment. There were 600 Nomad Troops, 462 Territorial Police, 100 Camel Corps, 90 guides; 50 were administration employees such as cleaners and chauffeurs, 6 were municipal guards; there were 50 teachers of Arabic and the Koran; the applications of Koranic law employed 27 Saharauis; 30 more were trained medical assistants; 20 were auxiliary interpreters. An unexpected category of 'wage-earner' was that of 'chief', of whom a round hundred were rewarded for unspecified services to the authorities. There were also some 2,500 workers outside the administration – these were employed in the development of the enormous phosphate mine, the port and road projects, and the housing industry.

At this date the minimum daily wage was 75 per cent above that in the peninsula. There was a labour exchange, with a couple of hundred looking for work, and there were pensions, paid holidays and unemployment benefit; this last, for example, was from 20 ptas a day for a single person – 14 per cent of the minimum daily wage – to 35 ptas a day if married with over four children. The Saharauis do feel themselves well paid.

## Saharaui Fishermen

The yearly rhythm of the fishing tribes has some similarity to that of the camel nomads, since for many it is geared to a natural cycle, in this case fish migration, and also, in closely similar fashion, to the supply of drinking water. The fishing year begins with the autumn rains, if any, the tributaries then going to the optimum points for fish and water; on Fuerteventura there is a very similar movement to that on the coast. Tents are set up, last year's shelters repaired. The peak of activity is reached in December and January, when captives would also be sent from the interior to fish. In February the nomad-masters themselves would arrive, especially if it were a bad year in the desert, and gorge on fish and fish oil, vitamin-rich. The wells then began to dry, and as the summer approached the fishermen and their poorly-preserved catch went inland to their masters' camps, to sell their surplus, or to the Guetna date-feast in July amongst the wild palms of the Adrar. Others, though still retaining the rhythm, have during the last ninety years taken temporary jobs at the European settlements, for example as dockers.

However, the fishing itself began to be affected from 1884 by the appearance of the Spaniards and, more markedly, by the establishment of Port Etienne in 1906. The tribes had long been in contact with the Canary fishermen, the former wading in the shallows, the latter in boats off-shore; in exchange for fish and provisions, the islanders were allowed to land to dry and repair nets, overhaul their boats and dig up bait. Tribes like the Ahel Laghzel and Berik Al-lah had long-standing relationships with Canary fishing families. So it was natural that from 1884 the Saharauis began to be employed by the Spanish, from 1906 by the French, the latter's intake being greatly increased by the formation in 1921 of the Soc. Industrielle de la Grande Pêche, also at Port Etienne. Some 'men of the gun' also joined the crews, making additional income in the close season by 'protecting' the Europeans' boats. The SIGP also acquired the tributaries' fish, in exchange for goods – buying and selling rates advantageous to the Europeans, as ever – and for authority-associated protection against their masters. It can be mentioned here that the French were no more effective than the Spanish in suppressing the tributary system; they formally declared it illegal in 1952.

The Sahara coast has never had seaworthy vessels of its own, a main factor being the lack of wood, and in 1951 the French set up the Soc. Indigène de Prévoyance de la B. du Levrier to fund boat-buying by the Africans themselves – of any caste – the loans to be repaid in fish over two years. The new captains usually began with a Canary partner as teacher, learning to fish in the island traditions.

Coming now to the techniques themselves, until very recently these had changed little since the time of the Portuguese Valentim Fernandes, 1506: 'The nets . . . are made from thread manufactured from a bark which is peeled off, beaten and carefully processed, and finally spun'. These nets were 'attached to rods pointed at each end, as big as a staff. The floats . . . are pieces of wood of *Figueyra do inferno* . . . weighted by balls of fired clay, dried in hot ashes and pierced'. Next 'the men go two and two to fish . . . they tie their two nets together, and, as soon as they see the fish . . . approach from either side, letting the net unroll gradually between them until they reach the shore. This takes place in the shallow water, hardly knee-deep . . . when the heat is at its height, because the fish are then . . .

drugged by the heat'. Fernandes added that 'They carry a harpoon in the right hand to spear the fish when, in trying to escape the net, it leaps in the air'.

The bark is from the *titarek*, a broom (*Leptadenia pyrotechnica* or *L. spartum*), now replaced by cotton; recently the size of the net, *chebka*, has been 30 m by 2 m deep, the mesh four fingers across for mullet fishing and otherwise finer. The floats, *tifa*, are made of *fernan*, the Portuguese Hell's Fig-tree (*Euphorbia balsamifera*); each is a 3–5 cm length of stalk, pierced and placed 5 cm from the next along the net's upper edge. The net staffs, *lbarat*, are polished. The round or oval weights, *idan*, can be found along the cliffs, near scatterings of fish-bones; the bricks of the Portendic fort were taken for shaping into weights, so Gruvel was told (1906). The weights were fixed along the net's lower edge, also at 5 cm intervals. Similarly-shaped cement ovals, weighing about 2 kilos each, are obsolete Spanish net-sinkers. The harpoon has been reported in use early this century at Puerto Cansado – with dolphins amongst the prey – and the rod in the mouth of the Saguiet-el-Hamra, a place with many bamboo clumps.

The most recent study (Anthonioz 1968) has described the use of dolphins, in fishing, by the Imraguen of the coast just below the B. du Levrier. In 1960 these 400 people had 84 tents. They also had 31 launches by then: still working the shallows, the wading techniques continued alongside net-casting from aboard, with the boats also used to bring partially-preserved fish to market and to take back goods and drinking water. The fish, mullet the most esteemed, are at their best on their south-going migration in September–April, on the way to the spawning grounds; in May–July the mullet return, exhausted, to be caught together with a species of sardine. August is used for repairing nets.

The man-dolphin symbiosis begins once a look-out spots a bank of fish. A child goes into the water and slaps the surface with sticks. The dolphins, recognising the call, according to Anthonioz, but equally probably imagining they are hearing the sounds of jumping mullet, come inshore, causing the fish to do so also. A single pair of fishermen, their turn having been decided in advance by a draw made by the elders, at once strip to their leather shorts and, taking an end of a net between them, holding its staff, they wade or swim rapidly – with one hand – out to sea, blocking the shoal's way. A second and a third net may be laid out. The dolphins apparently stop the fish escaping out to sea and frolic amongst the fishermen. The nets are dragged around the fish and then back to the shore. Emptied, with the aid of the women and children, they are taken out again, until the catch falls off. Once the first landing had been made, other waiting

15 The old Spanish fishing and trading post, La Guera, with the fortnightly steamer at anchor.

Passengers' barge being pulled into La Guera jetty by negroes. White-robed *beidane* and several Territorial Police.

(Below) Main street, La Guera. Sacks of contraband leaving for Mauritania, right.

16  The secondary school, Villa Cisneros.

A Senegalese selling carvings and jewellery to Spanish children, Villa Cisneros. Behind, Saharauis in the Spanish forces.

Islamic and western culture, Villa Cisneros

Imraguen could enter the water and try to net the fish roundabout. The shoals can be hundreds of metres long, 30 m wide and 1 to 2 m deep; a good session can bring in three or four tons of mullet and meagres. It is forbidden to kill the dolphin.

The families all help to gut the fish; some do so through the back. Part of the catch is dried in the sun, this *tichiar* later being sold to the nomads; it is the habitat of flies and other insects. The fish for sale to the SIGP are kept in brine – a recently-learned technique – and then sun-dried, each process lasting four days. The mullet roes are flattened, salted and dried; called *poutargue* now, this form of caviar fetches a high price. The Berik Al-lah appear to act as middlemen in the sale of the salted fish and *poutargue*, preserving the latter further by dipping it in melted beeswax. Anthonioz did not give the pro-portions of the profits taken respectively by the Imraguen fishermen and by their old masters, the Berik Al-lah.

## Spanish and Other Fishing Fleets

It has been described how, soon after C. Bojador was passed in 1434, European vessels began to fish the Saharan bank. The distance, how-ever, made this too hazardous a venture unless coupled with a local shore station: the Spaniards have always had the Canaries, the Portuguese used Agadir between 1505–41 and Arguin from 1448 to 1638. The year of the departure of the Portuguese saw the beginning of the custom, in the Spanish boats, that the first man to catch a fish after the C. Blanc latitude was crossed was given a bottle of wine by the captain.

Glas described the Canary fishermen at work off the coast in 1764, part of the reconnaissance for his Hilsborough base. There were 20–30 ships of 20–50 tons each, their crews of 15–30 men; most were from Grand Canary, a few from Tenerife and La Palma. The owners provided salt and biscuits, the fishermen the lines, hooks and other gear and also their own wine, oil, liquor, *pimento* and onions. Profits were divided as in the Mediterranean, being a share for the owner according to the boat's size, the rest being split up into two parts to the captain, one to each seaman, a half to every apprentice and a quarter to each boy. The whole coast was fished. Glas too stated that the Saharans had no boats; the Sultan's cruisers did not then venture so far south.

In the nineteenth century the French became very interested in the fish, with the stimulus of a study made by Berthelot, their Canary consul: 'A Canary fisherman takes 10 tons of fish a year compared with under half a ton caught by each man off Newfoundland'. In 1879 the French thought of re-occupying Arguin as a base, and in 1886 sent a naval vessel to chart from C. Blanc to the Senegal. In this same year, a Spanish boat, trying to estimate the potential of the new 'Protectorate', took 400 meagres averaging 16 kilos each in a single cast. By 1890 the Canary fleet was up to 50–60 sailers of 35–40 tons, the crews about 20 men each. These were the crews which were taking on the Saharauis. The Spanish-French treaty of 1900, the fishing grounds an important aspect, was signed against a horizon dotted with the vessels of many other European nations, busily investigating the Saharan bank.

Since then these waters have been fished intensively by the Spanish and French, with the primitively-equipped Villa Cisneros, La Guera and Port Etienne as bases. Gruvel's detailed study of the fish was made during the first decade. In the last years before the 1914–18 war, Spanish Sahara's main export was about 2,500 tons of dried fish annually. Each world war brought the fishermen of the embattled nations to the Sahara coast. The Spaniards learned little from these, being handicapped by a lack of capital, modern ships and techniques; their slow sailing boats were away a month at a time, but the Sahara bases had no accommodation for the men's families, though some settled at Port Etienne.

The last quarter-century has seen the depletion of many of the world's best-known fishing grounds, paralleling an accelerating international interest in the African bank. Beginning in 1958, by the nineteen-sixties the Japanese had 35–50 vessels based on Grand Canary, including two of 3,400 tons and two of 2,800 tons; the Russians, working direct from their home ports by a system of shuttling service and collection vessels, were rapidly increasing their Sahara fleet. Many other nations are also fishing alongside the Canary and Sahara Spaniards, including of course Mauritanians and Senegalese. As is to be expected, this bank is now being depleted.

If pirates are no longer present, politics and their gunboats have taken their place. In 1964 a Mauritanian minister referred menacingly to 'the precarious position of the Spanish who live at Port Etienne'. The Spaniards are well aware of the need for harmony with the southerners, whose B. du Levrier, fished under the 1900 agreement, yields a good part of the Spanish catch. By a treaty in 1964 the Spanish were allowed to build a fish-meal factory at Port Etienne. Fishing politics have to be seen against the wider issues involving the surrounding states, described in Chapters 13–15.

To the north, in fact, events have already been at crisis point. As an example of Spain's provocative posturing, vying with that of Morocco, the outstanding Spanish study of the Saharan bank (Garcia Cabrera 1964) labelled the ocean between Spain and the Canaries the

'Mar de España'. In 1967 Spain extended her territorial waters to twelve miles, as agreed by the European nations in 1964; however, foreign vessels would be given permits to fish the three to six mile zone if they had done so between 1953–62; the outer six miles were open to nationals of all countries with reciprocal agreements, one being signed in 1969 with Morocco. In 1972 the Instituto Nacional de Industria and the Office National de Pêche agreed to share equally in a fishing organisation to be set up in Agadir, with the building of a 700-ton tunny boat and five other ships of 150 tons each. However, early in 1973 the Moroccans decided to claim the sea for seventy miles around their shore – except opposite the Canaries and Gibraltar – and soon seized about 150 Spanish boats for fishing within this limit. A Spanish destroyer exchanged fire with Moroccan gunboats. In 1974 Morocco announced it would allow 200 Spanish vessels to fish within seventy miles of the coast; this still left some 600 fishing boats no choice but to go further afield, many to the hard-worked Sahara waters. The 1969 treaty, abrogated in 1972, was renewed. Hovering behind the Spanish diplomats in all issues such as this is the spectre of their departure from Spanish Sahara; this will be a great blow to the Canary fishermen.

Before coming to fishing techniques and the hauls, the bank's properties need to be summarised. The factors leading to the concentration of fish have been outlined in the opening chapter. An average fishing depth is 200 m though 500 m is commonly reached by the most powerful modern vessels: within this depth, off Spanish Sahara, there lies some 100,000 sq km of bed, its surface sandy and flat other than for that of the Arguin bank. The most prolific zone, once considered to be between 15°–30°N, has shrunk to 19°–26°N. These waters hold at least 300 species of fish; Spanish names are given here.

The Canary fishermen's catch, made at depths down to 300 m, consists to about 60 per cent of the *corvina*, sometimes called the meagre in English (*Johnius hololepidotus* according to Garcia Cabrera 1964); a bream, *sama* or, locally, *pargo* (*Dentex filosus*) totals 25 per cent; the grouper-like *cherna* (*Epinephelus aeneus*), 7 per cent; the *burro* (*Parapristipoma mediterraneum*), 5 per cent. The well-known *chacarona* (*Dentex canariensis*) is probably included with its close relative. The waters between 175–500 m produce the cod-family, notably *Merluccius m.* The chief migratory species sought are the tunny-family *patudo* (*Parathunnus thynnus*) and *rabil* (*Neothannus albacora*). The Moroccan and green lobsters (*Palinurus mauritanicus*, *P. regius*) are an important quarry. Species of big turtles are caught from C. Blanc southwards. Of all these, the immense quantities of meagre has dominated reports; these fish reach 1·50 m long and 60 kilos in weight, and it is said that, if one puts one's ear to the bottom of a boat, their hoarse grunting can be heard. So many fish are caught, of all species, that, dried, they have often been used as firewood.

Techniques in the nineteen-sixties fell into four groups. Twenty-ton sloops from the Canaries, equipped with hooks and *nasa* traps, fish inshore all the year round, down to eighty metres; the catch is preserved, though some vessels, known as 'freezers', have refrigerated plant. The meagre boats, equipped with nets, concentrate in the shallow B. du Levrier in spring and summer, follow the fish to the Villa Cisneros bight in autumn, finally join the first group of boats for the winter; perhaps 100,000 tons of meagre reach the Canaries in various states each year. Trawling forms a third division. The best catches of cod are made in the winter, the Japanese powerful enough to exploit the waters below 300 m, the Spanish working the 175–300 m zone. Small Spanish trawlers fish the inshore waters, down to about sixty metres, for the bream, *cherna* and *burro*. Finally, the tunny boats, many Japanese, get good results from May round to January, fishing between 22°–27°N; rods and lines are used, stationary or on the move, in depths of 100–300 m.

It is impossible to calculate the yearly haul by boats of so many nations. In the nineteen-sixties, the Canary islanders had 750 boats there, 17,000 tons, many antiquated; the sailers were taking five days to reach C. Blanc and longer to return; the islanders' total catch was about 44,000 tons a year, giving work to 22,000 people as crews and in the forty-four processing factories in the archipelago.

Table 6 gives available 1949–72 statistics for fishing actually based in the territory. This industry entered a new phase when it at last received official stimulus by the creation in 1948 of the IPASA fishery enterprise, with capital from the INI, from the ELCANO merchant navy concern and from Spanish ship-owners and industrialists. The stated aims of IPASA were to strengthen the Iberians' hold on the territory, to get fish for Spain and Guinea and to give employment. In summary, the IPASA brought down a mother-ship, the *Artico*, 1,300 tons, 3,800 tons laden, able to service the fleet and process or at least refrigerate its catch; obtained two fast corvettes for taking the frozen fish to the peninsula, then cut out the need for them by building refrigeration and processing plants at the desert ports and in the islands, thus keeping the work and fish in Spanish Sahara and the Canaries; intended that the factories at Villa Cisneros and La Guera should produce good-quality fresh and frozen fillets, dried fish, meal and oil, since until then their poorly-prepared products had only been acceptable to low-income Africans and Canary

Table 6: *Fish catches for boats based in Spanish Sahara, 1949–72*

| Catch in Tons | 1949 | 1950 | 1951 | 1952 | 1953 | 1954 | 1955 | 1956 | 1957 | 1958 | 1959 | 1960 |
|---|---|---|---|---|---|---|---|---|---|---|---|---|
| El Aaiún | 31 | 10 | 12 | 807 | 12 | 9 | — | 9 | — | 18 | 1612 | 114 |
| Villa Cisneros | | | 880 | 7 | 483 | 480 | 423 | 1086 | — | 499 | 3555 | 522 |
| La Guera | 626 | 2630 | 2649 | 2730 | 3094 | 3424 | 2705 | 2799 | 3957 | 1686 | 750 | 4591 |
| Total | 657 | 2640 | 3541 | 3544 | 3589 | 3913 | 3128 | 3894 | 3957 | 2203 | 5917 | 5227 |

| Catch in Tons | 1961 | 1962 | 1963 | 1964 | 1965 | 1966 | 1967 | 1968 | 1969 | 1970 | 1971 | 1972 |
|---|---|---|---|---|---|---|---|---|---|---|---|---|
| El Aaiún | 323 | 870 | 417 | 329 | 330 | 275 | 270 | 184 | 84 | 45 | — | 11 |
| Villa Cisneros | 460 | 1400 | 121 | 162 | 139 | 156 | 139 | 191 | 252 | 119 | 84 | 97 |
| La Guera | 4969 | 3700 | 1475 | 1806 | 4414 | 3440 | 3516 | 6286 | 3935 | 3488 | 3166 | 4904 |
| Total | 5752 | 5970 | 2013 | 2297 | 4883 | 3871 | 3925 | 6661 | 4271 | 3651 | 3250 | 5012 |

Islanders. Most of the aims were to some extent realised, sooner or later.

The increasing importance of the fishing industry, aided by the State's building of houses as part of its general development of the territory, produced a corporate strength amongst the fishermen. In the period 1950–55, said Lodwick, they would boycott one or the other of the two ports if they felt ill-treated by the authorities, gathering in an empty bay such as Angra da Cintra for their shore operations; this accounts to some degree for the statistical fluctuations. In 1964 they were promised State aid for boat purchase through the Fondo Nacional de Protección al Trabajo; the similar French scheme had begun in 1951, in Port Etienne. This aid followed the Spanish fishermen's agitation against their small share in the profits compared with that of the absentee boat-owner, the system comparable to the *latifundismo* which holds back Canary and peninsular agriculture. They also demanded the development of La Guera, many being well aware of their 'precarious position' at nearby Port Etienne. The year 1969 saw the opening of a Nautical and Fishing Professional Training School, with hostel, at Villa Cisneros.

The latest available Spanish Sahara figures value the total 12,700 tons caught in 1965–7 at 165 million pesetas. In 1969–72 the territory had still only some three dozen motorised vessels, no bigger than six-tonners on average; during this period 14,000 tons of fish were taken, 88 per cent being made into fish flour, 832 tons salted and the rest eaten fresh.

Lobster-fishing forms a separate division. The two species live in the breakers from Peña Grande to the south. The Canary Islanders, using the hooped *gueldera* net, have always caught a few of these, with the French intensively exploiting the species between the two world wars. At present, the Islanders have a few fifty-ton lobster boats off the coast; the French, modernised, have a fleet working around C. Blanc from March to September.

In the past, the lobsters caught by the Sahara-based Spanish had to be flown out, for example 40 tons in 1950. Refrigeration and also a live-transport ship, *La Mayonesa*, have eliminated this costly method. Between 1969–72 a total of 417 tons of lobsters was landed at La Guera and Villa Cisneros. The local boats carry six or seven men each, the usual gear being nets 35 m long and 3 m deep. In 1974, with lobsters selling at 400 ptas a kilo, the crew each received 10,000 ptas a month plus 5 ptas a kilo premium. A legal close season from 15 December to 15 March has been declared, with 18 cm as the minimum size to be retained, due to presently increasing exploitation.

Garcia Cabrera extensively discussed the need for the modernisation of Spain's Saharan fishing and processing industries – and suggested a search be made for new areas of development. He noted that the African shore, with cold low-salinity water, would be ideal for shellfish rearing.

## Seaweed Collection

The marine weeds have been worked since 1953; their uses are as food, fodder, fertiliser and in industrial products. During the first decade, three of the four zones into which the coast was divided were taken up, by two large groups, PRONA and IPASA; each exported 50 to 100 tons dry a year. In 1965 processing factories were being built at Villa Cisneros and El Aaiún, the whole then conceded to Algas de Sáhara SA for ten years, twice renewable.

The weed may only be cut from April to October, with the lowest third to be left attached; the machines have to be approved. The red weeds are pulled by hand. The labour force for this work is Saharaui, with payment by weight.

# Chapter 11

# Mineral Prospection and Mining

The Saharauis cheer themselves through life with a saying: 'What does it matter if the way is long, provided there is a well at the end'. But for many it is a mine that awaits them. During the near-century of Spanish activity in the territory, the most far-reaching occurrence has been the attention turned on it as a source of minerals for Europe and America. Geological fieldwork under difficult conditions between 1940–50 led to serious prospection from the end of the decade. Phosphates were located and, from 1972, mined; iron was confirmed but in 1964 exploitation was officially deferred, it was said, for economic reasons; the first period of oil prospection, 1960–4, was unsuccessful. Water and fuel were problems: the first was magnificently struck by the oil-seekers, flooding Villa Cisneros, whilst the use of eolian and solar energy for the second has been solemnly debated by the Spanish Association for the Advancement of Science. All this – and especially the oil prospection by American groups – has affected the Saharauis and their territory in the many ways, both obvious and subtle, common to such situations. For the Spanish, it brought such novelties as aeromagnetic survey, the acceptance of foreign capital in an overseas territory, the techniques of modern mining; the State had to pass appropriate laws, re-organise various related industries. Not least, the Spaniards have had to deal with the conflict between their own interests, those of foreign investment, of the Saharauis and of the Moroccans.

*Phosphates*
In 1945, the geologist Manuel Alia Medina collected samples from the northern *hammada* sediments in order to date the formations. Back in Madrid in 1947, it occurred to him to test the specimens for phosphate content and, with his brother José as chemist, he found he

had a 27 per cent sample. The Colonies Directorate sent him out on a further expedition, unpublicised. Collecting the Ifni chemist as analyst, Alia set up a laboratory in El Aaiún, and he has described the excitement as they awaited the yellow precipitate which would at once roughly show the phosphate proportions of the most likely samples. These yielded 50–60 per cent, worth mining. In October Alia met Franco and gave him a specimen of the deposit, since found to be part of the most extensive phosphate zone in the world.

The origins and deposition of phosphates have been much debated; Kazakov's theory, for example, is that the phosphorus in all dead matter sooner or later reaches the sea and is there eventually precipitated in water 50–200 m deep, the optimum. Phosphates have been discovered in the sedimentary basins of Upper Cretaceous and Middle and Upper Eocene age in Morocco and all along the North African coast, and at Dakar and, in Spanish Sahara, in the described El Aaiún and Tindouf Basins. Alia's finds were made in the former depression, south of the capital. Study by the State's prospection and research group, ADARO, with a pilot plant, rejected the first deposit, of three beds totalling 3·60 m at 30–47 per cent pure, in the walls of Wadi Labadilla. They next sampled 750 sq km of the Izic Meseta, 50 km south of El Aaiún and 40 km from the sea, and its eastern limit, Wadi Idgui; there were the handicaps of a 70 m capping of fossil dunes, a very hard siliceous layer and flooding by salt water. The bed averages were, reading down:

I     65 cm, 42·5% pure
II    1·50 m, 2·30–4 m, 7 m, according to zone. The last, at 133 m, was 45% pure
IIIab 1·35 m at up to 61% pure and 70 cm at 62·45% pure
IV    1·65 m, 51%. Outcropped on east wall but could not be reached by drilling, even at 244 m.

Levels IIIab, the richest, totalled 45 million tons with an average of 55% pure, levels II and IV 400 million tons at 45%. Too impure for use as it stood or for simple mechanical concentration, the deposit would have been exploitable had water and fuel been available for economic processing. Prospection near the sea at C. Bojador yielded nothing.

In 1962 the Empresa Nacional Minera del Sáhara SA, or ENMINSA, was formed, as an agency of the Instituto Nacional de Industria, the INI. Simultaneously the Bu Craa outcropping deposits were announced, up to 2,000 million tons over 1,200 sq km, 60 per cent pure at below 2 m; it was estimated that the region held 10,000 million tons. It has been said that the deposit was in fact found by US oil prospectors. Some 30 km east of the Izic Meseta, Bu Craa is about 100 km south-east of El Aaiún. The loading port was at first to be at Lemsid, the nearest point to the mine, but then the El Aaiún shore was preferred. Exploitation would involve the installation of the mine; a 96 km conveyor belt which would cross the mobile dunes on stilts; and the port plant and warehouses and, not least, a very long jetty to get out to deep water. Processing trials were carried out in Japan and at Fosfórico Español, the phosphoric acid plant in Huelva. In 1967 ENMINSA sought foreign capital and a contract was agreed with a consortium led by the International Minerals and Chemical Corporation of America (25 per cent), French and German companies (20 per cent) and the Spanish State (55 per cent); but early in 1968 the Americans withdrew because of the Spaniards' insistence that the phosphates should go for processing to the peninsula. The US Import-Export Bank loaned $2·2 million and backed a similar amount lent by the First Wisconsin National Bank of Milwaukee, these loans paying for 90 per cent of the mining gear bought from the United States. Estimates of investment in FOSBUCRAA fluctuate widely, but in 1975 the cost to various industrial countries has probably reached around 200 million pounds, half of this found by Spain. At the end of 1972 the concern employed 1,272 workers, expected to increase by half during 1973; Bu Craa itself, reached by a tarmac road off the El Aaiún–Smara highway, had a 500-person settlement, with mosque, whilst a new block of flats in the capital also bears the emblem of two crossed mining tools.

The ultra-modern mine began production in 1972, sending out 2–3 million tons a year; it is hoped to reach 10 million tons a year before the end of the decade. Two mechanical excavators, each weighing almost 3,000 tons, remove the top soil and then the underlying phosphate, in 75-ton pieces. Trucks take the phosphate to a treatment plant, after which it goes on to the conveyor belt. A silvery snake undulating across the sandy wilderness, this has the word 'Krupps' – a partner of the Spanish State in many an important enterprise since 1936–9 – in huge letters along its metal scales. Costing 20 million pounds, the belt is watched over at eleven stations; 55 motors drive its 150,000 rollers. Up to 2,000 tons of phosphates can leave the mine each hour, crossing the desert at 16 kph. In August 1974, fire destroyed 300 m of the belt, its cause said to have been heat from the friction of jammed rollers; in October, however, two burnt-out control stations were admitted to be the work of guerrillas.

The Aaiún Playa terminal, costing 20 million pounds, receives the phosphates off the belt. Here they are concentrated, using water from a desalination plant built by the Belwin-Lima-Hamilton-Babcock & Wilcox Corporation; yielding $3\frac{1}{2}$ million litres a day, very pure at 50 p.p.m., heat consumption is 1,000 B.T.U. to 8 litres of water. The storage hangar, $350 \times 58$ m, has a capacity of 300,000 tons. Belts in tunnels below move the phosphate out onto the jetty, 3,158 m long, to the waiting ships. The wharfs are graded to take vessels from 10,000 tons and 9 m draught to 100,000 tons and 17·50 m draught; up to 6,000 tons an hour can be loaded from the whole jetty. A pumping platform sends back seawater to the desalination plant on the shore. The gigantic security-encased construction contrasts with the coast round about, low and empty.

The Spanish Sahara phosphates are intended partially as fertiliser for the acid soils of northern Spain and partially for the world market, with Japan initially the largest foreign buyer. Both aspects affect Morocco, whose own phosphates represent 30 per cent of its exports – 20 million tons of the mineral in 1974 – and 10 per cent of its revenues. First, Spain has always imported Moroccan phosphates, a million tons in 1970, but this then became unnecessary. Secondly, Spain's mine, comparatively cheap to run, was finished just when world prices were falling but consumption was increasing only slowly; the US played a similar role in the decade to 1970. Nevertheless, in 1970 Morocco rejected a second time the Spanish offer of a common phosphate policy in exchange for the relinquishing of the former's claim to Spanish Sahara. Then, however, 1973–4 saw an increase in world demand with prices rising steeply to around £30 a ton, though the general boom did not of course reduce the intensity of Morocco's claim to the territory.

Needful of the support of the Saharaui people, the Spaniards in 1969 appointed a few of their preferred local chiefs to the Council of Administration of FOSBUCRAA . . . Saharauis have assured the author that the profits from the mine will all stay to benefit the territory.

*Iron*
The presence of iron-bearing deposits in the west Sahara has long been appreciated, the best-known being those of the unexploited Gara Djebilet, just south of Tindouf in Algeria, and of the Kedia Ijil, 50 km into Mauritania from the curve in the Spanish territory's south-east boundary, this ore being mined by the MIFERMA organisation. Spanish Sahara itself was known to have iron too, with early travellers noting its effect on their compasses, especially in the central zone. Iron, unlike the phosphates, can be exploited by processes not needing water.

In 1947 Alia reported the ferrugineous enrichment of the Lower
Devonian in the Smara Arc, in the Emsian fossil level. The bed outcrops over several hundred kilometres, on the eroded mesetas of
Ternit, Aserauit and Laglagla; the iron is an oligist, mainly in its red
haematite form but replaced by limonite in the upper part. Alia
suggested the whole Tindouf Depression might be iron-bearing, at
least in the extensive Lower Devonian. Nothing more was done until,
in 1961, the Gara Djebilet iron-bearing oolitic sediments were found
to extend closer still to Spanish Sahara – an aeromagnetic survey of
the north-east was then carried out. The Algerian iron is a magnetite,
but the Spanish survey did not show any concentrations, though
there were a few anomalies; the prospectors comforted themselves
by noting that the zone's known iron was, after all, non-magnetic.
Soundings were to be made next, but there is no further information,
either because the results were negative or for political reasons –
to avoid exciting nationalist and neighbouring claims. A later mention by the INI of a big iron deposit, 65 per cent pure, in the north,
may stem from this prospection.

Most investigation, publicly at least, has been done in a zone
130 km east of the Villa Cisneros bay, on the north-west limits of the
Tiris meseta; both this and the Kedia Ijil are part of the Pre-Cambrian basement. In search of a concentration, aeromagnetic survey
was carried out in the nineteen-fifties over a known iron-bearing
rectangle 60 km north to south and 30 km wide, its south-east corner
at 14°24'W and 22°58'N. A mass of hyperstene granite impregnated
with magnetite was rejected because the siliceous content was too
high for it to be workable. The largest of the four outcropping iron
masses lies two kilometres south-west of Agracha and, covering
30,000 sq m, was once estimated at 72 million tons but, soundings to
277 m having shown it to be in lenses rather than continuously, the
deposit is likely to total only 20 million tons; also, some of this is
reduced in value by being mixed with sterile rock. The deposit is a
metamorphosed Pre-Cambrian basic magma, probably gabbroid,
and the iron consists of magnetite and ilmenite transformed into
oligist with fine secondary ilmenite; analysis gives 57·3 per cent iron
and 13·6 per cent titanium oxide, with only 5·25 per cent of non-
metallic impurities. The titanium oxide cannot be eliminated by the
ordinary processes, but parallel researches by the Instituto del Hierro
y del Acero and by the Norwegian Elektrokemisk firm showed that
treatment in electric ovens would be effective. It was also thought
that the rock's 0·6–0·8 per cent of vanadium could then be recouped
too; one of the world's largest deposits of this strategic mineral, its
value would affect the viability of the exploitation. The route of a

160 km railway to the Villa Cisneros bight was surveyed and found feasible, with three possible terminals with 20 m of water. Production of three million tons a year was mentioned. Carrero Blanco made an official inspection of the Agracha zone in 1962. Nevertheless, in 1964 an INI commission stated that, as the world iron market was depressed, Agracha would not yet be developed.

The Kedia Ijil iron, known since at least the eleventh century, had long been studied by the French when, in 1951, the MIFERMA was formed, with 95 per cent European capital; the mine and its town of Zouerate – with 6,250 inhabitants by 1965 – were helped by an International Bank loan of 66 million dollars. Mauritania made a marriage of necessity with the French-dominated consortium; the clash between their interests and those of Spain and Morocco will be described in the last chapter. The Kedia Ijil ore, a magnetite 60–65 per cent pure, is extracted from a Pre-Cambrian quartzite massif, one of many in the region. Exports total nine million tons a year, 94 per cent of Mauritania's revenue. In 1974 the 'MIF' was nationalised.

About 1965 the Spanish were again thinking about iron: aero-magnetic survey of the centre of the territory threw up forty-six anomalies greater than that of Agracha, some by four times as much. As with the north-easterly prospections, reports have not been published on these.

*Oil*

Prospection was announced in 1950 and the next decade was taken up with the raising of the necessary finance; for the first time, foreign capital had to be let into a Spanish overseas territory. In 1956 agreement was reached with one or two interested international companies, but this was then vetoed at top level. The 1958 Hydrocarbons Law was then passed. The State's Servicio Minero now carried out an aerial survey of 180,000 sq km of the sedimentary deposits, both of the surface and of the beds, the latter to 5,000 m in the north and to 2,000 m in the south; this area was that most likely to hold oil. The whole of Spanish Sahara was divided into 108 rectangles of 70 × 35 km each, running 40' along the meridians and 20' along the parallels; coastal concessions would also carry with them the adjacent continental shelf. Prospection permits were to be for six years, possibly extended to nine years; the prospectors would be obliged to spend a minimum amount, elegantly fixed at two gold pesetas the hectare; exploitation permits would be granted for fifty years but only for half the concession, the other half reverting at once to the State; the royalty paid to the State on the companies' exploited halves was to be comparatively low; a 'Co-ordination Commission' would watch over all financial aspects. Following sale of the survey details for 60 million pesetas, forty-three concessions totalling 100,000 sq km of the sedimentary zone were taken by eleven groups, most or all being a mixture of US and Spanish concerns; the largest interests were held by Tidewater-Sohio Iberian and by Cepsa-Spanish Gulf Oil, and the Spanish State had direct participation in various groups through such agencies as the INI.

The first drilling gear arrived in 1960 and soon the triangle coast-wards of the territory's NE–SW diagonal was dotted with rigs and trucks, tents and caravans; similar prospection was then taking place down the coasts of Mauritania and Senegal. Some 10,000–12,000 workers are said to have arrived, mainly from the Canaries. Excitement grew with the first deep oil, in a concession on the coast halfway between El Aaiún and Villa Cisneros. Further small amounts were found in the north.

Frustratingly, elsewhere in Africa, the consolidated sediments of the same shallow marine transgressions were yielding oil in quantity. But special conditions are needed: a basal bituminous rock which, as a result of tectonic or other forces, distils its oil into an overlying porous bed which, in turn, must be sealed off upwards by an impermeable level. The territory's older marine sediments were known, by 1960, to hold both bituminous rocks and oil impregnations; and the tectonics were considered adequate. So the prospection teams had cause for optimism. Also, in 1960, traces of oil were struck as near as Tindouf by Algerian water-prospectors drilling to 2,100 m; most of the oil was at about 700 m in the Emsian stratum of the Lower Devonian, present of course in the extension of the Depression into Spanish Sahara. The Emsian's parallel role as an iron-bearing level has been discussed.

There were many administrative problems, since the Spanish mining authorities had never had to cope with such a massive-scale prospection under desert conditions. Local workers, reticent, were anyway few. Laws were needed to govern the peculiar labour contracts. The telecommunication network was minimal. The Hydro-carbons Law laid down that Spanish industry should benefit from the prospection, but the Americans and other foreigners preferred their own transport and materials, and the Spanish did equally want them to get on with the work with maximum speed and efficiency. Thus foreign aeroplanes were allowed free access initially, since Spain's civil aviation was not adequate, but various Spanish companies were soon formed for the purpose. The dynamite used in the seismic work amounted to 600 tons a month, and in quantity and quality that from the peninsula was at first inadequate, nor could the Spanish supply the mobile stores for the explosives.

Another form of problem came in 1961 when a force of Moroccan 'patriots', in Royal Army lorries, entered Spanish territory and kidnapped eleven Spanish and foreign employees of Union Oil, eventually handing them over to their consuls in Rabat. A day or two after their capture, four Italians of the AGIP prospection company, at work in south Morocco but forced by bad weather and lack of fuel to drive into Spanish Sahara, were delivered by the Spaniards to their consul . . . in the Canaries. This was done 'for their own sakes, in view of the dangers of the return journey by land'. The incidents must be seen against the background of the 1957–8 fighting and the subsequent guerrilla incursions from the Tarfaya Province – the latter having been reluctantly handed back to Morocco in 1958 – and of course against Morocco's general claim to Spanish Sahara and its minerals.

By 1964 it had become likely that, though twenty-seven traces of oil had been found, Spanish Sahara did not have a viable deposit. So most of the concessions were abandoned; discoveries in the peninsula and elsewhere in the world were more interesting. The Spanish had expected 10,000 million pesetas to be spent over six years but, prospected in four, the work had cost only half as much at the most, though this passed the agreed minimum; some 120 million pesetas had gone on dynamite alone, into sixty soundings totalling 103,000 m in depth. Noting that 60,000 pesetas was needed for adequate prospection of each square kilometre, a Spanish spokesman complained that, though 34,000 pesetas had been spent, the prospection value of this was only 20,000 pesetas since the companies had acted without co-ordination and thus much work had been duplicated; anyway two-thirds of the information had still to be gathered. The companies' reports would be secret if, added the spokesman sadly, they had submitted them.

However, interest was soon to be shown in the continental shelf. In 1966 the offshore concessions were officially demarcated; only Cepsa-Spanish Gulf had unlapsed coastal holdings, three around Villa Cisneros. Inland, the State agency, Ibérica de Sondeos, appears to have gone on drilling on behalf of ENMINSA, national custodian of 492,000 hectares of unwanted concessions. As with the other minerals discussed, recent information is extraordinarily sparse. The Africa Pilot of 1971 vaguely reported oil rigs, within the 200 m line, to north and south of C. Juby; since this headland is only 40 km from the frontier, some may be in Spanish waters, though they may all be part of the Texas Eastern prospection of the Sus region and thus Moroccan enterprise. Finally, in 1974 it was announced that the international oceanography research vessel *Atlantis II*, mapping the West African sedimentary bowl during the collection of data related to the continental drift theory, had evidence of likely oil and methane gas zones in the continental shelf from Gambia to Spanish Sahara.

## Miscellaneous Minerals

Travellers have been struck by the antimony vein in the Saguiet-el-Hamra wall but little else has been written on the territory's rarer minerals, probably due to the strategic value of some of the deposits. In 1950, Alia carried out heavy mineral analysis on sand from ten places along a traverse from Villa Cisneros to Aguenit in the south-east corner: hornblende could reach 67 per cent, garnet 56 per cent, with kyanite, epidote, staurolite, hyperstene, ilmenite, magnetite, rutile, tourmaline and zircon. In 1965 it was announced that the water-strike in the Villa Cisneros region would allow re-appraisal of the exploitability of various minerals needing concentration by water, notably of the Adrar Soutouf copper in the south-west, of nickel – this has been reported from the Tiris basement – and of deposits of wolfram, tin, beryl, chrome, platinum, gold, manganese, corindum and radioactive minerals. Silence, probably strategic, has since been maintained.

## The Salt-pans

In the Middle Ages salt was an essential link in the nomads' circular commerce: their slaves quarried it from the desert pans, they themselves took it south to exchange for more slaves, these then being marched for sale to the Maghreb and, from the fifteenth century, to Arguin Island also. Quiroga's expedition of 1886 recorded that a black girl of six to eight years was worth 4 to 6 bars, a young man 10 to 12 bars, a young woman 14 to 16 bars. Salt was a form of currency. The nomads themselves consumed little salt direct from the pans; their water is salty, their milk comes from animals grazing on salt-bearing vegetation. The most famous pan was at Taghaza, now in the very north-west corner of Mali; it was described by El Bekri, Ibn Batuta and Leo Africanus.

Ijil, once called Taghaza el Gharbie, or West Taghaza, is just in Mauritania and, as described, is responsible for the curve in the south-east frontier. The pan, likely to be an early tectonic depression, is up to 80 km long and 10 km wide. Around 1886, when the Spanish recorded crunching their way across, the output was some 4,000 tons a year. Prudhomme (1925) said the pan belonged to the Cunta of Wadan who leased the mining rights to the guild of butchers of the Adrar, at a yearly rent of twenty bars each, reduced to three bars if paid at Wadan; the butchers' slaves quarried the salt over six months of the year. The Cunta also sent out salt caravans themselves and sold to convoys come from north and south to buy; the tributary Agzazir quarried for the Cunta. Perhaps 60,000 bars a year were extracted: at an estimated 25 kilos each, this is some 1,500 tons a year. The salt increased in value the further it travelled; by the time it reached Walata or Nioro it was from five to ten times its price at the pan. During the French occupation their patrols watched over Ijil.

In 1974 a few men were seen working a zone about forty kilometres north-east of F'Derick, with the frontier marked by the peaked *gleibat* on the further side of the pan. The workers, each receiving a minute sum for every bar cut, could not leave without paying an impossibly-large indemnity to their employer; but perhaps it was better to be thus enslaved than to go and join Mauritania's semi-urbanised unemployed in the *bidonvilles* around Zouerate or Nouadhibou. The salt-cutters were living in low roofed windbreaks made of branches, slabs of stone and odds and ends from the MIFERMA, with one of their barrels, for water, at each entrance.

In spite of Quiroga's description, the surface of the pan is at present a pale brown lateritic clay, about 80 cm deep. Below this, interspersed with more seams of clay, come up to six bands of coarse salt, 7–12 cm thick, varying in clay-content and friability. The third down of these, 12 cm of white salt, was being exploited. To reach it, a curving trench about a metre wide had been dug through the overlying deposits, these thrown up as a multi-coloured spoil heap. The salt layer was attacked by making radial grooves in it with a chisel set in a 2 m handle, brought down vertically with great force, and with a hand chopper; the former was also used to prise out the separated blocks. These were about 90 cm long, 12 cm thick, and tapered from about 30 cm to 20 cm in width, the result of the deliberately-curving nature of the trench. A camel can carry eight bars, four corded together on each side, with the heavy ends high up on the animal's back, considered the best way. A black clay is used to mark the bars. Production, recently estimated as high as 1,000 tons a year, is certainly dropping, although parts of the Sudan still prefer the desert salt to that imported from Europe.

There is a marine salt-pan at Villa Cisneros, with a Saharaui labour force. The pan is organised in the normal European fashion, as a network of rectangles filled with sea-water by canals and using the sun's heat for evaporation. Output, 500 tons in 1948, was up to 2,000–3,000 tons a year in the nineteen-sixties, apparently rising as that of Ijil is falling.

*Wells*

The groundwater resources, with recent discoveries, have been described in the opening chapter. In the *bilad es attach*, the land of thirst, there is still no more than one well to 2,000 sq km, even after the Spaniards' water-seeking campaign. Before 1960 there were 130 water-points, most of them mere holes or scoops about three metres deep, yielding in total 1,000 cu m a day, 45 per cent 'undrinkable'. The best wells, averaging six metres deep and 50 cu m a day each, were at El Aaiún, Aguenit, Ausert, Bir Nazaran, Bir Gandus, El Farsia, Maatallah and Smara, all used since prehistoric times; the worst gave salty foetid water not even drinkable by animals. There was most water in the north, least in the central interior and on the south coast.

The wells have names according to their type: an *oglat* is down to 4 m deep, a *hassi* around 6 m, a *bir* to 10–12 m. A watercourse well is a *tilinsi*; a hole at the foot of an outcrop after rain is an *arguis*. Drought will probably mean deepening a well, merely postponing the day it dries up. The best wells were stone-faced inside and some-times had a low wall around the mouth; usually, however, they both fell in and silted up with dung and blown sand. The water was usually pulled up in a skin by hand or, if over 20 m down, the nomads used camel-traction through a pulley suspended from a forked acacia branch. Important as meeting places, 'the well at the end' made many a long march tolerable.

In the decade to 1970 the Spanish spent 170 million pesetas in increasing the water-supply to 50,000 cu m a day. A total of 175 water-points was announced; of these, 107 drillings, the average to 177 m, the maximum to 1,000 m, were yielding 98 % of the supply, three-quarters surfacing under its own pressure. About 90 % was 'usable for all purposes', 9 % only for animals, with only 1 % 'very salty'. The water is free to all; spread over ten years, its cost to the State will be a peseta a cubic metre.

El Aaiún, with 200 cu m a day in 1960, was receiving 3,000 cu m by 1970, this to be increased to 5,000 cu m a day shortly; in 1974, though drinkable, it was salty. Villa Cisneros used to rely on a cistern boat from the Canaries, the ration being five litres a day, to each Saharaui at least; the available supply is now limitless, though at the author's hotel it tasted somewhat of rotten eggs, perhaps not typical. La Guera, however, still relies on the 1,000-ton cistern in the main square, since no water-strikes have been made in its area. In the past, to try to help, the two coastal towns have had salt-water laid on, usable for some purposes; solar and solid-fuel distillation plants have each been used.

Legislation in 1965 underlined that the territory's water-supplies are under State control. The water-holding zones now appear to have a much-increased yield but the old arid regions are still ill-provided, with loss of grazing due to survival difficulties. Mauritania's wells were given modern superstructures by the French, notably sloping radiating channels with a trough at the end of each, thus keeping the animals spread out and the well clean. Most Spanish wells seen by the author do not have these, though one or two – such as Imililik and Gleibat Mosdat – are straddled by elegant arches. A water-point in the very centre of the territory, surmounted by a new pump-house, will be useless to the thirsty traveller not equipped with a pumping engine . . . one wonders what the *practical* increase in the water-supply has been to the nomads.

# Chapter 12

# Development of the Territory since 1940

The seventh chapter took the evolution of the territory to the key date of 1934, the year of the annexation of the interior. The Civil War delayed reconnaissance until 1940. In 1943 the newspaper *Arriba* commented that the territory's value lay in 'its strategic position, fishing, raw materials and minerals'. These last three aspects have been described, whilst the international politics and conflicts over Spanish Sahara will be discussed in the last two chapters. It is here intended to summarise the material developments which have in part come about to cater for the needs of the Spanish civilians, army, phosphate industry and other projects, and, in part, to benefit the Saharauis. In the latter case the reader must be left to choose, as motive, between the *quijotismo* associated by the Spanish with the pesetas with which Franco, 'the cloud who brings us . . . good things', has deluged the land, and their need to obtain the nomads' support at local and international levels.

Public money reaches the desert in the form of the State's almost total payment of the budgeted outgoings, and also in the shape of expenditure on the army, including pay. Chief imports are food, clothes and luxury goods, fuels, vehicles and machinery, construction materials – and military equipment. The ubiquitous administration pays higher wages and salaries than on the peninsula, in turn raising those in the private sector. The first return to the State has been the outflow, since 1972, of the phosphate.

The Spanish developments described below are either European conceptions or each consists of two parallel institutions, the long-established beside the Iberian. In the former category comes the idea of a single administration for the territory, with money to spend on all alike; the main sub-divisions are health, urban development and housing, communications and the dissemination of Spanish culture.

Tourism is another Spanish innovation. The second group consists of local government, justice, education and, also, the just-described well improvements. Accepted under pressure or voluntarily, slowly or rapidly, the developments represent centralisation at the expense of individual initiative and effort, with the disappearance of aspects of the established culture – sometimes for the better and sometimes, one may feel, for the worse.

However, it is possible to bring a people to dependence upon a materially more developed culture without making them capable of eventual independence. In 1974 the Governor-General of the territory said the Spanish had trained some doctors, mining engineers and lawyers; there was one officer-cadet at military school.

## The Budget

The accuracy of the official statistics depends on the intentions and abilities of their compilers. Figures in the foreign press vary widely. Until 1958, Spanish Sahara was grouped with Ifni as 'Spanish West Africa', their combined non-military budget for 1957 totalling 87 million pesetas, their shares in inverse proportions to their sizes; some 13 million pesetas were raised by the territories, the rest coming from the State. Petrol prospection began in 1960 and during 1961–4 the budget for Spanish Sahara, on its own, was each year between 200–250 million pesetas, in 1965 leaping to 464 million, and then increasing until, in 1972, it had reached 1,215 million pesetas. An analysis of the first Development Budget, 1961, gives Administration 6%, Education, Health and Posts 44%, Telecommunications 11%, Public Works 16%, Urban Construction 13%, Mines 1%, Miscellaneous 9% – odd groupings. In 1965 it was remarked that where 5,400 pesetas a year were spent on each peninsular inhabitant, those in Spanish Sahara enjoyed 18,000 pesetas. Although there are now vehicles to tax as well as camels, still no more than a tithe of the budget is raised locally, the rest being met by the government's subsidy, 'extraordinary credits', special Development Plan allocations and so on.

## Local Government

Unification of the territory under a single ruler was approached by the Almoravides and by Ma el Ainin; throughout there has been the claim to sovereignty by the Moroccan Sultan, with his intermittent attempts to assert himself. Below these rulers have always come the tribal chiefs, each usually subject to the will of the tribal assembly, the *yemaa*, which elected him. The *yemaa* is, moving downwards, in turn made up of the heads of the fractions, positions open to the eldest son of each family, by election. Courage, generosity and eloquence are important leadership qualities. Each fraction has its own *yemaa*, at which all men can speak. Decisions made by one or other of the two assemblies are binding on those whom they represent, expulsion the only alternative.

Following the Civil War, the Spaniards continued to hold the territory by military rule, without attempting to integrate with the existing tribal organisation. In 1958, following the short bitter war between Spaniards and Africans – described in the next chapter – Spanish Sahara and Ifni were parted and instead of 'colonies' became 'provinces'. In 1961, with international and local pressure building up parallel to the mineral prospection, laws were passed laying out a form of government which, it was hoped, would be able to cope with the new developments. The Spanish delegate to the UN was at last able to read out the formal report demanded by the General Assembly.

The new regime was to be based on the 'Fundamental Laws of Spain', with appropriate modifications. In charge would be a Governor-General answerable to Madrid in the shape of the 'Dirección General de Plazas y Provincias Africanas'. In practice always a military man, the Governor thus also commands the army; the navy and air force would operate autonomously in the territory; all three forces were under their respective commands in the Canaries. The Governor-General was to be seconded by a General Secretary, the working head of all departments except the military and the judiciary. Government delegates represented the Governor-General in the few settlements. These are the powers which effectively control the territory.

Nominal representation is provided by a separate hierarchy. At the top, a few *procuradores* at the Cortes, the Madrid government. At the head of the territory, a *cabildo*, the name familiar from the similar island councils in the Canaries and the parallel of the peninsula's Diputación Provincial under the Ley de Régimen Local. Installed at El Aaiún, the Cabildo was constituted with a president, automatically a *procurador*, and thirteen councillors; two of these are elected by the *ayuntamientos*, described next, six by 'commerce, industry and the professions', six by the 'nomad fractions'; any man or woman over twenty-one could stand for councillor.

Below the Cabildo came the two *ayuntamientos*, the town councils of El Aaiún and Villa Cisneros, each to be led by a mayor over twenty-five, that of the capital automatically a *procurador* too. The El Aaiún council had twelve members, that of Villa Cisneros eight; the qualifications were to be twenty-three years or over and also the head of a family or concern who were active in commerce, industry or the professions. Half the councillors were elected by the heads of the regions' families, the other half by commerce, industry and the professions again. Clearly, the town councils will consist only of Spaniards and sedentarised Saharaius, those dependent on the Spanish way of life. The *ayuntamientos* took the places of the old 'Local Juntas' in the two towns.

Further down the scale still come the 'minor local authorities', such as that of Smara. It has an appointed president and four local elected spokesmen.

The fourth and final grouping is that of 'nomad fractions', chosen apparently because of their close reflection of nomad feeling. Their function, left vague in the 1961 decree, appears limited to making suggestions over uncontentious matters and to electing their six Cabildo members. There was no provision for a General Assembly of Saharauis.

The law established general equality in matters such as education, and affirmed the nomads' traditional rights to the desert pastures. Some problems were not resolved: slavery, tribal minority and marriage, polygamy, collective responsibility. With a dozen departments – Justice, Property, Finance, Industry and Commerce, Labour, Public Order, Housing, Posts and Telecommunications, Information and Security, Education, Health, Mining – Spain planted its first tree in the desert, a leafy bureaucracy.

The first elections were held in May 1963, with a recorded 75–85 per cent turnout. The announced results were:

|  | Spaniards | Saharauis |
|---|---|---|
| Cabildo | 7 | 7 |
| Ayuntamientos |  |  |
| El Aaiún | 7 | 5 |
| Villa Cisneros | 4 | 5 |
| Minor local authorities |  |  |
| Smara | 2 | 2 |
| La Guera | 2 | 2 |

The elected President of the Cabildo was Khatri, long the chief of the Boihat, the leading Reguibat Leguacem fraction and 'faithful to the Spanish', according to *Africa*. A Spaniard was elected mayor of El Aaiún; Suilen uld Abdelahe, chief of a Delim fraction, became mayor of Villa Cisneros. On 17 July, all three in fact took seats in the Cortes in Madrid, Khatri veiled and in dark glasses, Suilen bearded and with a black turban, their white robes gleaming against the sombre suits of the peninsula *procuradores*.

In 1965 half the seats came up for re-election. With a 70 per cent poll, the various groups returned the candidates to be expected. Khatri – in and out of Spanish favour – was replaced as Cabildo President by Seila uld Abeida, also chief of a Reguibat fraction, the Chej. The territory's new leader was a thin-faced man with deep-sunk eyes and a large convex nose, clean cheeks, scanty moustache and beard and, though only forty-seven, white-haired; he was already a Gentleman of the African Order, a Spanish decoration.

Further local elections took place in 1967, slightly increasing the Spanish representation; only 38 per cent now voted. However, the *procuradores* at the Cortes were put up to six: the Cabildo President and El Aaiún mayor, both roles now held by Seila, the Villa Cisneros mayor, 'the national councillor of the Movement', together with two 'family representatives'. All over Spain there were then elections for the 108 'family representatives' in the Cortes, to which may be compared the 300 or so seats chosen by the ruling hierarchy; separatist Barcelona with 1·8 million voters had two seats, the same as the desert territory. In Spanish Sahara there was an 80 per cent vote.

However, the main event of 1967 was the inauguration of a general tribal assembly, a *yemaa* representing all Saharauis. To be elected every four years, it was to have eighty-two members, half being the tribe and fraction chiefs, with the Cabildo President and the mayors – if Saharaui – and the other half to be proportionally elected direct by the nomads from all levels. The minimum age for a councillor was to be twenty-one years. The Spanish Secretary-General sits in as 'assessor' but has no vote.

The allocations worked out to forty-nine Reguibat seats, the Boihat fraction holding eleven and the Suuad nine; ten Izarguien, seven Delim, five Arosien, four Tidrarin, two Ma el Ainin, two Lahsen, three others. Nearly the whole electorate voted. Having been elected as first president, Seila made one of his usual pro-Spanish speeches. The Governor-General, speaking in the tone of godfather to a new infant, told the tribes' representatives, one or two in European dress, that 'Your job is to tell us about matters of general interest to the territory . . .'. This was indeed the limit of their work, to produce opinions and suggestions. The importance and also the validity of the General Assembly was indignantly denied by Morocco, as will be described.

With the return of Ifni to Morocco in 1969, the Spanish-dominated desert was placed under a Dirección General de Promoción de Sahára; the journal *Africa*, short of news due to the diminishing number of territories, increased the size of its type-face and margins.

The second General Assembly election came in 1971, for the forty directly-chosen candidates. The fishing tribes were given a seat. A poll of 85–90 per cent was claimed in the towns, with 65 per cent overall; there were 280 candidates. The Reguibat Khatri, arrested not long before by the Spanish in connection with the 1970 clash, became President. A Delim, Baba uld Hasenna, became Vice-President. Commissions, each with 11 members, were set up in the shadows of some of those of the Spanish administration: Education, Agriculture, Livestock, Health, Commerce, Housing, Public Works, Wells, Tourism. In 1973 the Assembly was increased to 102 members.

Its meetings can last several days, the representatives coming in from all over the territory; in 1971 a building in Hispano-Saharan style was erected in El Aaiún for the Yemaa, Cabildo and Ayuntamiento. Recent issues discussed officially have been the choice of examiners for the posts of Arabic and Koran teachers, the limits to be set on livestock export, suitable places for new urban settlements, the continuing drought. It would be interesting to know what is discussed unofficially.

*The Legal System*
Laws of 1934 and 1953 extended the parallel lines of Spanish and local justice, the latter in its Koranic and *orf* sub-divisions. In 1961 the legal system was re-organised. As before, all Saharaui decisions are subject to Spanish acceptance.

The 1961 laws come under four headings: civilian, labour, military and Saharaui. Taking the first and starting at the bottom, there were to be Justices of the Peace in Villa Cisneros and La Guera; in 1972 this was extended to Smara, whilst Villa Cisneros, having reached 5,000 inhabitants, was given a District Court. A Municipal Court was installed at El Aaiún. Above all these came the Territorial Court, with its judge at the head of the judiciary in Spanish Sahara; this court combined the roles of the courts of First Hearing and of Instruction on the Peninsula. The territory's criminal cases would go before these courts, but civil suits involving a Saharaui on each side would only be judged by the Spanish on application by both parties.

Outside the territory came the Provincial and Territorial Courts of Las Palmas, giving second hearings, respectively, to criminal and civil cases from the Saharan Territorial Court.

The labour laws were to be as in Spain, with suitable modifications. As for military law, although stated to be separate from that applied by the judiciary, the Governor-General could take instant action over the judges' heads in matters of gravity such as discipline and public security. Decisions under Malikite and *orf* laws would need ratification by the Territorial Judge.

However, in 1955–6 more detailed laws had already been passed ensuring that the Spanish controlled the local legal system. A Malikite hierarchy had been formalised: minor judges spread over the territory, an appeal judge in El Aaiún, a High Court as final arbiter. The *orf* was dominated from within: District Native Tribunals, able to sentence to a month's imprisonment or 5,000 peseta fine, were subject to a Territorial Court in Villa Cisneros – headed by a Government Delegate – and to a High Court, composed entirely of Spaniards, in the capital.

Spanish statistics for civil and criminal cases are both fragmentary and unreliable. Between 1953–62 there were 940 arrests; between 1963–72 the published figure was four times as large. The peak year was 1970, with the repressed demonstration in June: 767 arrests and 54 sentences. But 1958, the year of the end of the minor war, has only 86 arrests and three sentences as its published figures. Throughout the twenty years, an average of 18 people is shown as in jail at the end of each December. In 1972 the Territorial and Municipal Courts dealt respectively with 83 and 20 cases. No details are available of the cases judged by Sancho Panza in the desert.

## Education

If one assumes it is desirable to take the children from the Sahara's delicately-balanced nomad society and train them to become a landless urban proletariat dependent upon a highly-artificial colonial organisation, then it can be said that the Spaniards' recent development of education in the territory has been admirable. In 1948 there were three schools only, two for Spanish children and one for Saharauis, with a total of ninety-one boys and girls. Table 7 shows the growth since, the figures as usual to be treated with caution; actual attendance in the nineteen-fifties was only one in three, but there are no recent estimates. The effects of the minor war can be seen on the figures for 1958–9: the local children were withdrawn at once but soon went back, whilst three out of five Spanish children appear to have been sent to safer places for the subsequent year.

Education is free, together with books, three meals a day and unlimited milk; the child is given shoes and clothing, these European, with a covering smock or *babi*. Grants are distributed – for example, fifty averaging 6,600 pesetas for the year 1966 – and Spain's General Trade Union pays for technical training on the peninsula.

The town child's education may begin at three to six years in a *crèche*, not yet widespread. The boy or girl then goes to an infant school and next to a graded primary, these in each case being subdivided into 'sections' spread around the settlement. If the child is

Table 7: *Education statistics, 1953–72*

| Year Ending | 1953 | 1954 | 1955 | 1956 | 1957 | 1958 | 1959 | 1960 | 1961 | 1962 | 1963 | 1964 | 1965 | 1966 | 1967 | 1968 | 1969 | 1970 | 1971 | 1972 |
|---|---|---|---|---|---|---|---|---|---|---|---|---|---|---|---|---|---|---|---|---|
| **PRIMARY** | | | | | | | | | | | | | | | | | | | | |
| Sections | — | 7 | 8 | 10 | 8 | 7 | 6 | 21 | 23 | 23 | 30 | 39 | 44 | 40 | 72 | 73 | 74 | 96 | 99 | 137 |
| Spanish Teachers | 6 | 6 | 8 | 10 | 8 | 9 | 6 | 16 | 17 | 18 | 30 | 40 | 37 | 37 | 76 | 73 | 72 | 104 | 113 | 144 |
| Saharaui Teachers | 2 | 2 | 3 | 3 | 2 | 1 | 1 | 5 | 16 | 16 | 16 | 22 | 15 | 15 | 30 | 30 | 30 | 30 | 58 | 60 |
| Spanish Pupils | 125 | 127 | 220 | 232 | 156 | 185 | 105 | 263 | 283 | 294 | 347 | 668 | 850 | 759 | 1230 | 1142 | 1364 | 1659 | 2144 | 2668 |
| Saharaui Pupils | 118 | 132 | 191 | 206 | 23 | 152 | 139 | 787 | 1009 | 1104 | 1031 | 1051 | 1162 | 821 | 1362 | 1304 | 1285 | 1328 | 1736 | 2516 |
| Sp and Sah. Adult Pupils | 108 | 116 | 136 | 250 | 62 | 108 | 122 | 84 | 130 | 117 | 365 | 300 | 294 | — | 2382 | 2128 | 1008 | 580 | 800 | 1292 |
| **SECONDARY** | | | | | | | | | | | | | | | | | | | | |
| Spanish Pupils | — | — | — | — | — | — | — | — | — | — | — | 217 | 273 | 435 | 507 | 755 | 933 | 932 | 1108 | 883 |
| Saharaui Pupils | — | — | — | — | — | — | — | — | — | — | — | 23 | 59 | 93 | 149 | 229 | 276 | 234 | 244 | 141 |

going on to secondary education, there are the National Institutes in El Aaiún and Villa Cisneros, opened in 1963; each has a hostel for children from the interior, housing forty and thirty respectively. There are all-Saharaui rural schools, taking all ages, at a dozen minor settlements across the territory; a new project is for ten teachers to move with the nomads, living in caravans towed by Land-Rovers and teaching in special tents.

The Spaniards describe how, before formal education can begin, the little Saharauis have to be taught 'the elementary notions of civilisation', together with the Spanish language. They have their own teachers of the Koran, religious ritual and Hassaniya Arabic. By 1967 it was estimated that some 44 per cent had school places and it was intended to offer a place to every child by 1974. Many details are lacking for secondary education but it seems likely that the two schools opened in 1963 with about 20 teachers, this reaching a staff of 74 by 1970. During the year ending in 1972, there had been 499 boys and 386 girls on the European register and 133 boys and 6 girls on the Saharaui; an evenly-spread two-thirds passed the year, including all five Saharaui 'Pre-University' boys out of the 35 pupils in this grouping. For 1968–72 there was on average one Saharaui receiving secondary education to four Spaniards.

In 1967 a technical School for Professional Training was opened in El Aaiún, followed by a second in Villa Cisneros. Simultaneously, nine-month courses were inaugurated at a Civil Service Training Centre; these taught local administration and trained Arabic teachers and Malikite-law judges. The spread of education within the territory was reflected in Madrid when, in 1972, the university opened its Institute of Oriental and African Studies.

The second half of the nineteen-sixties brought new life to adult education. Radio stations in the two main towns began to send out the daily programmes of 'Cultural Transmissions of the Sahara'; the 300 registered pupils, two-thirds being adult illiterates, were visualised gathered around transistors in tents in the desert, following the course for fifteen hours a week with the aid of free books. The Army, which had already opened its own primary school, announced a School for Applied Arts and was also given its own radio programme, this to educate soldiers for the baccalaureate or school-leaving examination.

Political education is not lacking, of course. The association of the Feminine Section of the Falange with the Saharaui girls and women has been mentioned. The usual para-military youth camps include Saharaui boys: they are often sent to Spain on these, to be 'freed from the fatalism brought on by an upbringing in tribal life'. The older people look on unhappily.

*Health*

Table 8 gives the most interesting available statistics. It too reflects the 1957–8 fighting and also the advent of the prospectors in 1961. The factor of up to eight times as many Saharaui as European deaths in hospital can be ascribed to their being comparatively few old Spaniards in the colony, to the departure of serious Spanish cases elsewhere and to the slowness of the Saharauis in reaching the hospitals.

For many years the only doctors were those of the army; it is said they would always treat the nomads, without charge. In 1972 there were 'hospitals' in El Aaiún, Villa Cisneros and La Guera, with 157, 75 and 12 beds respectively; there were 'dispensary-infirmaries' at Smara and Ausert, the former with ten beds; finally, there were fourteen 'dispensaries', some with beds, and three 'sanitary posts', these at Miyec, Amgala and Aguenit, remote places of importance to the traveller. Average time in hospital is about two weeks. Included in the staffs are interpreters and about twenty Salesian nuns. The ratios of doctors to the territory's inhabitants and of these to each hospital bed are both good. There are various forms of social security and sickness benefits.

The health authority has attacked both the endemic and the transitory diseases by campaigns of vaccination, immunisation and by other means. The incidence of tuberculosis, usually in the lungs, appears to be dropping; the sanatorium is in Las Palmas. Syphilis, usually already advanced when the sufferer comes for treatment, is certainly not conquered; and the Saharauis tend to give up treatment once there is a slight improvement. Until 1968 there were one or two leprosy cases a year, but none have been recorded since.

In most years there is a dramatic onslaught by a passing disease. In 1953 a plague panic spread, as many died from eating rotten camel-flesh, recorded Lodwick. Three years later the famine, due to drought and locusts, allowed a 'flu epidemic, filling the hospitals; this was repeated after a deluge in November of the following year. In 1962 the poor water and sewage systems produced thirty-one cases of typhoid fever. Some statistics can only have a cultural significance: appendicitis, in 1962, brought in 101 Europeans but only eighteen Saharauis. Presumably the forty-two cases of malignant tumour suddenly hospitalised in November 1967 are to be linked to the arrival of a specialist or new equipment. July 1972 produced seventy-four cases of trachoma, a complaint at its worst in summer. From the nineteen-sixties there has been some increase in injuries from work and traffic. The Spaniards fear the nomads' enormous and accelerating sugar consumption will have a bad effect.

Table 8: *Medical statistics, 1953–72*

| | 1953 | 1954 | 1955 | 1956 | 1957 | 1958 | 1959 | 1960 | 1961 | 1962 | 1963 | 1964 | 1965 | 1966 | 1967 | 1968 | 1969 | 1970 | 1971 | 1972 |
|---|---|---|---|---|---|---|---|---|---|---|---|---|---|---|---|---|---|---|---|---|
| Medical centres | 4 | 4 | 6 | 10 | 10 | 12 | 8 | 5 | 10 | 10 | 10 | 20 | 21 | 19 | 19 | 19 | 19 | 19 | 19 | 22 |
| Hospital beds | — | — | — | — | — | — | — | — | — | — | — | — | — | 193 | 202 | 204 | 236 | 226 | 262 | 262 |
| Qualified staff | 4 | 4 | 5 | 5 | 5 | 9 | 6 | 7 | 13 | 14 | 17 | 20 | 19 | 23 | 24 | 20 | 18 | 18 | 18 | 22 |
| Auxiliary staff | 12 | 12 | — | — | — | 34 | 25 | 38 | 85 | 90 | 87 | 78 | 79 | 87 | 88 | 91 | 81 | 78 | 102 | 107 |
| Hospitalised | 240 | 930 | — | 680 | 640 | 3600 | 1800 | 1200 | 1900 | 1900 | 1900 | 1900 | 2200 | 2300 | 2600 | 2500 | 2600 | 2300 | 3000 | 3200 |
| TB | — | — | — | — | — | — | — | — | — | — | — | — | — | 232 | 310 | 175 | 266 | 95 | 73 | 184 |
| VD | — | — | — | — | — | — | — | — | — | — | — | — | — | 81 | 122 | 102 | 170 | 153 | 102 | 126 |
| Bacillar Dysentery | — | — | — | — | — | — | — | — | — | — | — | — | — | 76 | 13 | 7 | 15 | 22 | 22 | 61 |
| Whooping Cough | — | — | — | — | — | — | — | — | — | — | — | — | — | 9 | 117 | 344 | 671 | 102 | 111 | 918 |
| Measles | — | — | — | — | — | — | — | — | — | — | — | — | — | 991 | 252 | 811 | 573 | 656 | 1266 | 1489 |
| Chicken Pox | — | — | — | — | — | — | — | — | — | — | — | — | — | 9 | 267 | 27 | 33 | 259 | 495 | 111 |
| Infectious Hepatitis | — | — | — | — | — | — | — | — | — | — | — | — | — | 265 | 405 | 241 | 587 | 339 | 174 | 146 |
| Trachoma | — | — | — | — | — | — | — | — | — | — | — | — | — | 44 | 24 | 8 | 2 | 3 | 7 | 112 |
| Influenza | — | — | — | — | — | — | — | — | — | — | — | — | — | 1217 | 1032 | 2528 | 3387 | 203 | 3015 | 3991 |
| Deaths per 1,000 Treated – Spanish | 48 | — | — | 2 | 9 | 22 | 3 | 12 | 6 | 15 | 7 | 6 | 9 | — | — | — | — | — | — | — |
| Saharaui | 24 | 6 | 29 | 15 | 26 | 20 | 24 | 34 | 27 | 37 | 22 | 48 | 34 | — | — | — | — | — | — | — |

There is a saying that the louse has *baraka,* so that all good Moslems have a few. To the nomads, the writing must have seemed on the wall as the first European fumigation teams moved into the tents.

## Urbanisation

Expansion into the interior in 1934 brought El Aaiún into being and led to the installation of the small military posts at key water-points. Since 1949 there have been land-laws which, on paper, safeguard the nomads' rights, rule over transfers to Spaniards and lay out the particularly-high authority needed to sanction land-acquisition by anybody else. From 1960 the three coastal settlements began rapid public and private development, together with expansion at the capital's landing place, Aaiún Playa; stone dwellings for Saharauis were put up at many of the inland posts, with a small town of a few hundred people being laid out at Smara. The settlements, designed for the most part in monotonous grids, have the characteristics of the typical small Spanish town, together with studied versions of some of the essential elements of north-west African communities, such as the mosques, *souks* and artisan quarters. Noticeable are a few buildings, in a new Hispano-Saharan style, and the overwhelming area occupied by the army. The towns have the public amenities normal to Spain, the important water-supply described already. By 1972 there were five power stations of 3,450 kW total output, in that year giving out some nine million kWh to consumers, including street-lighting, in the towns; one scheme to help solve the fuel problem was to cut a canal from the Atlantic to the vast salt-pan of Tah, fifty metres below sea-level, the falling water to turn turbines and, on evaporation, to yield various minerals too. Each town was given a coat-of-arms in the middle of the nineteen-fifties.

El Aaiún, now with 15,000–20,000 inhabitants, rises up the several shelly terraces of the southern bank of the Saguiet-el-Hamra. Its central square, faced by the frescoed façade of the hospital, the whitewashed church and other important edifices, holds a small well-watered park with refreshment kiosks. By Franco's wish in 1950, the churches of both El Aaiún and Villa Cisneros were designed by the architect responsible for the Valle de los Caídos outside Madrid. The ochre-coloured government buildings and the *parador,* the State hotel, are significantly reminiscent of the south Moroccan *ksour,* fortified dwellings; parades are frequent, including the regular changing of the guard. Religious processions are now more frequent than in the past. Moving outwards and upwards from the centre, the traveller passes through piecemeal and planned quarters of Spanish and Saharaui houses, with much construction in progress; the airfield is clearly indicated but the patch of ground where the 1970 bloodshed occurred is discreetly enclosed by a barbed-wire fence. In the opposite direction, the steep rubbish-festooned drop below the lowest terrace leads the intrepid to the edge of the foetid lagoon. This is a centre for wild-life, from the bacteria around the sewage pipes through leeches, crustaceans and mullet to the ruddy shelduck and flamingoes. Goats hunt for food along the garbage-coated shores. The lagoon is ponded up by rippling yellow dunes, the sand also lying in sheets against the further wall of the canyon. Little white towers, in fact ringing the whole town, were once the Spaniards' look-out posts; abandoned, they are used by the local youths for practices such as the illegal *kif*-smoking. The Morocco-bound road crosses the lagoon on a causeway, there passing through the last barracks, the cement works and a nomad camp, to disappear up a dry north-going *wadi*.

The long narrow peninsula on which Villa Cisneros is built, with its beaches, cliffs and marine fauna, contrasts with the desert and dry watercourse setting of the capital. Villa Cisneros has some 5,000–10,000 inhabitants; clean, very regular in plan, it looks down on a good harbour and the excitement of the returning fishing boats and the Canary Island steamers. The vantage point is a square of richly-coloured exotic plants and trees, backed by the modern architecture of the church and, in a corner, by the Spaniards' first fortress, now holding the post office and a games pitch; there is no longer a field-gun pointing at the Moors' Door.

La Guera, with 500–750 people, is characterless but for the ancient and weathered fort-cum-fishing-factory on the end of a curving spit of sand-drifted rock; the arms of the Marcotegui company, a shark and a dolphin, still crown the entrance that leads off the platform above the breakers. In the afternoon, figures appear amongst the dunes to the north, on a broad track which makes a wide detour around the customs post in the centre of the peninsula. Single or in little groups, silent and purposeful Mauritanians pad into the main street, usually making for the 'Bazaar Brahim'. Each fills a sack with boxes of cigars, cigarettes and other high-duty merchandise. Then, in the dusk, the figures plod away again across the cooling sands. The goods go to Nouadhibou, Atar and Zouerate; these more active towns, respectively with 11,000, 10,000 and 16,000 inhabitants in 1970, underline La Guera's somnolence. To its south stretches C. Blanc: the monk seals off the tip are usually visible, whilst the gigantic MIFERMA mine's loading terminal, Point Central, the dunes puce with its drifted ore-dust, is conspicuous at all times.

Table 9: *Construction work, 1953–72*

| Built | 1953 | 1954 | 1955 | 1956 | 1957 | 1958 | 1959 | 1960 | 1961 | 1962 | 1963 | 1964 | 1965 | 1966 | 1967 | 1968 | 1969 | 1970 | 1971 | 1972 | Totals |
|---|---|---|---|---|---|---|---|---|---|---|---|---|---|---|---|---|---|---|---|---|---|
| Houses | 13 | 14 | 7 | 4 | 7 | 3 | 20 | 157 | 289 | 84 | 102 | 202 | 1070 | 996 | 758 | 446 | 146 | 587 | 48 | 92 | 5045 |
| Misc. | 3 | 5 | 6 | 0 | 4 | 2 | 24 | 99 | 25 | 15 | 28 | 46 | 23 | 21 | 71 | 53 | — | 51 | 11 | 14 | 501 |

*Housing*

After seventy years as a colony, the territory had some thousand buildings, 700 of these being dwelling houses; these figures included Tarfaya and Tan-Tan, then the largest settlements after El Aaiún, and in Moroccan hands since 1958. Table 9 shows the immense construction programme under way since 1960, one of the indications that the Spanish have been intending to stay some time in this desert. The 1972 figure of 5,000 houses is difficult to relate to the population since different dwelling needs are ascribed to Spanish and Saharauis, the latter's 'fourth-class' houses being 'suited to their way of life' rather than inferior, it is explained.

The architects have described the problems of construction in the desert. A great part of the materials has had to be imported, those for El Aaiún landed in amphibians for lack of a deepwater quay. The structures had to be made resistant to the wide temperature range and to damage from internal condensation; air spaces, cement blocks and a minimum of metal were normal. Remote places such as Tifariti, Guelta Zemmour and Ausert – the last was once called 'the garden of the Sahara' because of its acacias – saw the erection of prefabricated buildings.

The streets are preferably laid out to cut the north wind. The Spaniards live in modest flats and villas, the latter with gardens. The 'more civilised' Saharauis get houses, some with domes and with patio-ventilation in the old Andalucian style, others shaped like Nissen huts. The most innovatory are the hexagonal buildings forming an irregular cluster on the southern side of El Aaiún: for the newly-sedentarised nomad who is still inseparable from his flock, each face of the hexagon holds two wedge-shaped dwellings, with alleys leading to individual animal pens in the centre. Roads were not laid to these houses, to make the transition from the tents easier. There was an extensive *bidonville* on the south side of El Aaiún in 1975: the preceding stage to receiving the little house in Calle Reguibat is for the nomad to spend a last period – used for reconnaissance and acclimatisation – in a tent or hut on the town's edge.

*Communications*

The three most important frontier posts are at Tah, on the route between Tan-Tan and El Aaiún, and in the middle of the C. Blanc peninsula and at Guelta Zemmour. From Tan-Tan a tarmaced road runs along the coast as far as Wadi Chebika – it will eventually reach Tarfaya, then being 250 km long – after which drivers make their way up and down a few more deep ravines, then across the soft dunes and so, either by way of the edge of the Tah pan or of the coastal Tarfaya, to the frontier and its line of lice-infested cardboard shanties. The post is most easily passed through on the days set for the exchange of goods between the Moroccan and Saharaui lorry convoys; in 1974 this was taking place on Mondays and Thursdays. The Spanish side is tarmaced over much of the distance to El Aaiún, the route being through the strategic post of Daora. From the capital a good road covers the twenty-five kilometres to Aaiún Playa, the port, through oil-controlled dunes; the track down the coast to C. Bojador is being improved. Inland from El Aaiún runs a tarmaced road to Smara, 245 km, with the surfaced side-road to the Bu Craa mine.

In fact, tyre-marks radiate in all directions across the desert from El Aaiún. The many Land-Rovers, usually made at the Santana works on the peninsula, can go almost everywhere. Even off the more or less cleared routes it is normal to keep up an indicator speed of 75 kph for long stretches.

The key interior routes are all unsurfaced. Smara is linked through Mahbes to Tindouf; the tempting itinerary of Foum el Hassan–Tindouf–Smara suffers from its first leg being mined, a remnant of the 1963 Moroccan–Algerian war, and a Volkswagen and its Australian passengers were recently blown up. The route to Guelta Zemmour is across the desert from Bu Craa; on the other side of the frontier lies the Imperial Way, along its stretch of Tindouf–Ain ben Tili–Bir Moghrein–F'Derick.

From Villa Cisneros an astonishingly-broad highway runs north to the level of Herne Island at the back of the bight, there linked by a black strip of shattered macadam to the satellite development at Argub. In the very south, the military post of Bir Gandus has a surfaced road to La Guera and this is joined to Nouadhibou by a busy nine-kilometre highway; further into Mauritania, from Nouadhibou, there are only desert tracks. It will be a long time before the projected La Guera–Villa Cisneros–El Aaiún road is in existence.

The number of vehicles licensed in the territory each year is given in Table 10; during 1955–71 a total of 5,500 vehicles was imported, compared to a thousand newly registered with the 'SH' in 1972. Public transport overland is assured – in its discomfort and uncertainty – by three classes of vehicles. Maximum contact with the desert can be enjoyed by riding for a day or two on the cargo of a long-distance lorry, exposed to the 24-hour alternation of heat-dust and cold-damp – with luck witnessing the year's only rain – and sharing the frequent breakdowns, sand-mirings and route-altercations with the voyaging Saharauis and their animals, with sleep wherever the crew or the lorry choose to stop; so far the known maximum number of passengers carried in the back of a single smallish lorry has been

Table 10: *Vehicles licensed, 1953–71*

| | 1953 | 1954 | 1955 | 1956 | 1957 | 1958 | 1959 | 1960 | 1961 | 1962 | 1963 | 1964 | 1965 | 1966 | 1967 | 1968 | 1969 | 1970 | 1971 |
|---|---|---|---|---|---|---|---|---|---|---|---|---|---|---|---|---|---|---|---|
| Cars | 25 | 29 | 10 | 29 | 29 | 89 | 134 | 102 | 325 | 412 | 505 | 792 | 1196 | 1447 | 1846 | 2233 | 2759 | 3289 | 3885 |
| Lorries and Coaches | 23 | 23 | 19 | 24 | 24 | 31 | 56 | 146 | 378 | 404 | 187 | 204 | 221 | 217 | 197 | 221 | 250 | 284 | 322 |
| Motorcycles | — | — | 1 | 2 | 2 | 10 | 11 | 2 | 14 | 35 | 114 | 138 | 150 | 174 | 199 | 213 | 217 | 223 | 229 |
| Bicycles | 3 | 14 | 16 | 13 | 12 | 25 | 37 | 50 | 61 | 70 | 85 | 70 | 120 | — | 191 | 208 | 228 | 195 | 425 |

forty-three, all foreigners. A place in a rapid Land-Rover taxi, which takes thirteen adults inside, costs about double a lorry place. As a guide, Tan-Tan to Tah takes a minimum of twenty-four hours on a lorry, with the mentioned problems together with brawls and military activity extending this endlessly; a Land-Rover driver will insist he can do the journey in twelve hours.

The coach service is tolerable but scanty. On the two frontier days a coach leaves El Aaiún around 6 a.m. for Tah, returning by noon. On Mondays, Wednesdays and Fridays there are early coaches to Smara from El Aaiún and Mahbes, the following day returning to these. There is a frequent service from El Aaiún to its port. The Villa Cisneros bight is partially circled by the coach to Argub. Hitch-hiking is only possible in non-African vehicles; a Saharaui will usually stop but will ask for payment.

The approach by sea, with the unceasing swell, is usually made from the Canaries aboard the aged steamers of the Ciá Trasmediterranea, for example the *Leon y Castillo*; there are two itineraries, weekly via El Aaiún and Villa Cisneros, fortnightly via Villa Cisneros, La Guera and Nouadhibou. There are seven lighthouses down the territory's coast.

The desert shore has few natural anchorages. The only semblance of shelter at El Aaiún is a patch of sunken rocks at the present port. In the middle of the nineteen-sixties a 250 m jetty, with only 1·40 m of water at low tide, was built to take loads from three launches which were to shuttle to and fro to freighters anchored out at sea; the water deepens at the rate of five metres to a kilometre. However, it has been found simpler to continue to use a fleet of amphibious vehicles from World War II for unloading cargoes and passengers. The enormous phosphate quay receives official freight of large size.

Villa Cisneros has a good harbour, though it is subject to silting. The bay is entered over a six-metre bar, the deepest of several channels, about 500 m off the peninsula, then leading to the 100 m-long outer wharf of an F-shaped quay about 450 m in length; the maximum size of vessel is 6,000 tons with six-metre draught. La Guera has a small calm jetty sheltered by the factory promontory, landings being by launch and towed-barge from vessels anchored out at sea. Small-boat jetties are projected for Angra da Cintra, Puerto Rico, Morro del Ancla and C. Bojador.

The Iberia airline links the three coastal towns to the Canaries and the peninsula. There are also flights from Nouadhibou to Morocco and to France. The small company CANAIR flies a route Canaries–El Aaiún–Smara. There are military airstrips at the interior posts. Fog at Dakar occasionally brings foreign airlines' planes into Villa

Cisneros; the first jet airliner to land, German, was forced down at El Aaiún in 1966. The Spaniards' hopes that Villa Cisneros would become an international halt between Europe and South America have not been realised.

The limited telecommunications network has always been in the hands of the army. In 1966 a few public call-boxes were installed and in 1970 work was begun on private telephones for the towns' residents. Telegraphy, until recently by radio transmitter, is now modernised; international co-operation is still however at a primitive stage, since telegrams from La Guera to Nouadhibou go by way of Madrid, Paris and Nouakchott.

*Culture*

When, a couple of decades ago, the nomads first became interested in goods like detergents and toothpaste, some did believe there was a 'power' behind each. Spanish culture, using the word in its narrowest sense, is now available in many of its aspects to all the inhabitants of the coastal desert. In fact, it was as long ago as 1963 that Muley Ali uld Mohamed Fadel had a maximum win, nearly two million pesetas, on the pools; a waiter who had never seen a football match, he announced that he would enter commerce. Many an old Saharaui warrior must have shaken his head, knowing that a true son of the clouds can only become rich from camel-rearing, pillage and shipwrecks.

In 1966 Franco pressed a button in the Pardo Palace and the Saharauis were able to see a television programme on their own land and way of life, the first transmission to the desert; this was relayed from Izaña in the Canaries. Radio Sáhara, a 5kW transmitter on 641 Kc medium wave, sends out programmes in Castilian and in Hassaniya Arabic. The main towns each have a cinema. In 1963 the periodical *Sáhara* was first published, a thousand copies: the 'excusable lack of news' was made up for by many articles by army officers.

The towns have small libraries. A museum has been projected for El Aaiún; there is a 1965 law against removing artistic or historic objects from the territory . . . other than to museums in Spain, of course. There are the usual peninsular 'cultural circles' with art exhibitions, lectures and occasional festival of documentary films. The 'Queen of Spring' *fiesta* included a battle of flowers – these presumably imported – and fireworks, a procession, the Maria Rosa ballet company and a beauty queen.

*Foreign Travellers and Tourists*

'The doors of Spanish Sahara are open to the whole world', a Spanish journalist wrote recently. However, the intending traveller will soon find that the Spanish authorities, tourist offices and transport companies – both inside and outside Spain – are part of a conspiracy of silence and unhelpfulness aimed at ensuring that the rest of the world does not get into the territory. It has long been so: Lodwick waited three months for a visa in 1955. However, it is now usually a waste of time to apply for a visa other than in the Canaries or at the land-frontier posts themselves. Tickets to travel to the territory by Spanish boat or plane will usually not be issued unless visas are produced.

The popular Tah approach route is also the most difficult. A preliminary to leaving south Morocco is the thorough search for arms made at the King's army post of Tenuachad, usually in a gale and, due to the schedule of the vehicles, by headlamps in the night. It is essential to travel in a vehicle passing through Tarfaya, in order to obtain a Moroccan exit stamp to show at the frontier post twenty-five kilometres away, not entrusted with the work. Equally essential are the varying vaccination certificates demanded by the Spanish immigration control; these could be obtained, by the tyro, at Tarfaya, by paying a high price to the one man in the market who holds the blanks and a further sum to the hospital orderly who signs them, with or without the injections themselves. For north-going travellers, Moroccan entry stamps are best obtained at Tarfaya, though it may be possible to get these at Goulimine.

At Tah, the Spanish Secret Police will give the average non-African foot-traveller a four-day 'safe-conduct' to go to El Aaiún and get the first boat out to Las Palmas. His passport will be checked again at Daora, a third time at the town's entrance; within, he must at once report to the Secret Police, well known in their unsignposted office behind the Iberia building. Africans can be kept waiting indefinitely at the frontier, or merely refused entry, even for transit.

Alternatively, foot-travellers will arrive on the steamers. At El Aaiún they will be given a rotting life-jacket each and, clambering down the ladder of the pitching steamer, go ashore in one of the wallowing amphibians, the spray and perhaps the waves washing across the open platform. Passengers for Mauritania will do best to leave the steamer at La Guera, being towed ashore and then rapidly removed to Nouadhibou by the Territorial Police.

Some of the means and problems of travel within the territory have been covered already. The inter-town flights miss each other by an hour or two, so that it takes a couple of days to fly down the coast, presumably to make the route unattractive. Travellers going overland should have a sleeping bag and carry food, preferably also a tent or plastic dew-sheet; it is a good idea to ally with other voyagers, bargain

out the hire prices in advance, then pay only on arrival – or there can
be a threat of abandonment somewhere in the desert unless more
money is produced – and to turn to the Spanish police for help. The
Saharauis, for whom caravan-interception, pillage and ransom were
the highest arts, expect argument and only respect strength.

Travellers in vehicles wishing to drive across the territory have to
wait for special authorisation, most easily obtained at Tah rather
than at the other frontier posts. Printed conditions of entry include
the possession of a minimum sum of money, £100–£200 according to
intended length of stay, and the employment of an official guide from
frontier to frontier, at the traveller's expense. If transit is granted, the
routes allowed will depend on any military actions at the time; it may
be necessary to travel in a protected convoy. On each side of the
frontier, the driver may be asked: 'Have they got any tanks up?'
The writer, after waiting for a week at La Guera for permission to go
overland to Villa Cisneros, resorted to a telegram, to the British Consul in the Canaries, denouncing the delay as a breach of the Human
Rights Charter; read of course by the tight-roping Spanish authorities, the visa was granted later the same day.

Almost needless to say, all vehicles should be in first-class condition, equipped with sand-runners, spare parts, fuel reserves and
adequate water. In August 1973, an ill-prepared Land-Rover taxi
carrying eleven Saharauis lost the Route Impériale between Bir
Moghrein and F'Derick, then broke down, with no survivors; a
Saharaui can last about two days without water in this area in midsummer. The main settlements have pumps and repair shops: fuel
is usually cheaper than on the peninsula. The maps lack adequate
detail; a 'road' or 'track' often indicates no more than the general
direction taken between two places.

Accommodation is not only poor and expensive but also limited,
since the few beds are taken by development workers and by soldiers
on leave from the interior posts. The El Aaiún *parador* was opened in
1968; costing 32 million pesetas, it has a swimming pool and the full
*folklórico* atmosphere. The tolerable Hostal Barcelona is always full
and the traveller will normally find himself with the agonising choice
between a night in the open and the Pensión Mensahud; combining
all roles, Mensahud himself is said to be an ex-slave who has become
a millionaire and recently lent the Spanish money for local development. At Smara there is a single room in González's Bar. Villa
Cisneros has the excellent 'Casa de los Curas', run by the missionaries;
its name is forbiddingly mispronounced 'Casa de Locura' by the
Andalucian population. The traveller may hear of the seventy-bed
*parador* built by Iberia in 1948 at Villa Cisneros, in the expectation

that the airport would become an international halt: the airline now uses the building for its own purposes. La Guera has two pensions; if Villa Cisneros has bad water, at La Guera any at all should be gratefully accepted. At Nouadhibou, assuming the traveller's funds have survived the application of Mauritania's latest currency laws, there is the Hotel Imraguen: in 1974 it was charging 900 *ouguiyas* or £9 for a double room. Alternatively, in the *bidonville* beside the football pitch there is a Senegalese called Ahmed, his old career in oriental dancing, who gives full board and lodging for under a pound a day.

In sharp contrast to the travellers whom the previous pages will interest are the elegant, clean tourists who arrive on expensive package flights from the Canaries. Driven along an airport road brightened, as usual, with lavishly-tended shrubs of a luxuriance unrecognisable to a nomad's camel, they are given a carefully-monitored programme of 'typical attractions' and then flown back the same day. The lush oasis of Meseyed, camel rides across Sahara dunes, tea in a nomad tent, perhaps with a little traditional singing and dancing, and then back to civilisation for supper. Mainly Scandinavians, the first 'Miss Turismo', in the 1969 Autumn Fiesta, was a Swede; there is also a 'Day of the Tourist'.

In 1968 it was decided to build a tourism complex, the Costa Brava in the desert, at Tifariti, 130 km south-east of Smara. Perhaps the region's clashes between the guerrillas and the Foreign Legion, involving bazooka and machine-gun fire, can be avoided during the tourist season.

# Chapter 13

# Internal Conflict, 1956–74

'We treat the native as a brother, a coloured Spaniard to be christian-ised and raised to our level', said an article in *Africa* in 1944. Thirty years later an Arab or a Berber was still *el moro* to the local Spaniard, a black man *el negro*; in La Guera, a negro will always be hailed as 'Samba'. Secondly, the *moro* and the *negro* are irreconcilable amongst themselves: black man equals goat, says the nomad, presumably measuring himself against the noble camel, whilst in the negro regions of Mauritania, mothers menace bad children with 'The Moor will come and take you away'. Internal politics have forced the Spaniards to leave the social positions largely untouched, even had they equality in mind; the black people cannot sit in the General Assembly since the tribes would never elect them, they are never to be seen in official photographs, they 'know their place' in queues, they carry out the lowest-grade manual work. Incoming Sudanese, notably the spirited richly-dressed curio-sellers, are bargained with good-humouredly by the Spaniards but ignored by the *beidane* or whites, as the nomads call themselves. The latter are however in turn sub-divided by tribe incom-patibilities and by the barrier between the sedentary and the wanderer. In these various divisions lies the deepest-seated source of conflict.

Closely associated with these racial and other barriers are various cultural differences, with religious beliefs beyond reconciliation. '*Nasrani*', shouts the Saharaui urchin at the passing European: 'christian', an insult. Each group considers itself spiritually the sup-erior: Cervera wrote in 1886 that the Saharauis felt the Spanish culture 'to be better . . . in a material sense, but . . . utterly to be condemned on all that relates to destiny and the future life of the spirit'. Within the desert community, the black people are feared for their knowledge of the occult, associated with their homeland to the south. Both African groups envy the wealth of the Europeans.

The return of the major African nations to independence rapidly polarised the territory's various differences. And, by the nineteen-seventies, the Spaniards realised it was the wall they could feel against their backs. However, those Saharauis whose priority has become material culture do see that they live better at present than they would under Morocco or Mauritania and so prefer to retain the Spanish and their economic support. These Saharauis include the old, who remember the difficulties of the past, and the sedentarised who have a share in the developing economy; the aim of the sedentarisation programme is of course to attach the nomads to the Spanish economy. A second group of Saharauis is demanding independence, no matter what the outcome. A third faction sees absorption by Morocco as the preferable future. Mauritania's claim to at least the south has support too, including amongst the black people: in Mauritania, the *beidane*, up to four-fifths of the population, have their backs turned to the Senegal and its black people – in fact the more evolved citizens, having been sedentary and thus easier to teach during the French administration – and would be nominally strengthened by the addition of the Saharauis and their vast desert. Resistance to the Spanish is strongest amongst the young.

This chapter will describe the sequence of internal politics – and the resort to violence by various factions – which have led to the interior tension and crisis of the time of writing.

*The Spaniards are Woken Up, 1957*

In 1950 Franco visited the territory. There had been a bad drought during the few previous years and the starving nomads were being given free barley and *gofio*, together with steamer tickets to the Canaries. At the frequent parades, the field guns and armoured cars rumbled past the saluting podium; the bedecked beasts of the Camel Corps filed docilely by, bearing nomads dressed in cloaks over white tunics, their pennant-adorned lances unlikely to lead to a revolt. The 'supreme dream' of the Saharaui was, apparently, to enjoy the status and comforts of service in the Spanish Army. Journalists and their cameras could be openly excluded – but then they rarely wished to enter. It did not matter much that, though the press referred to the 'wild enthusiasm' greeting the Caudillo, the photos showed only a few, serious Saharauis. Back in Madrid, Franco had the phosphate sample which Alia Medina had just given him, a fair exchange for the barley. All was well.

Then, in 1956, came Moroccan independence, part of the emergence of African nationalism. Spain had to agree to return the two Protectorates. However, Spanish Southern Morocco – 25,000 sq km with an estimated population of 6,000 people – was in fact held back because Spain feared the close presence of the Moroccan Army of Liberation, formed primarily to combat the French: whilst half had joined the new Royal Moroccan Army, the other half had gone south to help in the struggle against the Spanish and the remaining French administrations. The Spaniards, working from a colonial premise less widely accepted than in 1912, said that the 'anarchy' in Morocco meant they had a duty to continue in control; it was for the Sultan's own sake.

On 10 April 1956 there was an anti-Spanish demonstration in Ifni, the clash referred to as a 'vulgar brawl' by the Spaniards. Open hostility gradually developed, with intermittent murders of Spaniards and their supporters; a Spanish plane was hit over the Sahara territory. On 23 October 1957 the Army of Liberation talked to the Moroccan government in Rabat and then drafted 1,500 *moukhahidines*, freedom fighters, to Goulimine, and 600 to Bou Izarguen, towns near Ifni; the commander was Ben Hammu. Throughout November the force prepared for attack. The King – as the Sultan was now called – was involved in international negotiations over various other issues and would have preferred to be seen to be moderate but the Liberation Army, recently successful against the French, was not in the mood for compromise; it was also the means of expression of the extreme Istiqlal party and its 'Greater Morocco' territorial ambitions, described in Chapter 14.

On 21 November an informer brought the Ifni Spanish the news that the 'freedom fighters' were arming their volunteers at nearby Tafraut and that an attack was imminent. Morocco later claimed that the assailants were the Ait ba Amaran tribe of Ifni itself, and in 1974 a book was published describing their 'resistance': the Spanish reflex-claim has always been that their subjects are on their side . . . but on this occasion the press, not yet practised, did let out a single brief statement that, before the fighting began, it was noticed that Ifni tribesmen were leaving the territory, so it is likely that a number did fight against the Spaniards.

During the night of the 23rd the telephone wires to the frontier posts were cut and attacks launched on their garrisons and upon the airfield and arsenal of the capital itself, Sidi Ifni, built in the middle of the coast. The *moukhahidines* numbered 1,000–1,200 men. The Spaniards claimed their arms included Czech weapons, allowing them to raise the usual cry of 'Communists'; apparently the Liberation Army included veteran communists from the Civil War's International Brigade. The Spanish also said that 'peace-keeping guns given to Morocco' were used against them, permitting the accusation of ingratitude. The Liberation Army's weapons included automatic arms and mortars. The resident Spanish forces were small, due, it was claimed, to a moderate policy: three infantry battalions, the native police, three batteries of field artillery, in total 1,500 Spanish and 500 Ifni soldiers.

The greater part of these were in Sidi Ifni and here the attacks failed; significantly, it was thought necessary to disarm the local people and impose a curfew. At the isolated frontier posts the Spanish fought desperately; there is no information on the enthusiasm of the local troops. The only workable solution was seen to be to withdraw all the outlying garrisons to the capital, but this was to take two weeks; by then two posts had been lost to the Moroccans. The main actions were fought around the Tiliuin post in the very south. In co-operation with the air force in the Canaries, it took a week to organise a parachute drop in relief. At this point the archipelago was covered by some seventy planes, Junkers 52 and a few DC-3 of the 35th and 36th Transport Wing and the Heinkel 111 bombers of the 29th Group. The besiegers around Tiliuin were first bombed and then subjected to low-level gunning by five H-111, then five J-52 dropped the parachute Legionaries and a sixth a consignment of arms and supplies. The Spanish then re-took the Tiliuin airstrip long enough for an ambulance plane to evacuate their wounded, then fought their way back overland to Sidi Ifni. A second drop, to the Telata post, was inaccurately carried out and, after a twenty-five kilometre march, the paratroops were cornered when still five kilometres from their comrades, relief only coming after nine days. A special drop was made of *alpargatas*, light shoes, to a Legion unit; from the photographs of the troops crossing the desert, the uniforms appear designed for use in a Pyrenean winter campaign. The aviation was important because of the notorious difficulty of landing from the sea at Sidi Ifni; bad weather handicapped the aeroplanes during the fighting.

By 9 December the Spanish troops had all retrenched to the capital. The more conservative estimate of the garrison, by now re-inforced, was 7,500 men, with three cruisers alongside; the navy had anchored off Agadir for a day, resulting in a Moroccan protest. The Spaniards admitted to fifty-five dead, 128 wounded and seven missing. As fast as the outposts had been evacuated so they had been occupied by the 'freedom fighters', these claiming this as a victory . . . the Spaniards announced a successful retreat. The *moukhahidines* suffered many dead and wounded, filling the hospitals of Goulimine, Agadir and other towns. The Moroccan press claimed the Spanish air force had killed humans and animals near Agadir.

The Moroccan force now ringed Sidi Ifni. The Spaniards settled down in the role of besieged, using their local troops in sporadic but useless sorties 'because they knew the appropriate tactics'. In June a part of the garrison was withdrawn. Henceforth there was total press censorship over the Ifni siege. The moderation of the Spanish policy was due to a wish to avoid a major war with Morocco and, in fact, the Spaniards never re-occupied the outlying territory; in 1969 came the total abandonment of Ifni to Morocco.

The desert territory had been attacked simultaneously, though in a less effective manner. The garrisons at Tan-Tan, Villa Bens and Argub – this post on the approach to Villa Cisneros – were assaulted, as were garrisons in the interior; the Spanish at once fell back to the coast and their pre-1934 positions. The C. Bojador lighthouse, with its plaque to Gil Eannes and Henry the Navigator, was attacked and put out of action, its Saharaui keepers taken as prisoners to Morocco and still there over a year later; the Villa Bens–El Aaiún mail jeep was taken, though defended by a Saharaui corporal; tracks were mined by the attackers. In December, El Aaiún itself was approached, patrols and convoys being involved in pitched battles. The assailants were the Liberation Army together with contingents of the Spanish territory's Tekna and Reguibat tribesmen; the Spaniards later admitted this, though at the time their nomads were said to be demonstrating *en masse* hostility to the 'invaders'.

January 1958 saw continued fighting around the towns, and on the 12th El Aaiún was openly attacked. The incensed Legion was let loose and caught up with the *moukhahidines* at Edchera, close by to the south-east, and, in one of the war's major battles, inflicted a severe defeat, killing 241 against their own losses of fifty-one dead and wounded. The Spanish press henceforth referred to the 'Sahara Liberation Army', to avoid direct conflict with Morocco. It was said that the Saharauis were demanding arms to repel the 'invaders'. Spanish Sahara and Ifni were now turned into 'provinces', partly to demonstrate Madrid's intention to stay in the desert.

The Spaniards were at this moment engaged in an unmentionable negotiation. Traditional peninsular politics were to be seen as friends of the Arab countries . . . nevertheless, military necessity now pointed to a joint operation with the French of Mauritania. Simul- taneously the subject of the Liberation Army's attentions, it was equally clear to the French that the whole desert would need to be 'pacified', not just their own in the south and east. So, on 10 February, without publicity, the two European powers began a concerted campaign against the opposition in Spanish Sahara.

The Spaniards had by now increased their local air strength to about a hundred machines, including sea-planes and helicopters; some had to be flown down from Seville, amidst great excitement since their range only just allowed them to reach Ifni in one leg. Though a 1950 military study, underlining the lack of cover, had seen speed as the key to success, a further reminiscence of the Civil War was the plodding lines of soldiers and mules; the Santiago Cavalry Group was used. The Spanish forces were grouped under the Captain-General of the Canaries, Lieut-General López Valencia. The European assault used 9,000 Spaniards and 5,000 Frenchmen, respectively supported by 60 and 70 aeroplanes.

The first attack was upon the northern zone. Following aerial photographic reconnaissance, the Liberation Army strongholds between Tan-Tan and the Saguiet-el-Hamra were assaulted. The focus was Smara and, after preliminary bombing, this was taken by Spanish forces from El Aaiún and Villa Bens and French convoys from Ft Trinquet. Rocket-firing planes raked cave-strongholds in the banks of the Saguiet-el-Hamra; in spite of the apparent lack of cover, the Liberation Army was able to hide so well that low-level flying into the wind was needed to spot their units, resulting in some aeroplanes being hit. The Liberation Army lost 150 men and a large amount of materials.

On 21 February the Liberation Army concentrated between Bir Nazaran and Ausert was similarly defeated, this time by the Spanish from the capital and Villa Cisneros and by the French from Ft Gouraud. By early March the Europeans had 'pacified' the whole region again. It was estimated that camped around Agadir there were 12,000 tribesmen from Ifni, Spanish Southern Morocco, Spanish Sahara, Mauritania and Tindouf. The Moroccan press accused the Europeans of killing 600 men with a gas.

The Spaniards later published a few figures on the war. The air force carried out 354 bombing and gunning missions, using up 43,000 cartridges and 222 rockets; reconnaissance flights totalled 341; 427 men were dropped from 31 planes, 20 tons of material from 29 planes; a further 1,218 transport missions landed 900 tons of materials; nine crew were killed. The territory's hospitals took in 450 Europeans and 190 Africans in 1957, with four and five deaths respectively, the hospital cases rising to 3,246 Europeans and 349 Africans in 1958, with 71 and 6 deaths. The Spanish said that, in August 1959, the the Liberation Army held 39 prisoners, including the lighthouse family, and that all were being well treated; the Spaniards did not disclose information on their prisoners.

The Nationalists' Victory Parade on 4 May 1958 included para-troopers from the African Provinces' recent campaign. In 1966 the highest military award, the Cruz Laureado de S. Fernando, was posthumously awarded to two Spanish soldiers for covering their comrades' retreat at Edchera, after long hand-to-hand fighting, against an enemy five times the size of the Spanish force. A special

'Ifni-Spanish Sahara' medal was struck, the award conditions summarising Madrid's impressions of the war: three months service
during the 'general' period of hostilities, 11 August 1957 to 28
February 1958, or service during the entire 'active' period, 23 November to 22 December 1957 for Ifni and 12 January to 28 February
1958 for the desert, or actually fighting, flying missions over the
provinces, giving naval support, preparing campaigns or being
injured.

Now aware that Bens' sugar-lump policy would no longer be
effective, the Spaniards began to mix in manoeuvres used by other
European powers with those elements of their own naïve palaeo-
colonialist policy which they could not bring themselves to abandon.

## Internal Policy, 1958–74

The Spaniards have tried to stimulate a local sense of 'nationalism'
together with a fear of the surrounding states and of 'the red threat';
in 1963 they published a map of Africa showing communist domination to be 70–90 per cent in Morocco, 60–80 per cent in Mauritania
and Mali, 50–70 per cent in Algeria. Economic support has been
lavish, the graphs' curves highest during crises. Spaniard-Saharaui
brotherhood is underlined; a primitively-executed mural at the
entrance to a Villa Cisneros barracks shows a Spanish officer at the
apex of a human triangle, one of the lower corners – each a nomad
soldier – with his hand caressing his superior's cuff, whilst the other
corner pours out the mint tea. The sedentarisation programme was
inaugurated as the best long-term approach.

The leaders have been bought, with Khatri's nomadisations, for
example, apparently waited upon with help and supplies by the
administration; however, in traditional Saharaui fashion, the chiefs
manoeuvre uninhibitedly for their own ends. Prestige is also dis-
bursed: in 1966 Carrero Blanco gave out a total of sixteen Africa
Orders and twenty-five Imperial Orders of the Yoke and Arrows.
General hand-outs range, as described, from blankets to jet flights to
Mecca.

The pliant support this has usually engendered in turn allowed the
Spanish to announce local puppet representation in 1961 and its
'revitalisation' ten years later. A feature of the period since the
creation of the general *yemaa* has been the dialogue between this
assembly and Franco, an alternation of supplications by the former,
desperate to stay with the Spanish, and of reassurances by the latter
that he will never abandon his desert people. International pressure
for a self-determination referendum, discussed shortly, led to this
being scheduled for 1971: policy was to avoid all reference to it

internally, including in the press, and it was never held. Continuing international insistence and local resistance led to Franco's announcement, in September 1973, of 'progressive participation' for the Saharauis, as a 'necessary preparation' for self-determination; the programme would, as ever, be worked out according to principles to be laid down by the Spanish government. The Spaniards had already considered nominal independence with Seila as leader, but had decided the risks were too great. However, in 1974 the administration had again to announce a referendum, due early in 1975 – but again not held. Spain hoped to get a favourable vote, with the aid of the chiefs; a negative vote would leave it to try for a form of association with the territory, assuming this remained independent of its neighbours.

Policy over the phosphate discovery of 1947 was to remain silent, with phrases such as 'were mineral riches to be found' used in the mid-sixties. Eventually the vast mining complex could be hidden no longer: propaganda concentrated on two aspects, that it was a Spanish miracle of modern technology in the desert and that the wealth would remain in the territory. Though even if Spain wished to spend the profits in the desert, it is doubtful if this is the intention of the various foreign investors, their participation as enormous as that of the colonial administration. The mine is estimated to have a life of 85–170 years at the scheduled 10–20 million tons a year output.

Finally, there are various more or less subtle aspects of internal politics. The photo of the first elected Cabildo, in 1963, placed the Saharauis at the centre and the Spaniards at each side; in 1967 the Saharauis began to be referred to by the Spanish title of 'Don' rather than the Arabic 'Sid'; in 1970 the El Aaiún mayor appeared in a European suit. Carefully worded articles pour out, starting in 1958 with 'Independence, a Problem of Our Age'; the El Aaiún secondary school was opened with a lecture 'The Legal and Historical Rights of the Spanish Presence on the West Coast of Africa'. The voting urns at the various elections are placed upon typical Saharaui blankets. In 1963 there was created the Gold and Silver Camel Awards to the arts and sciences, in 1966 the Gold Medal of El Aaiún City to outstanding Africanists . . . its first recipient being Franco.

*Armed Conflicts, 1958–74*

A month after the combined Spanish–French 'mopping-up' operation, the Protectorate of Spanish Southern Morocco was returned to the King, on 10 April; the Spaniards affirmed that their terms had been accepted. The 'Villa Bens' garrison of 1,500 men was evacuated. However, the Moroccan motorised convoy of 1,000 soldiers, on its way to occupy 'Tarfaya', tried to use the route which crosses into Spanish Sahara and passes through Hagunia and Daora: needless to say the Spanish turned them back, protesting against the provocation. Morocco simply stated that it now did not recognise the latest frontier – that of the present territory – and to incite the Spanish further, installed a renegade from their own administration as first Tarfaya governor.

The loss of this buffer zone was immediately paralleled in the south and east: in November 1958 France acceded to Mauritania's demand for independence. The Spaniards were alone. To toughen the resistance, José Vásquez, at fifty-four the youngest division general, was made Governor-General: a model for the men, he had three sons, did not drink or smoke and had been wounded in the chest in the Civil War.

The appearance in 1960 of the Spanish and foreign oil prospectors, with the threat of their exploitation of the Saharauis' unlocated and therefore limitless wealth, brought on the next of the always-imminent crises. By January–February 1961 the Liberation Army was building up again along the northern frontier, the aerial reconnaissance estimate being a thousand men. By now the desert was patrolled by the Territorial Police, created the year before: offspring of the army and the Civil Guard, its members wear sand-coloured uniforms, dust-goggles and head-cloths, their arms including rifles and cartridge belts and their transport stripped-down Land-Rovers. The third Legion, 'Don John of Austria', was stationed throughout the north, together with the Nomad Group 'Saguiet-el-Hamra'; the Fourth Legion, 'Alexander Farnese', with the 'Capt. Gandara' Nomad Group, flew the red and yellow flag in the southern desert. There had been a big pay-rise for the Saharan army. The 1961 crisis brought the troops officially to 9,000 men, with as many again in Ifni; the navy and air force took up their active stations.

On 11 March a Union Oil prospection team was at work some twenty-five kilometres north-west of Hagunia and two kilometres from the northern frontier – in fact right on the track taken by the Moroccans in 1958. A Moroccan Army truck with armed and uni-formed men crossed the border and captured the prospectors, five Spanish, three Americans, two Canadians and a Frenchman, taking them and their lorries and gear to Tan-Tan. Rabat claimed the affair as the work of patriotic tribesmen. On 21 March the prospectors were handed back to their respective ambassadors in Rabat and the seized property returned to the Spaniards. In the meantime, however, on 14 March a jeep with four Italian prospectors in the pay of Morocco, and on its way from Tan-Tan to Puerto Cansado, had lost the route in bad weather and, short of fuel, decided to cross the border to seek help at the Union Oil camp. This apparently innocent coincidence was too good a chance for the Spaniards to miss so, perhaps with tongue in cheek, they delivered the Italians to their representative in the Canaries 'for their own sakes, in view of the Liberation Army activity along the border'. These prospectors were back in Morocco by 16 March. After returning the Union Oil men, Morocco relaxed the tension by a statement that it would rely on negotiation over the desert.

Subsequently, for almost a decade no serious incident appears to have occurred in the territory. The Moroccan and Saharan irregulars were still camped around the frontier but could not take effective action against the Spaniards' superior forces. These were demonstrated from time to time: in March 1968, for example, the air force carried out manoeuvres over Edchera, including rocket-firing 'with great precision' at targets in the Saguiet-el-Hamra bed. It was not chance that, in the same year, the firing squad of the 'Don John of Austria' Legion won the national shooting competition.

The most important incident since the 1957–8 clash occurred on 18 June 1970; it appears to have provoked the subsequent wave of anti-Spanish guerrilla activity. The colonial administration had organised a routine demonstration in favour of continued links with Spain. Moroccan and other opposition sources have claimed that a Saharaui group, 2,000 strong, turned up to demonstrate against Spain and for the King: the troops had opened fire, killing twelve and wounding several dozen of the counter-demonstrators. The terse Spanish statement was that the demonstration was disturbed by people from outside the territory, then shots were fired to which the police had to reply, killing 'two individuals of Negro race'. Repressive measures included many arrests, not least that of Khatri, of whose dissidence rumours had escaped during the previous years. Direct information in 1974 from a Smara legionary, not a Spaniard, was that whole 'villages' had been destroyed by the administration's forces, following the incident. Many fled across the borders; a young Mauritanian described to the writer the arrival of one fleeing Saharaui at his door in Bir Moghrein, exhausted and his feet lacerated from an unbroken crossing of the desert.

The Spanish troops were at once raised to 20,000 men, with accelerating modernisation and increased pay. A great parade of military strength was held: the Legion, Artillery, Engineers, Service Corps, Ambulance, Paratroops, Territorial Police and Nomad Troops. Air and naval manoeuvres were carried out simultaneously. Tanks were on show in 1971. Later, six native soldiers were sentenced for arms theft and the attendance of unauthorised meetings, probably of a movement called the 'Defence of the Saharan People'; the soldiers were said to be amongst the organisers of the counter-demonstration. However, 'credit' for the incident was also claimed by the equally-unknown NIDAM group, apparently established in 1969 and working from Algeria. These were the first two of the soon-proliferating and mostly ephemeral 'liberation movements', their number reminiscent of the tribes' inability to combine to resist the Europeans at the turn of the century.

In 1971 a new type of Saharaui appeared to oppose the Spaniards. Referred to in the Moroccan press as Edouard Moha, he was born in 1943 near Smara, in a Reguibat fraction. Educated in Morocco and France, in 1971 he formed a resistance movement which included a number of young intellectuals, some being students at the Mohammed V university in Rabat. Known as MOREHOB, the group's full title was the Mouvement de Résistance des Hommes Bleues. Recognised by the Organisation for African Unity, its creed – independence for the Blue Men – was however unacceptable to Morocco. Soon restricting MOREHOB's activities, Rabat eventually withdrew Moha's passport, so that in April 1973 the movement transferred its headquarters to Algiers. Not necessarily by coincidence, this town is also the base of a Canary Island independence movement, under the lawyer Antonio Cubillo. MOREHOB's political activities include, in November 1972, denying the population statistics submitted to the UN by the Spanish, these figures being relevant to the proposed referendum; in January 1973 appealing to the Pope to stop the Spanish church persecuting Moslems; in June 1973 calling on 'Arab progressive youth' to create an international brigade to help 'the Moslem peoples oppressed by Franco'; and a general cry for joint military action by the three countries surrounding Spanish Sahara. In the desert itself, and in spite of its declared intention to use guerrilla tactics, MOREHOB does not seem to have been active, unless one includes its claim to have met in 1973 at La Guera, there deciding that the flag of the future 'Republic of the Arab Sahara' would be a blue crescent and star on a white background.

After a lull in 1971, guerrilla activity began in earnest in 1972, to continue to the present. On 7 March 1972, anti-Spanish manifestations in El Aaiún and Villa Cisneros were reported, with ten Spaniards and eight Saharauis killed, and a hundred arrests; a further armed clash took place in the capital on 17 May. In July the Spanish press was forbidden to mention the territory, though little enough had been published in recent times anyway. It was said that a further 1,200 nomads had fled to Mauritania. This was presumably linked with anti-Spanish demonstrations in Tindouf and other towns just across the frontier. Significantly, in Tan-Tan the Moroccan police clashed with demonstrators, arresting fifteen; probably the tribesmen were supporters of complete independence rather than of a Moroccan Sahara. Morocco's guerrillas had not been heard of for some time and when, in 1973, a new group appeared, the 'Movement of the 21 August', it was referred to by the Mauritanian guerrillas, described next, as 'a Moroccan machination', formed to support the King's claim.

The most active opposition was at first based on Nouakchott, the Mauritanian capital: FRELISARIO, from the Spanish name of the People's Front for the Liberation of the Saguiet-el-Hamra and Rio de Oro, formed in 1973 on behalf of the '280,000 inhabitants' of the territory. Its close relationship to the Mauritanian state makes it interesting to summarise the strength of the country's official military forces: not only because these will be lending support to FRELIS-ARIO but because, upon the 'independence' of Spanish Sahara, Mauritania is likely to dispute the occupation of the territory with Morocco, the latter's armed forces standing around 50,000 men in 1974.

The French organised the forces of the southern state in the years 1961–5; these have since been modified. A recent estimate of the volunteer army, based on two-year service periods, was that there were 1,600 soldiers, including paratroops and rapid-movement motorised groups, the latter using all-terrain vehicles equipped with ground and air radio, machine guns and mortars. Spread out over the vast country – the north-east half, 500,000 sq km, holds 110,000 people – are nomadic units in radio-contact with headquarters; the units are in touch with the people, dealing in passing with social problems, giving medical aid and so on. The air force has a few reconnaissance and transport planes, for example the French Brous-sard. Not mentioned in the quoted estimate, a navy existed by 1974, in the shape of a few small gunboats.

FRELISARIO has claimed numerous clashes since May 1973. In late October its several actions in the north-east excited general un-rest. On 11 November, it said, a thousand Saharaui workers were sacked after a demonstration; it was reported there had been a series of arrests and ill-treatments for tract distribution and contact with FRELISARIO, and also for illegal entry into the territory. The Spanish lost men, weapons and vehicles in the conflicts.

On 28 January 1974, when the writer was staying in the military hospital in Smara, the building quartered reinforcements brought up from El Aaiún for a protracted clash, on the 26th–29th, in the nearby

Tifariti region; the Smara legionaries, using machine guns and bazookas, routed and eventually caught a band of guerrillas. These had been distributing tracts, said to have been printed in Algiers, which included condemnation of the lack of support by other Arab countries, including Morocco, for the resistance to the Spaniards. The Smara legionary mentioned earlier stated that military orders were to destroy the settlement, the dissidence focus, if necessary; the people were kept in fear, following the measures taken by the Spanish after the 1970 incident. They did not use camels in the Foreign Legion any longer, he added.

The most effective guerrilla strike took place on 26 October 1974, against the most obvious target: the phosphate belt. It had been announced that, on 4 November, the general *yemaa* would elect four members to a council formed to prepare the way to autonomy, officially defined as an 'Independent Saharan State under Spanish guidance'; Saharauis in the Spanish administration began to spread the slogan 'Independence, yes, but with Spain'. Not surprisingly, FRELISARIO was not invited to the *yemaa*. So, as a protest, in a dawn manoeuvre it burnt out two of the motor and control stations along the belt. The Spaniards, bridging the gap with lorries, forecast that repairs would take several weeks; the opposition, hoping to shatter the confidence of Spain's foreign customers, claimed that shipments would be halted for six months. Whilst the 96-kilometre belt will always be vulnerable to sabotage, disruption of the industry will be counter-productive to the guerrillas if it results in unemployment for the Saharaui labour force, increasingly dependent on wages in its way of life.

As 1975 opened, the Spaniards were sending away their families to the safety of the Canaries and the peninsula. The military presence was at its highest level in the territory's history, its personnel well rewarded; anti-aircraft guns now ringed the capital's airport. Movement was strictly controlled, the Saharauis having to carry identity cards, vehicle drivers having to keep logs of their movements. There were, however, no signs of major mobilisation by the neighbouring countries. It seemed likely that there were as many Spanish military in the territory as there were able-bodied Saharaui men. The effect of the guerrilla actions would clearly be to hasten Spain's acceptance of one or another demand put forward by the interested groups at international level.

# Chapter 14

# International Politics, 1956–74

Spain's case – to begin by summarising the positive assertions of each of the claimants – is built upon its presence on the coast during the Middle Ages, on the 1884–6 treaties with the Saharauis and 1900–12 treaties with the French, on the Spaniards' 'civilising' and anti-communist role, on the assertion that the Saharauis desire the continuation of the colonial situation.

Morocco, independent in 1956, thereupon claimed not only Spanish Sahara but also Mauritania, western Algeria and north-western Mali: this 'Greater Morocco' was the conception of Allal el Fassi, leader of the nationalist Istiqlal party. The various Spanish zones along the Mediterranean and Atlantic coasts were of course also claimed. The Moroccans' demand for the desert is based on ethnic and cultural identity and upon the Sultan's alternating acceptance by or conquest of the Saharan people throughout history; documents ranging from acts of homage to tax demands have been produced to support this affirmation.

Mauritania became independent in 1958 and, in spite of Morocco and the Arab states, with support from France and from black Africa managed to enter the UN in 1961; thereafter the 'Greater Morocco' claims became muted. Mauritania's case over Spanish Sahara is also based upon ethnic and cultural continuity; on the assertion that, during history, the desert was never divided politically, and that, geographically, Spanish Sahara is a continuation of Mauritania. Recently the Mauritanian claim has been reduced to the south of the territory.

Algeria, sharing thirty kilometres of frontier with Spanish Sahara, has had a lesser role in the developments. Its support for one or another of the rival factions has been offered in exchange for satisfaction of its own political demands over other matters. Secondly, it has a direct economic interest, in its future need for an ore-transit route to the Atlantic from the still-unexploited Gara Djebilet mine near Tindouf: this transit concession has been essential in obtaining Algerian support.

Finally there is the possibility of Saharaui independence. This would hand the European investment over to the Saharauis, though with the inevitable deterioration in the territory's economy. Independence-supporters wish to avoid simply changing masters, perhaps for the worse, certainly so economically. It could be claimed that the Spanish administration has produced a different culture from that of the surrounding states. But the chief justification for independence is simply that its supporters wish it.

The arguments used to refute these various claims may already be obvious from the earlier chapters of this book. With international politics theoretically condemning war, claims based on one-time conquest are not at present respectable. No nation can show that its involvement with the Saharauis – between the Middle Ages and the present – has been due other than to self-interest.

Spanish treaties with the French are not binding on the Saharauis or on their neighbours. Had a majority of the Saharauis wanted the Spaniards to remain, then the referendum would long ago have been held. The Spanish assertion that Moroccan–Mauritanian and intertribal bloodshed would follow their departure may well come true, but present preference is to accept this probability as an essential stage in human and political evolution in Africa.

Morocco's ethnic-continuum claim is tolerably accurate but culturally, apart from the Tekna tribes north of the Saguiet-el-Hamra, the similarity is much less obvious. Neither is the sovereignty case strong. For within Morocco itself there have been the *insoumis* of the Nun and the Sus, as a guide to the likely attitudes of the nomads of the W Sahara . . . tax demands do not equal tax payments. At the most the nomads acknowledged the Sultan's *de jure* rule when it suited them: any practical demands on them were always unacceptable. As one example of Morocco's image, the Arosien tribe's traditional founding came when Hamet el Arosi had been 'caught by the Sultan of Morocco', another saint then lifting him into the air to freedom in the desert. Clearly the nomads have always manipulated the situation; for example, they did ask help against the French, help which equally significantly was not apparently to be automatically expected from the Sultan. The Almoravides may have held the whole of north-west Africa, but it was from Mauritania, not from Morocco, that their conquest stemmed. And the Arab tribes which colonised the desert late in the Middle Ages had in fact been chased out of Morocco.

Mauritania appears to have the best case on traditional arguments. On ethnic, cultural and geographical grounds, the greater part of the country is a continuation of Spanish Sahara; events, climatic to political, have always rippled to and fro across the western desert.

It has been said that the most sound modern argument is the mere wish for independence. Yet 50,000–100,000 Saharauis could hardly form themselves into a lasting state.

*Evolution of the Political Scene*
Manoeuvres by the adjoining nations began, then, following their independence late in the nineteen-fifties. The conflicting territorial claims made agreement on other issues impossible, with the MIFERMA mine and its railway the ,earliest outlet for dissent. The Mines de Fer de Mauritanie consortium was formed with 56% French, 19% British, 15% Italian, 5% German and 5% Mauritanian capital. Coming within 'Greater Morocco', the development was the subject of ineffectual protests by Rabat, not invited to participate. The Spaniards, equally, had long been nursing their hatred over the 'loss' of the Adrar zone by the 1900 treaty and had always avoided marking out the Ijil frontier: they did so in 1956, to consolidate the breakdown of negotiations with the MIFERMA. Earlier in the decade it had been intended to lay the railway from the Kedia Ijil magnetite massif to Villa Cisneros, but the Spanish terms together with the limitations of their harbour, shallow at the side of Port Etienne, then brought discussion to an end. The railway was there-fore laid over the less suitable frontier land; thirty kilometres of the Azefal dunes had to be stabilised with heavy oil. Worse, since the boundary corner lay at the foot of the Adrar massif, the company had to blast through two kilometres of granite bluff at a cost of three million pounds. The Spaniards employed Gibraltar-tactics, causing all manner of problems: passage below the massif was refused to construction vehicles, these being seized if they attempted the circuit, transit permits were delayed, labour was made difficult to recruit from Spanish Sahara. The Spanish garrisons were increased along the frontier. And, at this point, they of course marked out the hated boundary.

Between Morocco and Mauritania the tension was heightened in 1958 by the public departure of five important Mauritanians for Rabat, there to be given official posts. One was a son of Ma el Ainin, another was the Emir of Trarza; as a sign of the vassalage so much claimed by Morocco, the Emir formally surrendered his title to the King, then received it back. The Mauritanians explained that they did not wish to be a part of black Africa . . . by coincidence, the new Mauritanian state was then abolishing the emirate system.

For the Spaniards, the 1957–8 war in the territory was paralleled by the first open aggression in the field of international politics. At the UN there was pressure by African countries for the statutory information which the Spaniards had never provided on their territory. Spain saw it would be necessary to make friends of its neighbours. In 1959 a permanent Spanish–Moroccan commission was set up to deal with mutual problems. Relations began again with Mauritania, reaching an exchange of diplomats in 1962. The same year the National Museum of Hispanomusulman Art was opened in Granada.

Attention was now paid to how the territory itself looked from outside. Thus, apart from the internal politics intended to tranquilise the Saharauis themselves, there was propaganda aimed at the exterior: the 1960 Declaration of Loyalty, the 1961 support for the reorganised administration. Franco reassured himself in the Cortes: 'Our nation has never practised colonialism, and nothing is more eloquent of this . . . than our conduct over the centuries in America'.

The few published general studies of Spanish Sahara have been of official origin. The majority appearing in 1962, the most significant (Hernandez-Pacheco 1962) being written by the unusual combination of the Keeper of Madrid's Natural History Museum and the President of the International Politics Section of the Institute for Political Studies. The former's contribution concentrated on the poverty of the territory, apparently lacking in natural sources; the second author, insisting that the Saharauis were not Arabs but merely Arabised, devoted himself to showing that the Spanish presence was essential. From 1963 the magazine *Africa* passed trivial matters such as locust plagues over to *Sahara*, the new local periodical, filling itself instead with endless propaganda, including articles by Saharauis.

The year 1963 brought a diversion in the form of the Morocco–Algeria frontier war; Tindouf, the Reguibat town, was the most southerly of the settlements which the Moroccans unsuccessfully attempted to occupy. Rabat's attention was temporarily moved away from Spanish Sahara but Algiers now found it advantageous to enter into discussions with Spain and Mauritania over the territory. Mauritania pressed its own claim not only from a desire to take over the whole desert but in order to avoid loss of the buffer zone between it and Morocco; both Nouadhibou and the Choum tunnel are within gunshot of the border. In 1964 Spain gave Mauritania technical aid, and worried about the Chinese helping to construct Nouakchott.

In 1965 came the first of the UN resolutions against Spain's presence in the Sahara; throughout the next decade the Moroccan and Mauritanian delegates have repeatedly recited their countries' claims. In 1966 the OAU asked Spain to allow political evolution in the territory. There were various Spanish counter-moves. They emphasised that the public exchequer spent several times as much on each Saharaui as on a peninsular dweller and twenty times as much as the Mauritanians could find for each of their subjects. And, in parentheses, there is no doubt that Spain has brought the Saharauis nearer to 'civilisation', a step automatically approved by many; the modern business mind, one alternative approach, will see and approve a normal capitalist relationship. Otto of Hapsburg took up the job of press officer in Europe, describing the Saharauis as 'miraculously lifted into the atomic era', with the old barrier between the whites and the negroes now removed. There was a suggestion that Ifni and Spanish Sahara, or at least a share in the phosphates, might be given in exchange for unconditional acceptance of the Spaniards' occupation of Ceuta and Melilla. The town of Ricote, in Murcia, put up a monument to the Arabs of the Middle Ages.

However, Spain's main counter was the petition, apparently signed by all the chiefs, sent to the UN on 21 March 1966. In it the Saharauis drew attention to the absence of consultation over their wishes – other than by the Spanish, of course – and asserted their desire to retain the situation unchanged. There was no subjection; their religion, laws and customs were respected; they had a representative body; they were able to keep the territory's limited resources to themselves though, thanks to Spain, they had reached a high level of civilisation. They would defend their land against foreign intervention and, if they ever felt strong enough to become independent, would work this out with Spain and with nobody else. The signatories asked that the UN should send a commission to verify the authenticity of this model declaration.

In October an individual vote was taken; referred to as a 'refer-endum', the choice was to sign the document or to abstain. The Saharauis held *yemaas* during the preceding days. Eligible to sign were 16,433 men over the age of eighteen, of whom 14,637, or 90 per cent, now declared themselves in favour of Spain. The administration admitted that two fractions were opposed to the petition. Scrutiny of the lists shows that only half the Reguibat Leguacem supported the petition; for example, only 430 signed out of 1,475 Boihat, the main fraction; in one small fraction only 10 out of 163 signed. Some small tribes dissented also. The Delim, now a tribe of civil servants, signed unanimously. So, less explicably, did the Tekna confederation and the Ma el Ainin, both usually determined opponents of the Europeans. In November, Seila and the other official Saharaui leaders took these results to the UN's Commission on Non-Autonomous Zones. The delegation also met Franco, one of its members apparently saying, on their return to the territory, that the Caudillo's pronouncements were 'words from the mouth of God'.

In 1966, in fact, the nomads were showing great awareness of national issues too, since over 90 per cent turned out to vote on Franco's Organic Law on the succession of the head of the Spanish state. Naturally the Saharauis were in favour of the proposals, 95 per cent so.

The last years of the nineteen-sixties brought little but ineffective threats by Morocco: King Hassan promised action 'on all planes, economic, military, political and territorial', thus reversing the policy of negotiation announced in 1960. Rabat's UN delegate stated that not only was Spain not preparing a referendum but, rather, it had since 1965 been busy expelling dissident Reguibat; the 1966 petition must have helped them to sort the sheep from the camels. Spain preferred not to see any inconsistency between its attitudes over the territory and over Gibraltar, pointed out by Morocco. In 1969 an unthinkable event occurred in Spain itself: the Chief Inspector of the Armed Forces came out in support of the Moroccan claim to Spanish Sahara. He was at once dismissed by Franco and his action kept out of the press; in Morocco, which he then visited, he was warmly received personally and on paper, triggering off a further fusillade of recriminations against Spain. Spanish Guinea had been given independence in October 1968, and in the following year Ifni was passed to Morocco, some 10,000 Spaniards leaving the enclave, this 'consummating a process of generosity, something which, given the course of history, is inevitable'. In 1970 Spain handed an anti-monarch plotter over to Morocco in order to improve relations. Hassan suggested that the Spaniards would be allowed to keep military bases in the desert after their departure.

From 1967 the neighbouring countries have come gradually closer in their attitudes over Spanish Sahara. Between 1967–72, Morocco and Algeria drew nearer again: the frontier was delineated, leaving Gara Djebilet in Algeria but agreeing on its joint exploitation, with the shipment of the iron ore westwards, probably through the northern desert once this was in Moroccan ownership. Morocco's military conscription and increasing armaments, the result of the hostilities with Algeria, now gave the king courage to face up to the Spanish. The 1969 Islamic Conference at Rabat discussed the possibility that the north, with the phosphates, would go to Morocco, and the south, with the iron and any off-shore oil, to Mauritania; Morocco at last recognised Mauritania as a state. Then, in 1970, there was held in Nouadhibou the first of several conferences by the heads of Morocco, Algeria and Mauritania: joint action to free Spanish Sahara was pledged.

*One of the Last European Colonies*
This agreement amongst the neighbouring states, in 1970, brought Spain the disapproval of several wider organisations. At the UN, the writing on the wall was in many languages other than Arabic, with the perennial resolution being passed by 108–0, with 23 abstentions, in 1974; this year the motion had 'Called for independence . . . and invited Spain to hold a referendum . . . for the purpose, in consulta-tion with . . . Morocco and Mauritania'. The majority of the General Assembly seemed to have had as little idea of the purpose of a referendum as had the Spaniards in 1966. The resolutions had stressed, between 1970–4, that the consultation should only take place after the return of political exiles and then under UN supervision. There was an attempt at economic sanction, but the territory was in no way dependent on the hostile countries. Support at the UN for the Spanish came from Portugal, South Africa and a few Central American states.

At various times, since 1970, Spain has summarised the defence case. The Saharauis live as freely as Spanish citizens – not a promising opening – but themselves own the territory's wealth. The Spaniards administer through a Governor-General and look after defence and foreign relations. The Saharauis fear annexation. Tongue in cheek, a Spanish spokesman affirmed that his government 'energetically supported' the principle that 'self-determination . . . is the only valid solution'. A referendum on UN lines, scheduled for 1971, never mentioned in the Spanish press, was replaced in that year by a promise to hold it in the future 'if requested to do by the Saharaui people'.

The Organisation for African Unity avoided the referendum question in 1972, as Morocco – preferring to take over the territory without consultation, an indication that it has not a majority any more than have the Spaniards – was the host country. The King declared that Morocco would not use violence. However, the 1973 OAU meeting demanded a referendum. In 1974, at Mogadishu in Somalia, the Organisation called for the withdrawal of Spain.

In 1970 the Canaries Independence Movement condemned the Spanish, together with assertions that the territory's chiefs were in their pay. In 1972 the foreign ministers of the 'Non-Aligned Coun-tries', meeting in Georgetown, Guyana, asked Spain to hold the referendum. The same year, Libya offered aid to Mauritania in its liberation of the territory; in 1974, the Libyan prime minister, visiting Spain, rejected the idea of the referendum, saying that the Saharauis were Arabs – and, by implication, could not possibly be associated with the Iberians. King Faisal of Saudi Arabia, in a visit to Mauritania, demanded Spanish evacuation of the desert. Yasser Arafat has pledged the support of the Palestine Liberation Movement to King Hassan. In 1973 Madrid was given a tangible excuse for retelling the story of the red bogeymen: the Spanish Communist Party, in a joint statement with the Moroccan 'Party for Liberation and Socialism', added its weight against the colonialists, with the statement that there were 50,000 Spanish soldiers in the desert.

Morocco's various tactics during this final period have had varying success. The 1971–2 attempted *coup d'états* have led to increased emphasis on the Spanish Sahara issue as a distraction from home problems; the King's failure to obtain Tindouf in 1972 brought the same manoeuvre. Since 1973 the Moroccans have stated that they will not accept the independence of the Saharauis; the only acceptable referendum would ask for a straight decision between Spain and Morocco. But the Moroccans go further still, for they demand also that the Spaniards should anyway leave the territory before the referendum is held, surely the source of a wan smile in the Pardo Palace. Following Morocco's contribution to the October war in the Middle East, the King has claimed support for his campaign from the other Arab countries; however, he and his cause are not unanimously popular.

Throughout 1974 the Moroccan press kept the 'Spanish-Occupied Moroccan Sahara' in the headlines, in a daily reshuffling of claims, insults and threats; the logic was usually so absurd as not to merit discussion, with invocations of irrelevant treaties, for example between the English and the French, and rejection of those others which were being invoked, usually equally inappropriately, by the Spaniards. Radio propaganda was being beamed across the frontier to the Saharauis; in November, Morocco's National Theatre Company produced a new work, 'The Pillaged Sahara'. The King had the support of all Moroccan parties, with some demands for a military offensive. In July a delegation, claiming to represent the Saharaui tribes – apart from the Delim – paid homage to Hassan in Rabat. In August the King nominated the notorious Col Dlimi as chief of the military region on the southern frontier; Spain claimed there was a build-up of Moroccan troops along the border during the summer.

King Hassan's last manoeuvres in 1974 were to send members of his family – his sister, Princess Malika, and then the crown-prince, Mohammed – on tours to stir up the southern towns and, as far as possible, the Spanish-held desert. The press claimed the Spaniards refused exit-visas to Saharauis wishing to meet 'the Prince of the

Sahara', as Hassan's son was apparently greeted by the Tarfaya populace in January 1975. With Spain's expenditure on Saharaui welfare in mind, the royal family promised development of the southern region and, with tongue in cheek, of El Aaiún too.

As for Mauritania, in 1974 it was still holding to its claim to at least the southern zone. It too was using radio propaganda to raise support in the territory. In 1972, to help reach agreement with Morocco and Algeria, Mauritania asked to join the Maghreb Permanent Consultative Committee as a full member; however, in early 1974 it was pressing its claim alone. Algeria was seen to have swung towards a preference for an independent Saharaui state. The 1973 tripartite meeting did not, in fact, produce a joint plan of action and it seemed that, in 1974, all three countries were again acting more or less independently.

Finally, the Spanish moves in the last few years. The political attacks by the Arab countries from 1970 have led to an attempt at ingratiation, so that co-operation treaties in various fields were signed with Morocco, Mauritania, Algeria and other states aligned with the opposition. A conference of Catholics and Moslems was held in 1974 at Córboba, announcing co-operation between them and also supporting the Arab cause in Palestine. The news embargo was again tightened, in 1972, although the desert *yemaa*'s repeatedly-expressed fears of 'foreign interference' were always well publicised; it seems likely that these fears are in fact held by a majority of the Saharauis, though this does not of course imply that they wish the Spanish to stay. In mid-1974 the administration promised 'internal autonomy'. Morocco naturally recognised the flavour of this aged carrot and, referring to 'a puppet state', announced that 1975 would be devoted to the liberation of the territory. This led the Spanish delegate at the UN to protest that Morocco was taking a very dangerous line. Then, in August 1974, following Spanish–Moroccan talks, Madrid announced a referendum for the first half of 1975, to be held 'under the auspices and guarantees of the UN'. Simultaneously the Spanish stated they would continue the high level of contribution to the Saharaui budget, around £400,000 a year. Spain continued in the Sahara.

# Chapter 15

# The Year of Climax, 1975

By the autumn, the nomads and their desert were the still-unpicked bones of a contention marshalling the diplomats and armies of four countries and their more or less openly-sponsored local opposition groups – intellectual, puppet and guerrilla – and the International Court of Justice, a UN mission and the representatives of Libya, Egypt, France and the United States. The Moroccan King had referred to a possible 'second Vietnam' and the UN Secretary-General to 'the threat to world security'.

*At the International Court of Justice*
The breakdown of Spanish-Moroccan talks in mid-1974 had led Spain to reiterate its intention to hold a referendum, whereupon Morocco decided to bring in the International Court. Following a secret agreement between Morocco and Mauritania, the December UN General Assembly was persuaded to pass Resolution 3292 (XXIX): Spain should not hold the referendum but, instead, the Court's advisory opinion should be sought and a UN fact-finding mission should visit the territory. This resolution diverged from the last decade's sequence of straightforward 'self-determination' resolutions on Spanish Sahara, and a third of the delegates abstained, including several African countries.

The Court was to give its opinion on whether, at the time of Spain's colonisation, 1884, the western desert was a land without an owner and, if not, upon its legal ties with Morocco and Mauritania. Early in 1975, statements were lodged by the three countries, and also by France and seven Latin American states. The preliminary sitting in May brought Morocco the right, by ten votes to five, to appoint a judge *ad hoc*, but not Mauritania, by seven votes to eight: choosing the leading Ivory Coast judge, Morocco asserted the Court clearly felt it was the leading claimant to the desert.

In June and July the sixteen judges listened to the many delegates of the three countries and of Algeria and Zaïre; the MOREHOB group was not allowed to speak. Putting its case first, Morocco stated, as did Mauritania later, that the zone above the Saguiet-el-Hamra belonged to it, below came an area of overlap, the south was Mauritanian; including the Bu Craa mine, the overlap, 'not worth further definition', would clearly be fought over outside the Court later, the united front being concerted against the Spanish case. Morocco's claim was based on assertions that it had appointed or received homage from the desert's leading figures, had levied taxes on them and marshalled them against invaders; the Nun area, long known as the Moroccan south, extended to C. Blanc, or at least to C. Bojador. Though, as the 'immemorial possessor', its case hardly needed to be proved. Finally, since 'territorial integrity' outweighed 'self-determination' in international law, the desert should be re-returned to Morocco without a Saharaui referendum.

The Mauritanians spoke logically and calmly, in spite of the judge *ad hoc* setback. First they asserted a pre-independence existence as the 'Bilad Chinguetti', an entity of west Sahara people centred upon Chinguetti, an ancient town and undeniably the region's cultural focus. Though credibility was not strengthened by the statement that '. . . confrontations leading to loss of human life and to protracted hostilities were avoided'. Vincent Monteil, a specialist on the area, sent in a contribution to demonstrate the similarity of the inhabitants of the Spanish-held desert to those of Mauritania. Though making the same 'overlap' statement as the Moroccans, the Mauritanians were clearly taking no chances, giving their full case for ownership of the south. But there was an immediate divergence of opinion in Mauritania's continuing support for a referendum, this however to include the options of association with or attachment to Morocco or Mauritania, and not merely a choice between Spain and independence; it may be relevant that the most popular guerrilla group, POLISARIO, once FRELISARIO, is Mauritanian in origin at least. However, a direct confrontation with Morocco has to be avoided, in spite of President Ould Daddah's firm statements.

Zaïre spoke next, fervently describing African life and its identification with its land. The concept of 'a land without a master' was a European invention only possible by ignoring 'the populations of unadvanced civilisation'. The delegate supported partition between Morocco and Mauritania.

The Algerian contribution, though partly in conflict with that of Zaïre, was also in terms of human beings rather than based upon 'the cold creaking clockwork' of international law. Colonisation, with its justifications and laws, from Roman to European, was despatched in front of the Court. Denying any territorial interest itself, accepting only that the western desert had been a part of Dar el-Islam, the speaker for the Democratic Republic of Algeria insisted that 'self-determination' outweighed 'territorial integrity' and that the UN resolution had been passed against a background assumption of a future referendum. Algeria's agreement with Spain over this was simply the association of 'a profound conviction of the principle of self-determination with political opportunism'. It was underlined that Hispano-Arab friendship and Maghreb unity were both at stake.

Spain came last before the judges. Both at the preliminary hearing and in July Spain attempted to halt the proceedings. First, the decade of self-determination resolutions bound the UN; secondly, having earlier refused Morocco's request that they should go together to the Court to settle 'a dispute', this unilateral request for 'an opinion' was a way of going round the international rules and getting Spain there anyway; thirdly, as there was no 'dispute', there were no grounds for allowing judges *ad hoc*. Spain insisted that referendum preparations were under way and, in fact, the Governor-General had a month earlier given April or May 1976 as the date; the others in turn remarked that, if it ever did take place, it would be 'prepared', so they proposed safeguards.

But, with little hope that the Court would refuse to go on with the hearing, the Spanish had to put a case: the desert had been *terra nullius*, without an owner, though 'populated by independent tribes possessing full external political power'. It was never subject to Morocco or to Mauritania – the latter did not even exist until 1958. The delegate denounced Hassan's numerous threats of violence as a breach of the UN charter, adding that sixty-one Moroccan soldiers had in fact been captured in the territory since February.

Finally, it was necessary to explain to one of the judges a statement by Franco, on 23 May, that Spain might 'precipitate the transfer of powers'. The other countries saw this as a preliminary to the installation of a puppet government should the Court and the UN mission produce unfavourable opinions. The Spanish explained that it meant they would have to leave if guerrilla activity became out of control. The Court's 'opinion' was expected in October 1975.

## The UN mission

To report to the General Assembly in September, the mission consisted of observers from the Ivory Coast, Cuba and Iran. In May and June it visited the desert. The Spaniards produced their own pro-independence party, the new PUNS, described shortly, but the mission apparently asked: 'Where are the people?' It seems the authorities then more or less allowed a large anti-colonial demonstration by POLISARIO at Smara, registered by the mission. Morocco made numerous accusations: Spain had put thousands out of the way in concentration camps and had turned their garrisons into 'peaceful villages' complete with soldiers disguised as Saharauis, with a further 30,000 men sent out in disguise to cry pro-Spanish slogans. The troops had been ordered to shoot down any Saharaui who showed pro-Moroccan feelings, said the King's press, and a girl who had waved a Moroccan flag in front of the UN team had been beaten up.

The mission went next to Tan-Tan, in south Morocco, to be met by the many denunciations, by eye-witnesses, including the very subjects of the arrests and brutalities imputed to the Spanish, who had been careless enough to have deported them into the path of the UN observers. Camps said to be of refugees were visited, the Cuban woman meeting the women in a special tent. At Zag, fifty kilometres north of the frontier, there were slogans such as 'Neither autonomy nor referendum, we're all Moroccan Saharauis'. Nearby Amskroud apparently held 6,000 refugees. An aged Reguibat chief told the press that he and his family of seventy-three were in exile. Finally the FLU, in fact Moroccan army guerrillas replacing the 'Movement of the 21 August', made an 'unexpected' irruption, armed and motorised as if illegal in Morocco, to impress itself on the UN team as a Saharaui and, of course, pro-Moroccan liberation movement.

The mission went last to Algeria; Moroccan journalists were not allowed in. At Tindouf the team met POLISARIO representatives; the group was no longer working from Mauritania, it seemed. These men wanted independence and, in turn, alleged Morocco had arrested their members in advance of the UN mission's arrival there. A number of captive Spaniards said they were well treated. The team was taken to a camp of 3,000 'Saharaui refugees', coincidentally supporters this time of POLISARIO and of self-determination; the grandson of Merebbi Rebbu said, privately, that these were specially-imported Touareg.

The mission over, the leader apparently went so far as to say there was 'a certain similarity or identity between the people of Mauritania and those of Western Sahara'. In June the UN Secretary-General visited the contestant countries. Once the UN has both the Court's opinion and the mission's report, it will put forward a procedure for decolonisation.

*Opposition groups in the desert*

A new Spanish tactic was, in March, to form the Saharan National Unity Party, PUNS. Run by four Saharaui graduates, its secretary was Henna ould Er-Rachid, aged twenty-seven; moustached and suited, he had trained as an engineer in Las Palmas and Madrid. In his El Aaiún office, provided by the Spaniards, he said that the party stood for peaceful decolonisation followed by co-operation with Spain. A few days later, in Rabat after having defected with PUNS funds to the FLU, he said 'We are conscious of having chosen the difficult path of action and of the holy war under the leadership of HM Hassan II'. It was said he had left PUNS because it was so much less popular than POLISARIO but, if independence had really been his aim, the FLU was the last party to join – so probably he had sooner or later gone on to a double role, in local tradition. As an example of the limited actions of PUNS, in June it held a demonstration against Moroccan attempts to stop the referendum, with slogans hostile to Amin's offer of a suicide-squad for use against the Spanish.

POLISARIO is lead, from Algeria, by EL Ouali, a Moroccan exile. Aid comes from Libya and Algeria, since its manifesto – self-determination, autonomy, a socialist state – opposes the Moroccan expansionism so much feared by the others. Though equally in conflict with the Mauritanian case, other than on the referendum issue, this may turn out to be more apparent than real, given POLISARIO's origins in the south.

Nevertheless, about May, and coincidentally with Er-Rachid's departure, it was suggested that Spain was showing some tolerance of POLISARIO; perhaps it had suddenly realised that here was a *genuine* independence movement, as it seemed, that could be wooed and used, eventually, for the same ends as the PUNS group, to lead to independence in association with Spain. Simultaneously there seems to have been a general move by PUNS to support Morocco, stemming from or causing Spain's change of heart towards POLISARIO. Franco's threat to 'precipitate the transfer of powers' led the two groups to fight it out in El Aaiún and Smara in July: 'The streets of the desert capital were littered with sandals, banners, bloodstains, rocks and sticks, as well as stains left by the coloured water . . . squirted on the demonstrators'. The PUNS office was attacked, not for the first time. However, the majority of the hundreds of arrests were of POLISARIO supporters, suggesting Spain's courtship had soon ended; in August the Saharaui police were on strike as a protest over Spanish repression of POLISARIO.

In May the Moroccan Army commandos became active again, as the Front for Liberation and Unity, to counter POLISARIO, especially in the eyes of the UN mission. Attacks were made all along the north border, notably on the closed Tah frontier post – repelled by mortar fire – and at Hagunia and Sequen. Rockets were fired at helicopter and aeroplane patrols, routes were mined. In early June forty men of the 7th Camel Battalion, with written orders from the King, were caught whilst trying to occupy the old Mahbes fort in the extreme north-east; Hassan II, speaking to the OAU Liberation Committee, said they were an FLU group made up of Saharauis recently demobbed from his army. A new tactic claimed by the FLU was to organise 'a meeting of a thousand Dutch political and trade union militants' at The Hague, just before the opening of the Court.

To add to the many fires between which the Spanish are caught, the Saharaui soldiers began to mutiny in May, going over to Morocco or to POLISARIO and taking Spanish officers and men with them by force. The army at once paid off 200 local troops. Their own forces were estimated by foreign journalists at 20–50,000 soldiers, whilst they themselves assessed at 25,000 men the Moroccan frontier army. The death toll in action rose steadily on each side.

Terrorist alerts, mainly over bombs, were almost nightly in the capital, with a curfew from February. A bomb killed the child of one of the Saharaui *procuradores*. Saharaui medical and other students in the Canaries were arrested for having illegal Saharan propaganda, leading to the return home of all Saharaui students in Madrid. Arrests were made amongst Radio Sahara employees. The situation was increasingly intolerable.

In midsummer, with the comment that a week's fighting was costing five years' phosphate revenue, Spain announced its future departure, preferring this to a protracted Portuguese-style struggle. With the Governor-General mentioning an 'emergency evacuation plan', the Spanish women and children continued to leave the desert; the dust from the Sahara storm reached the Canaries and the people there agitated at events in the territory, only seventy miles from Fuerteventura. Saying it might have to transfer the desert to the UN, Spain asked for a military observer. Tension developed between the Government and those officers in favour of resistance.

The Yemaa of Spanish Sahara heard the Governor affirm, in May, that it should prepare to take over; though he soon afterwards announced the referendum date, 1976. . . if Spain were still there. Morocco said there must be enough 'settled' Spaniards, then, to out-vote the nomads. Khatri, the President of the Assembly, declared that Spain must guarantee them against annexation. It had been Khatri who, earlier in 1975, had stated that, once independent, the new state would claim lands at present in Morocco, Algeria and Mauritania, notably as far as the Draa and the town of Bir Moghrein.

*International manoeuvres*
Parallel to its military alignment, Morocco built up its international preparations throughout 1975; this nationalist extrovertism con-

tinued to be effective in keeping attention away from internal problems. In January the decolonisation of the Spanish-held Mediterranean enclaves was placed on the UN agenda; henceforth clashes and tension escalated in the *presidios*. Oil rights in the Canaries channel were a new subject for argument with Spain. Propaganda aimed at the desert included claims of a split in POLISARIO, of a pro-Moroccan swing in MOREHOB – certainly on tour about then in search of aid – and the attribution of incidents such as the July 1974 conveyor-belt disruption to its own FLU. Libya thereupon affirmed Morocco was claiming actions by POLISARIO, to which it was then itself giving generous radio time, and added that the FLU fought POLISARIO rather than Spain, an echo of the turn of the century. Hassan hastily invited Khadafi to Morocco, and ten days later it was said that Libya had offered Morocco military aid. In June three 'Saharauis' on Moroccan television were recognised by French viewers as veterans of Morocco's own independence struggle of the nineteen-fifties.

In 1974 the Bu Craa mine had only produced 650,000 tons of phosphates instead of the forecast 1·7 million tons, due to 'technical problems'. Capacity was 3·3 million tons and a second processing plant in action in 1975 and a third by 1980 was to bring output to 10 million tons a year. Spain put its investment at £200 million by 1975. It was reported that in May a joint exploitation agreement had been reached by the Unión Explosivos Rio Tinto and the Office Chérifien des Phosphates, but the accelerating conflict led to its abandonment.

The 1974 understanding between Morocco and Mauritania brought talks, in March, on the sharing of the high-grade phosphate mine. Then, in July, a combined support-raising mission toured Arab and other influential countries; Moroccan envoys also reached the USSR, while the Chinese increased their activities in Mauritania. In spite of the understanding, weather-forecast maps on Moroccan television no longer showed the Spanish Sahara frontier, other than that with Mauritania.

To the east, however, Morocco did not have even a temporary ally, Algeria bluntly opposing the King's claim, denouncing his secret agreement with Ould Daddah and accusing him of destroying Maghreb unity. Algerian envoys circled Spanish Sahara. No mention was made of the Gara Djebilet ore-export route. Morocco, decrying Algeria's interference and 'mercenary gangs', threatened it would re-open the border dispute if it did not get the western Sahara; it told the UN that it would take over if Spain left. It was said in May that UN observers had taken up positions on the disputed Morocco-Algeria frontier, with the 1963 war in mind.

During the summer many other countries had become involved. The Egyptian Foreign Minister negotiated to keep the peace. Senegal, a declared supporter of Morocco, now proposed a federation with it and Mauritania. The conference of Islamic Foreign Ministers favoured partition, as did the Tunisian President. The French and United States leaders took an interest, thinking of 'the balance of power in the Western Mediterranean'.

In August the OAU at Kampala found the problem too difficult to tackle; there was concern, however, at the prospect of Morocco and Mauritania 'carving up' the desert. It was suggested that the OAU should soon admit the nomads. The lawyer Antonio Cubillo, representing the Guanche Republic – aimed at by the Movement for the Self-Determination and Independence of the Canary Archipelago – offered the Saharauis an equal-shares confederation.

Finally, Spain has several times, since May, suggested a four-power talk on Spanish Sahara. This has been welcomed by Algeria and agreed to by Mauritania, but Morocco will neither accept Algeria at the conference nor talk until it hears the opinions of the UN mission and of the Court. There was thus maximum disagreement amongst the African countries, both actual and, in the event of an attempt at implementing the Morocco–Mauritania pact, to be expected in the future.

As autumn 1975 begins, Spain is still manoeuvring, though with increasing desperation. The inducements are not only the heavily-invested phosphates but also the fact that, once the desert is in African hands, the pressure will be fully turned on Ceuta and Melilla – and eventually on the Canaries. In mid-1974 the tolling of the bell for the colonial system had been heard in Portuguese Africa, leaving the Spaniards to share the last stages with the whites of Djibouti, Rhodesia and South Africa. If open invasion of Spanish Sahara is as unlikely as it would be unwise, the escalating guerrilla activity and increasing international pressure have left the Spaniards with little more to hope for than an association with the Africans which will allow them some share of the phosphates and also provide guarantees for the future of the Mediterranean enclaves – and, not least, permit them to make their inevitable withdrawal from Africa in as graceful a way as possible.

# The Descendants of Ma el Ainin, 1934–75

In 1934 Merebbi Rebbu and El Mamun had wisely 'submitted' to the Spanish rather than to the French, going to live in the nascent El Aaiún. The former, given the title of 'Iman' of Spanish Sahara by the administration, died in 1942. Agdaf, then sixty-six, became head of the north, with his warrior-brother El Ueli, who had quarrelled with Rebbu, leading the south from Villa Cisneros. In the nineteen-fifties, however, the Spanish preferred to treat El Mamun, then in his seventies, as the leader of the whole territory. In 1955, with the family's disproportionately-large number of Spanish posts officially explained as due to their culture, Saharaui resistance to the Spanish and French must have seemed remote. One of Ma el Ainin's descendants then referred to Franco, in a press interview, as 'the cloud who brings us rain and good things, the shooting star that fills our world with light'. The nomads had been 'pacified' for twenty years.

However, the comparatively-objective Caro Baroja, also writing in 1955, said that Ma el Ainin's descendants 'never give up scheming for a better future, in the meantime machinating for advantages over their rivals with the authorities'. In fact, the 1957–8 war saw these important Saharauis on the opposite side to the Spaniards. Members of the family already lived in the surrounding countries, others now left Spanish Sahara and joined them. In 1960 the Spanish press mourned the death of the aged Agdaf, at Tan-Tan, by then Moroccan; the Spaniards had earlier made him 'Grand Vizier' of their Southern Morocco Protectorate for his collaboration.

If the Spanish said little over the support of the Moroccan branch of the Ma el Ainin family for the 'Greater Morocco' concept – specifically, for its proposed annexation of Mauritania – they did react openly to their active support, in 1967, for King Hassan over Spanish Sahara. A demonstration had been organised in Tan-Tan by one of Ma el Ainin's grandsons, Abadilah the son of Agdaf, with a view to exciting regional feeling against the Spanish; it was attended by King Hassan, then playing the part of Minister for Saharan and Mauritanian Affairs, and by General Oufkir, Minister of the Interior and later to administer one of the failed *coup d'états*. The Moroccan press said the chiefs of the Saharaui tribes were present. Abadilah was then also the leader of the 'Sahara Liberation Front'; seemingly evolved from the Liberation Army, it was the Moroccan government's unofficial guerrilla movement at that time.

Indignantly denying the involvement of the Saharaui chiefs, the Spanish launched a campaign to villify Ma el Ainin and his descendants. In addition to character judgements and the label of 'political opportunists' on the whole family, the Spanish underlined their Sudanese origin, in the Hodh, and their present residence in Morocco and Mauritania. Nevertheless the tribe is always represented in the lists of signatories to the many petitions and declarations, in favour of the Spanish presence, which are regularly drawn up in the territory. This is just one of the mistakes commonly made by the Spaniards' propaganda machine. In 1974 the son of Merebbi Rebbu told the author's companion that the Spaniards would not let him back into the territory.

It is clear that the present descendants of Ma el Ainin are to be numbered amongst the opposition to the Spanish. However, though used by Morocco as symbols, for their fame and *baraka*, they appear to be now no more influential in the desert itself than the chiefs of various other tribes and are certainly secondary to those of the Reguibat.

# Bibliography

*Africa* (Revista de Acción Española), Instituto de Estudios Africanos.
*África Contemporary Record.*
*Africa Diary.*
*Anuario Estadístico de España.*
*Archivos*, Instituto de Estudios Africanos.
*Boletín de la Sociedad de Historia Natural*, Madrid.
*Cuadernos de Estudios Africanos*, Instituto de Estudios Políticos.
FAO publications:
*Keesings Contemporary Archives.*
*MIFERMA Informations*, Mines de Fer de Mauritanie.
Moroccan press: *Maghreb Informations*, *Maroc Soir*, *Le Matin*, *L'Opinion*.
*Revista de Geografía Comercial*, Madrid.
UN publications
Aceytuno Gavarrón, M. F., 'Una tribu del Sáhara: Ulad Delim', *Africa* (1961).
Africanus, Leo, *History and Discovery of Africa*, trans. Pory, J., ed. Brown, R. (1896).
Alcobé, S., 'Grupos sanguíneos en nómadas del Sáhara Occidental', *Inst. Bernadino de Sahagún*, 1 (1945).
Alcobé, S., 'The Physical Anthropology of the W. Saharan nomads', *Man*, 47 (1947).
Alia Medina, M., 'Las Aguas Superficiales y Subterráneas en el Sáhara Español', *Africa* (1943).
Alia Medina, M., *Características Morfográficas y Geológicas de la Zona Septentrional del Sáhara Español* (Madrid, 1945).
Alia Medina, M., 'El Cuaternario en el Sáhara Español', *Bol. Real Soc. Esp. Hist. Nat.*, 43 (1945).
Alia Medina, M., 'Resultados de una Expedición Geológica al Sáhara Español', *Africa* (1946).
Alia Medina, M., 'Enriquecimiento Ferruginoso en el Devónico del Sáhara Español', *Estudios Geológicos*, 6 (1947).
Alia Medina, M., *Contribución al Conocimiento Geomorfológico de las Zonas Centrales del Sáhara Español* (Madrid, 1949).
Alia Medina, M., 'Estudio Mineralógico de Algunas Muestras de Arena del Sáhara Meridional Español', *Archivos* (1950).
Alia Medina, M., 'El Descubrimiento de los Fosfatos del Sáhara Español', *Africa* (1950).
Alia Medina, M., 'Formaciones de Hamada Neógena en el Sáhara Meridional Español', *Archivos* (1954).
Alia Medina, M., 'Sobre las Variaciones Climáticas durante el Cuaternario en el Sáhara Español', *Africa* (1955).

Alimen, H., *The Prehistory of Africa* (London, 1957).

Allison, A. C., 'Blood Groups and African Prehistory', *Actes Cong. Panaf. Préh.*, 2 (1952).

Almagro Basch, M., 'El Arte Prehistórico del Sáhara Español', *Ampurias*, 6 (1944).

Almagro Basch, M., 'Un Yacimiento de Tradición Capsiense del Sáhara Español: Las Sebjas de Taruma', *Ampurias* 7–8 (1945–6).

Almagro Basch, M., *Prehistoria del Norte de Africa y del Sáhara Español* (Madrid, 1946).

Almagro Basch, M., *El Estado Actual de la Investigación de la Prehistoria del Norte de Africa y del Sáhara* (Madrid, 1968).

Almagro Basch, M., 'El Arte Rupestre del Norte de Africa en relación con la Rama Norteafricana de Cromagnón', *Anuario de Estudios Atlánticos*, 15 (1969).

Almagro Basch, M., 'Las Representaciones de Carros en el Arte Rupestre del Sáhara Español', *Trabajos de Prehistoria*, 28 (1971).

Almagro Basch, M., 'Unos Objetos Háchiformes representados en el Arte Rupestre del Sáhara Occidental', *Muñibe*, 23 (1971).

Almonte, E. d', 'Ensayo de una breve descripción del Sáhara Español', *Bol. Real Soc. Geog.* 56 (1914).

Alvarez Pérez, J., 'En el Saguiet-el-Hamra', *Rev. Geog. Comm.* 2 (1886).

Andrés Andrés, C., 'Características Económicas y Legales de las Concesiones Petrolíferas en las Provincias Africanas', *Archivos* (1961).

Anon., *Dictionnaire Français-Berbère* (Paris, 1907).

Anon., 'El Sig, un juego del Sáhara', *Africa* (1944).

Anon., 'El Pueblo Saharaui ha elegido su Destino', *Africa* (1966).

Anon., 'El Verdadero Pueblo Saharaui quiere decidir su Futuro', *Africa* (1966).

Anon., 'La Yemaa o Asamblea General del Sáhara', *Africa* (1967).

Anon., 'Mauritania: Un Ejercito que ha encontrado su estilo', *Africa* (1968).

Anon., 'Maurítanie' and 'Province de Sahara', *Le Million*, 181 (1972).

Anthonioz, R., 'Les Imraguen', *Bull. I.F.A.N.*, Sc. H., 30 (1968).

Arrojas, E., 'El Coronel Bens', *Africa* (1946).

Arrojas, E., 'A.O.E.: 50 años de labor administrativa', *Africa* (1951).

Balbín Behrmann, R. de, *El Meran I*, unpublished Ph.D. thesis (Madrid, 1969).

Balbín Behrmann, R. de, 'Excavación de un túmulo Preislámico, en la zona de Guelta Zemmur, Sáhara Español', *Trabajos de Prehistoria*, 30 (1973).

Bataillon, C., *Nomades et Nomadisme au Sahara*, UNESCO, Arid Zone Research Series 19 (1963).

Batuta, Ibn, *Travels*, ed. Défrémery, C., trans. Gibb, H. A. R. (1958–71).

Bekri, El, *Description de l'Afrique Septentrionale*, trans. de Slane (1965).

Benéitez Cantero, V., 'Algunos Usos y Costumbres de nuestro Sáhara', *Africa* (1971).

Biberson, P., 'Stations Palaéolithiques du Dra Inférieur', *C.R. Séances Soc. Sc. Nat. du Maroc*, 2 (1954).

Biberson, P., 'Notes sur le Palaéolithique du Maroc Meridional', *Zephyrus*, 17 (1966).

Biberson, P., 'Observations sur le Pléistocène et la Préhistoire de Tarfaya', *Actes Cong. Panaf. Préh.*, 5 (1965).

Biberson, P., 'Recherches sur le Palaéolithique Inférieure de l'Adrar de Mauritanie', *Actes Cong. Panaf. Préh.*, 5 (1965).

Biedermann, H., Nowak, H., 'Altkanarische Kultur, Nordwestafrika und felsmalereien der Spanischen Sahara', *Mannus* (1974).

Bisson, J., 'Le Nomadisme des Reguibat L'Gouacem', *Trav. Inst. Rech. Sah.*, 20 (1961).

Bonelli, E., *Nuevos Territorios Españoles de la Costa del Sáhara* (Madrid, 1885).

Borras, T., 'Los "Liberadores" del Sáhara', *Africa* (1967).

Borras, T., 'Los Saharauis son Españoles', *Africa* (1967).

Bullón Díaz, G., 'Los Ulad bu Sba del Sáhara', *Africa* (1945).

Ca da Mosto, A. de, *Voyages*, trans. and ed. Crone, G. R. (1937).

Caillié, R., *Journal d'un Voyage* (Paris, 1828).

Camps, G., 'Le Néolithique de Tradition Capsien au Sahara', *Et. et Docs. Tchadiens*, 1 (1966).

Camps, G., 'Le Néolithique de Tradition Capsienne dans le Sahara', *Trav. Inst. Rech. Sah.* 26 (1967).

Carcopino, J., *Le Maroc Antique* (Paris, 1948).

Caro Baroja, J., 'La Exploración del A.O.E.', *Africa* (1954).

Caro Baroja, J., *Estudios Saharianos* (Madrid, 1955).

Caro Baroja, J., 'La Historia entre los Nómadas Saharianos', *Archivos* (1955).

Cauneille, Capt, 'Les Nomades Regueibat', *Trav. Inst. Rech. Sah.* 6 (1950).

Centre Culturel A. de St. Exupéry, *L'Art du Cuir en Mauritanie* (Nouakchott, 1973).

Cervera Baviera, J., 'Expedición al Sáhara', *Rev. Geog. Comm.* (1886).

Chamla, M-C., *Les Populations Anciennes du Sahara* (Algiers, 1968).

Clark, J. D., 'The Prehistoric Origins of African Culture', *J. African History*, 2 (1964).

Cola Alberich, J., 'Magia y Superstición en el Sáhara Español', *Africa* (1953).

Cola Alberich, J., 'El Aain en el Sáhara', *Africa* (1955).

Comba Ezquerra, J. A., 'Posibilidades Mineras del Sáhara Español', *Africa* (1960).

Comba Ezquerra, J. A., 'Investigación Minera en el Sáhara Español', *Africa* (1960).

Comba Ezquerra, J. A., 'La Investigación Minera en la Provincia del Sáhara', *Archivos* (1961).

Comba Ezquerra, J. A., '25 Años de Investigación Geológica y Minera de las Provincias Africanas', *Archivos* (1965).

Comba Ezquerra, J. A., 'Trabajos y Planes de desarrollo de las Investigaciones mineras y geológicas en la provincia de Sáhara', *Africa* (1966).

Commission on Non-Self-Governing Territories, *Report A/4785* (1961–2).

Conejo García, A., 'La Sanidad en los Territorios del A.O.E.', *Africa* (1949).

Coon, C., *The Living Races of Man* (London, 1966).

Crawford, O. G. S., *The Eye Goddess* (London, 1957).

Crova, B., 'Essai de classement des Pointes de Fléches de la Mauritanie', *C.R.VII Cong. Préh. de France* (1911).

Crova, B., 'L'Age de la Pierre en Mauritanie', *Rev. d'Eth. et de Sociol.* (1912).

Dangelzer, R., 'Préhistoire de la Mauritanie Occidental Saharienne', *Bull. Soc. Préh. de France*, 8 (1911).

Davidson, B., *Africa* (London, 1966).

Deasy, G. F., 'Spanish Territorial Boundary Changes in NW Africa', *Geog. Review*, 32 (1942).

Denis, Lieut, 'Cultures en *maader* dans l'Oued Dra', *Trav. Inst. Rech. Sah.*, 9 (1953).

Doerr, H., 'La Agresión al Territorio Español de Ifni', *Africa* (1958).

Domínguez Ortiz, A., *Plazas y Provincias Españolas en Africa* (Madrid, 1962).

Douls, C., 'El Sáhara Occidental', *Bol. Soc. Geog. Madrid*, 2 (1887).

Douls, C., 'Voyage dans le Sahara Occidental et le Sud Marocain', *Bull. Soc. Géog. de Paris*, 9 (1888).

Eannes (de Azurara), G., *The Chronicle of the Discovery and Conquest of Guinea*, trans. and ed. Beazley, C. R., Prestage, E. (London, 1896).

Farine, B., 'A la rencontre du passé en Mauritanie', *MIFERMA Informations*, 20 (1971).

Fernandes, V., *Das Ilhas do Mar Oceano* (Portugal, 1507).

Fernández Duro, C., 'Exploración en busca de Sta. Cruz de Mar Pequeña', *Bol. Soc. Geog. Madrid* (1878–9).

Findlay, R., 'The Rio de Oro: an Airman's Impression', *Cornhill Magazine*, 74 (1933).

Flores, A., Ensayo Geográfico sobre el Sáhara Español', *Africa* (1950).

Flores, A., 'La Religión en el Desierto', *Africa* (1951).

Flores, A., 'El Erróneo Artículo 3° del proyecto de tratado de 1902', *Africa* (1952).

Flores Morales, A., 'Razas del Sáhara Español', *Africa* (1948).

Flores Morales, A., 'Tipos y Costumbres del Sáhara Español', *Africa* (1949).

Forde-Johnson, J. L., *Neolithic Cultures of N. Africa* (London, 1959).

Furon, R., *Geology of Africa* (London, 1963).

Gallo, M., *Spain under Franco* (London, 1973).

García Cabezón, A., *Establecimiento de la Agricultura en el Sáhara*, Coll. Monograficas Africanas, 5 (Madrid, 1967).

García Cabrera, C., 'El Banco Pesquero Canario-Sahariano', *Archivos* 18 (1964).

García-Fuente, S., 'La Investigación Petrolífera en el Sáhara', *Archivos* 59 (1961).

García Guinea, M. A., 'Grabados Rupestres inéditos de Smara', *Zephyrus* 17 (1966).

Gatell, J., 'Viajes por Marruecos', *Mem. Soc. Geog. Madrid*, 1 (1887).

Gauthier-Pilters, H., 'Le puits pastoral dans le désert', *MIFERMA Informations*, 23 (1972).

Gerteny, A. G., *Mauritania* (London, 1967).

Gellner, E., *Saints of the Atlas* (London, 1969).

Gil Crespo, A., *Plazas y Provincias Españolas* (Madrid, 1962).

Gil Montaner, F., 'Notas sobre el Sáhara Español', *Bol. Soc. Geog. Madrid*, 71 (1931).

Glas, G., *The Discovery and Conquest of the Canary Islands* (London, 1764).

Gómez Moreno, P., *Rutas del Sáhara* (Madrid, 1958).

Grébénart, D., 'Antilope gravée sur coquille d'oeuf d'autruche (Tarfaya, Sahara Atlantique Marocain)', *L'Anthrop.*, 77 (1973).

Greenberg, J. H., 'The Languages of Africa', *I.J.A.L.*, 29 (1963), in Coon, *ibid*.

Gruvel, A., *Les Pécheries de la Côte Occidentale de l'Afrique* (Paris, 1906).

Guinea, E., 'Vegetación del Sáhara Español', *Africa* (1944).

Hamet, I., 'Les Marabouts Clairvoyants du Saguiet-el-Hamra', *Chron. Mauritanie Sénégalaise* (1911).

Harrison-Church, R. J., 'Problems and Development of the Dry Zone of W. Africa', *Geog. J.*, 127 (1961), 128 (1962).

Harrison-Church, R. J., 'Port Etienne: A Mauritanian Pioneer Town', *Geog. J.*, 128 (1962).

Hernández-Pacheco, E. and F., *El Sáhara Español* (Madrid, 1942).

Hernández-Pacheco, E. *et al*, *El Sáhara Español* (Madrid, 1949).

Hernández-Pacheco, F., *El Sáhara Español* (Madrid, 1962).

Hernández-Pacheco, F., 'Características Fisiográficas del Litoral y Costas del Sáhara Español', *Archivos* (1961).

Hertslet, E., *The Map of Africa by Treaty*, Vol. 3 (London, 1909).

Hugot, H. J., 'Mission à l'Ile de Tidra', *Bull. I.F.A.N.*, B, 28 (1966).

Ibáñez, E., 'El Culto a los Igurramen (Santones)', *Africa* (1950).

Instituto de Estudios Africanos, *Atlas Histórico y Geográfico de Africa Española* (Madrid, 1955).

Instituto Nacional de la Vivienda, *African Homes* (Madrid, 1966).

Jordá Cerdá, F., 'Los problemas de la investigación prehistórica en el Sáhara Español', *Archivos* (1955).

Jordá Cerdá, F., 'Notas sobre el levallois-musteriense del Yebel Zini (Sáhara Español)', *Archivos* (1955).

Juega Boudón, J., 'La Aviación Española en las Operaciones en el Africa Occidental', *Africa* (1958).

Julien, C-A., *Voyages de Découverte* (Paris, 1948).

Julien, C-A., *Histoire de l'Afrique du Nord des Origines á la Conquête Arabe, 647 A.D.* (Paris, 1951).

Khaldun, Ibn, *An Introduction to History: The Muqaddimah*, trans. Rosenthal, F. (London, 1958).

Labat, J-B., *Nouvelle rélation de l'Afrique Occidentale* (Paris, 1728).

Lafuente, D., 'Algo sobre la Coloniá de Rio de Oro', *Africa* (1945).

Lafuente, D., 'La Costa de la Zona Sur de Marruecos', *Africa* (1946).

Lafuente, D., 'Ma el Ainin, Señor de Smara', *Africa* (1946, 1947).

Lafuente, D., 'Ma el Ainin frente a Gouraud', *Africa* (1948).

Lafuente, D., 'De la zona al sur del Draa: su orografía y hidrografía', *Africa* (1950).

Lafuente, D., 'Gouraud en la Cudia Iyil', *Africa* (1950).

Latan, R., 'Un Campamento Neolítico a Tarfaya', *Bull. Arch. Maroc.* (1968).

Legum, C., *Africa* (London, 1961).

Legum, C., *Africa Handbook* (London, 1969).

Lhote, H., 'Problèmes Sahariens', *Bull. Arch. Maroc.*, 7 (1967).

Lhote, H., 'Le Cheval et le Chameau dans les peintures et gravures rupestres du Sahara', *Bull. I.F.A.N.*, 15 (1953).

Lodwick, J., *The Forbidden Coast* (London, 1956).

Lombardero, Col, 'Toponimia del Sáhara', *Africa* (1949).

Lotte, Lieut, 'Coûtumes des Imraguen', *J. Soc. Africanistes*, 7 (1937).

Lozano y Rey, L., 'Una Excursión Científica a la Costa del Sáhara Español', *Bol. Soc. Geog. Nacional*, 75 (1935).

MacBurney, C. B. M., *The Stone Age of Northern Africa* (London, 1960).

MacKenzie, D., *The Flooding of the Sahara* (London, 1877).

MacKenzie, D., *The Khalifate of the West* (London, 1911).

Maire, Sieur Le, *Voyages aux Isles Canaries, Cap-verd, Sénégal* (Paris, 1695).

Marmol y Carvajal, L. del, *Descripción General de Africa* (Granada, 1573).

Martínez Santa-Olalla, J., *El Sáhara Español* (Madrid, 1944).

Mateu, J., 'Nuevas aportaciones al conocimiento del arte rupestre del Sáhara español', *Ampurias*, 7 (1945).

Mateu, J., 'Grabados Rupestres de los Alrededores de Smara (Sáhara Español)', *Ampurias*, 9 (1947).

Mauny, R., *Gravures de l'Ouest Africaine* (Dakar, 1954).

Mauny, R., *Les Navigations Mediévales sur les Côtes Sahariennes antérieures à la Découverte Portugaise (1434)* (Lisbon, 1960).

Mercer, J., *Canary Islands: Fuerteventura* (Newton Abbot, 1973).

Mocquet, J., *Travels* (London, 1696).

Molina Campuzano, M., *Censo del Sáhara Español* (Madrid, 1954).

Monod, T., 'Gravures, Peintures et Inscriptions Rupestres du Sahara Occidental', *Bull. C.E.A.O.F.*, A, 7 (1938).

Monod, T., 'La Structure du Sahara', *Trav. Inst. Rech. Sah.*, 3 (1945).

Morales Agacino, E., 'Grabados e Inscripciones rupestres de la Alta Saguiet el Hamra', *Act. Mem. Soc. Esp. Antr. Etn. Preh.* (1944).

Morales Agacino, E., 'Las Gacelas de Rio de Oro', *Africa* (1945).

Morales Agacino, E., 'Jornada de Marcha en el Desierto', *Africa* (1947).

Morla, V. de, 'Rio de Oro, Sahara (1884 a nuestros días)', *Africa* (1971).

Morla, V. de, 'La primera occupación de la costa del Mar Menor de Berbería por los españoles (1476–1524)', *Africa* (1971).

Mulero Clemente, M., 'El Sáhara Español: Notas para su Estudio Militar', *Africa* (1950).

Murdock, G. P., *Africa, its peoples* (New York, 1959).

Navy Hydrographer, *Africa Pilot, West Africa*, 1 (1967), Supps (to 1972) *O.A.U.* Scientific, Technical and Research Commission, *West African International Atlas* (1968).

Oliver, R., Atmore, A., *Africa since 1800* (1967).

Ortega Cañadell, R., *Provincias Africanas Españolas* (Barcelona, 1962).

Pastor y Santos, E., 'Gestiones que precidieron a la ocupación de Rio de Oro', *Africa* (1949).

Pélissier, R., *Los Territorios Españoles en Africa* (Madrid, 1964).

Pericot García, L., *Manual de Prehistoria Africana* (Madrid, 1962).

Pinto de la Rosa, J. M., *Canarias Prehispánica y Africa Occidental Española* (Madrid, 1954).

Porras Zavala, A. de, 'Artífices del Desierto', *Africa* (1949).

Prudhomme, –, 'La Sebkha d'Ijil', *Bull. C.E.A.O.F.* (1925).

Puigaudeau, O. du, Senones, M., 'Gravures Rupestres de l'Oued Tamanart (Sud Maroc)', *Bull. I.F.A.N.*, 15 (1953).

Quiroga, F., 'La Geología del Rio de Oro', *Rev. Geog. Comm.*, 2 (1886).

Rennell, Major, 'The Captivity of Alexander Scott', *Edin. Philos. J.*, 4 (1821).

Revol, Lieut, 'Les Imraguen', *Bull. C.E.A.O.F.*, 20 (1937).

Riley, J., *Loss of the American Brig 'Commerce'* (London, 1817).

Rioja, L. de, 'Mauritania en la O.N.U.', *Africa* (1961).

Robin, J., 'Moors and Canary Islanders on the Coast of the W. Sahara', *Geog. J.*, 121 (1955).

Roncière, C. de la, *La Découverte de l'Afrique au Moyen-Age* (Cairo, 1925).

Rumeu de Armas, A., *España en el Africa Atlántica* (Madrid, 1956).

Sabau Bergamín, J., 'Las Telecommunicaciones en las Provincias Españolas de Africa Occidental', *Africa* (1965).

Saez de Govantes, L., *El Africanismo Español* (Madrid, 1971).

Saez-Martin, B., 'Sobre una Supuesta Edad del Bronce en Africa Menor y Sáhara', *Act. Cong. Panaf. Préh.*, 2 (1952).

Santamara, R., 'La Cultura, Arma de Paz en el Sáhara Español', *Africa* (1972).

Sanz y Díaz, J., 'Breve Historia de Sta. Cruz de Mar-Pequeña', *Africa* (1950).

Scott, A., in Rennell, *ibid.*

Tabernero, H., 'Libro Blanco y Libro Verde', *Africa* (1961).

Tabernero, H., 'Mauritania esta dispuesta a un acercamiento con España', *Africa* (1963).

Térrasse, H., 'Les Monuments de Smara', *Rev. Geog. Maroc.* (1932).

Thomas, H., *The Spanish Civil War* (London, 1965).

Trewartha, G. T., *The Earth's Problem Climates* (Wisconsin, 1961).

Valverde, J. A., 'Aves Paleárcticas en el Sáhara Español', *Africa* (1955).

Valverde, J. A., 'Charcas y Patos del Sáhara Español', *Africa* (1956).

Valverde, J. A., *Aves del Sáhara Español* (Madrid, 1957).

Valverde, J. A., 'Expedición Zoológica en la Provincia del Sáhara', *Archivos* (1965).

Verneau, R., 'Ethnographie ancienne de la Mauritanie', *Act. Soc. Linné-enne Bordeaux*, 65 (1911).

Vidal Box, C., 'Significación geológica de los territorios centrales de Rio de Oro', *Africa* (1946).

Vidal y Lopez, M., 'Materiales Saharianos en Valencia', *Preh. Levantina*, 2 (1945).

Vieuchange, M., *Smara: the Forbidden City* (London, 1933).

Vilar Ramírez, J. B., *El Sáhara y el Hamitismo Norteafricano* (Madrid, 1969).

Viña Villa, J. la, 'La Investigación de Fosfatos en el Sáhara', *Archivos* (1961).

Yanguas Miravete, J., 'Marruecos limita su frontera sur', *Africa* (1958).

Yanguas Miravete, J., 'El Nuevo Régimen de Administración Local de la Provincia de Sáhara', *Africa* (1963).

Yanguas Miravete, J., 'Todo por la Juventud Saharaui', *Africa* (1965).

Zeuner, F. E., 'Líneas Costeras del Pleistoceno en las Isla Canarias', *Anuario de Estudios Atlánticos*, 4 (1958).

# Index

Numerals in **bold** refer to plate numbers, those in *italic* to line drawings